GAME CHANGER

PAUL McNAMEE AM is the only professional tennis player to have changed mid-career from a one-handed to a two-handed backhand. He became the Australian number one in singles, reaching the semi-final of the Australian Open, and in doubles won five Grand Slam titles and held the world number-one ranking.

As co-founder of the Hopman Cup, Paul helped turn the tournament into a prestigious international event. He is credited with invigorating the Australian Open, positioning it as the Grand Slam of Asia/Pacific and instigating the night final—still the highest rating program in Australian television history.

Paul coaches the Taiwanese player Su-wei Hsieh, winner of the 2013 Wimbledon ladies' doubles, and is a professorial fellow at Monash University. He lives in Melbourne with his wife, Lesley, and their son, Rowan.

paulmcnamee.com.au

GAME CHANGER
MY TENNIS LIFE
PAUL McNAMEE

t

TEXT PUBLISHING MELBOURNE AUSTRALIA

textpublishing.com.au

The Text Publishing Company
Swann House
22 William Street
Melbourne Victoria 3000
Australia

Copyright © Paul McNamee 2013
Foreword © John McEnroe 2013

The moral right of Paul McNamee to be identified as the author of this work has been asserted.

All rights reserved. Without limiting the rights under copyright above, no part of this publication shall be reproduced, stored in or introduced into a retrieval system, or transmitted in any form or by any means (electronic, mechanical, photocopying, recording or otherwise), without the prior permission of both the copyright owner and the publisher of this book.

First published in 2013 by The Text Publishing Company
Reprinted 2013

Cover and text design by Chong Weng-Ho
Typeset in Sabon by J & M Typesetting

Printed and bound in Australia by Griffin Press, an Accredited ISO AS/NZS 14001:2004 Environmental Management System printer

ISBN: 9781922147387 (paperback)
ISBN: 9781922148414 (ebook)
Author: McNamee, Paul, author.
Title: Game changer: my tennis life / by Paul McNamee;
foreword by John McEnroe.
Subjects: McNamee, Paul.
Tennis player—Australia—Biography.
Tennis coaches—Australia—Biography.
Tennis—Tournaments—Australia—History.
Other Authors/Contributors: McEnroe, John, 1959–
Dewey Number: 796.342092

This book is printed on paper certified against the Forest Stewardship Council® Standards. Griffin Press holds FSC chain-of-custody certification SGS-COC-005088. FSC promotes environmentally responsible, socially beneficial and economically viable management of the world's forests.

CONTENTS

Foreword *by John McEnroe*   IX
Introduction   1

PART I

1. All In   7
2. A Rude Awakening   21
3. Changing Tack   32
4. Going Pro Again   38
5. The Man in the Mirror   51
6. McEnroe and Me, Macca and Me   62
7. London Life   74
8. Match Point   86
9. Jumping Jack   95
10. Mixing It with Martina   111
11. Comeback   122
12. Where to Now?   134

PART II

13. On the Hop   147
14. How the West Was Won   159
15. The Next Big Thing   168
16. Open for Business   184
17. The Great Australian Dream   199
18. Legends of the Game   213
19. The Roof, the Whole Roof, and Nothing But the Roof   220

20.	Star Power	226
21.	Trouble in the Ranks	233
22.	The Millennium	242
23.	The Dokic Factor	254
24.	Embracing Asia	261
25.	The Holy Grail	271
26.	The Centenary	283
27.	Moving On	294
28.	And Now	306
	Postscript	315
	Acknowledgements	319

FOREWORD
JOHN McENROE

PAUL McNAMEE is very intense, has loads of nervous energy, can be annoying and brilliant at almost the same time, is extremely competitive, and has an undeniable love and passion for the sport of tennis. Hey, that sounds a lot like me!

Despite growing up at opposite ends of the Earth, we were similarly influenced as we made our way to the pros. Both of us have those fiery Irish roots, and both were inspired by the late great Australian Davis Cup captain Harry Hopman, who instilled in us a respect for the traditions of the game and a belief in our abilities, so that we believed we could have an impact in this sport.

Paul and I go way back, and we certainly had our ups and downs as we battled for turf and titles on the professional circuit. I remember watching Paul early on in my career in practice one day in the sweltering heat of Washington, DC, where he was working on going from a one- to a two-handed backhand. I had never seen it done that late in someone's career, nor have I ever since. I had always respected Paul's work ethic from a distance, and this was crazy, but it worked.

I thought, I can't lose to a guy who pulls a stunt like this. But sure enough, as we battled our way up the singles and doubles rankings, we fought, we clashed, we trashed-talked and we tried (successfully, I'd say) to get under each other's skin.

Needless to say, Paul handled himself far better on the court than I did, and I believe that came in handy for him in some of our biggest matches. Don't ask me to name them; I am sure Paul will later on. But I will say that his switch from the one to the two hands exemplifies Paul's uniqueness, his doggedness and his willingness to think outside the box.

It certainly served him well post-career. He kept the Hopman name alive by starting the Hopman Cup in the late '80s, and I was certainly happy to eventually be able to go down under and play the event, and even be at Paul's wedding to Lesley there. Talk about killing two birds with one stone!

He also did a great job as tournament director of the Australian Open, helping increase its stature, and making it feel closer and closer to the level of the other three. Hell, he even brought a Yankee from the States (yours truly) to liven things up a bit, and I would like to think it worked.

On a personal note, I would like to think it allowed Paul and me to have a relationship where we were on the same side of things, namely improving our sport, and for that I am happy. Because I was able to transition pretty successfully to the broadcast booth, and because Paul's mind was once again working overtime, we were able to forge a partnership. The old theory still holds true—if you can't beat them, join them. Yes, I worked for a tournament that defaulted me!

Soon after, Paul went in a different direction (how could you go to golf, Paul?) and our paths rarely crossed, except for the occasional seniors' event, so while the fire was still there, boy, there was a whole lot more grey hair (at least yours is still full). I can say this—it was quite a ride for the two Maccas, and I hope there is still more to come.

Enjoy the book!

**GAME CHANGER
MY TENNIS LIFE**

INTRODUCTION

MY TENNIS life began in 1962, when I was seven. I'd get the yell from Mum and Dad's bedroom at 7.40 a.m. in the middle of the Melbourne winter—the Wimbledon report with Alf Chave was on ABC Radio. I'd listen to the scores and all the different names, like Gulyas and Pietrangeli and the Aussies: Emerson, Fletcher, Fraser and Mulligan. And the great one, Rod Laver, who won his first Grand Slam that year and did it again in 1969, the only player in the history of tennis to twice win all four major championships in a calendar year. Rocket was my hero.

I learnt that the Australian Championships was one of those majors, because ours was one of the first four nations to win the Davis Cup (along with France, Great Britain and the United States) and we'd produced a succession of champions. I swear I never missed Alf Chave's report: year after year I would marvel at the exploits of legends of the game.

I never imagined that I would not only play in the biggest arenas around the world, including Centre Court at Wimbledon, but enjoy a career lasting fifteen years. In the early days I played against Rosewall and Sedgman, had the honour of a hit with Lew Hoad, was tutored by the great Harry Hopman ('Mr Hopman' to players like me) and got to play against my hero, Rod Laver. Then I played with Borg, Connors, McEnroe, Gerulaitis, Noah and the Aussies, led by Newcombe and Roche, Alexander and Dent, McNamara and Edmondson. Near the end of my playing days I shared a court with Becker, Edberg, Cash and even Michael Chang—who at age fifteen became the youngest man to win a singles match at the US Open, by beating me.

To traverse those eras—with the changes in playing styles, racquet technology and court surfaces, from an amateur era when I wrote letters to seek invitations to tournaments, to the professional tour with prize money you could only dream about and advisers to tell you how to spend it—I was indeed lucky. But these pages are not just about my rollercoaster playing career: they're about the journey I embarked on the day after I retired, commencing with the Hopman Cup, my forays into coaching and later the opportunity to help the Australian Open take its place at the top level of international tennis.

As chief executive of the Open I often needed to draw on the experiences and inspiration I garnered during my years as a player. I knew instinctively there was only one way the Australian Open could be perceived as equal to Wimbledon, the French Open and the US Open. We needed to raise the bar, if not at everything (for example, French cuisine), then in as many areas as possible—from transport and hotel arrangements to the all-important scheduling.

We needed to remove the Aussie cringe that sometimes reared its head, the slight inferiority complex that, in tennis, meant copying Wimbledon. At the risk of offending my British counterparts, whom I respect greatly, I even introduced the concept of how *not* to do it like Wimbledon. Not because there was anything wrong at all with the Championships, but because the British way is not the Australian way. We needed to be ourselves as a Grand Slam—uniquely Australian, proudly egalitarian—and to celebrate it. This meant we had to recognise that, notwithstanding our British roots and our desire to respect the rights of the displaced Indigenous community, we are married by geography to our Asian and Pacific neighbours.

Back in 1998, after the Kennett government had agreed to build a second stadium at Melbourne Park, I went on a whistlestop tour promoting the new venue. At a media call at the US Open I was asked an innocent question. 'Would you consider dedicating your new stadium to a champion, as has happened here [Arthur Ashe Stadium]?'

I gave my standard reply. 'To help the Victorian government raise the money, the new arena will be given commercial naming rights.'

Then it dawned on me. How would we distinguish between the two stadiums? So I broke from the script. 'Actually, maybe we still have an opportunity. I'd love to see Centre Court dedicated to an Aussie great.'

No surprise about the follow-up question. 'Which Aussie do you think Centre Court could be named after?'

I could have been diplomatic and dodged it, as the decision wouldn't be mine, but instinct overpowered me. 'Only one player in the history of tennis has won two Grand Slams...I'd love to see Centre Court named after Rod Laver. Rocket's record stands alone, and he's such a humble bloke.'

That moment began a process that led to Rod Laver Arena becoming the centrepiece of Melbourne Park. Tennis would be front and centre, enshrined in the name of a stadium used for the sport only two weeks of the year.

Welcome to my journey down a road full of potholes and risky sidetracks, with sometimes mischievous and irreverent solutions, hopefully egalitarian, with tears, fears and fun—does that sound like an Aussie just being an Aussie, mixed up in the joy of sport, our national pastime?

I got into a taxi in Sydney one day and started talking about tennis with the driver. Out of the blue he said an amazing thing. 'Do you know why I love sport so much? Because you can't script it.'

He was right, and I've been lucky enough to fulfil my dreams in the theatre of life that we all know doesn't have a script and with characters who wouldn't follow one.

PART I

1.
ALL IN

I GREW up in the Melbourne suburb of North Essendon with a tennis club within walking distance of our home. It was called Doutta Galla, and I am still not sure of the origins of the name. Conveniently I had an older brother and sister to accompany me across the big street, Bulla Road, after which I could get to Doutta Galla on a scooter without crossing another street. If my siblings weren't around Mum would get me across. Later on I took my bike.

Every night after school I'd be at Doutta Galla. I was lucky that a number of like-minded boys and girls congregated at the club. I was the youngest (until my younger brother wanted to tag along) but I seemed to fit in, and what an advantage it was to be playing with older and stronger kids if you wanted to improve. If someone had had enough, I'd move on to another court and mix in—you never wanted for a partner on those three humble suburban courts. It was freewheeling tennis, where we hit thousands of shots randomly. I don't remember playing games or sets.

I was always the last to leave—when it was too dark to see the ball! Mum would be waiting for me on Bulla Road and I'd be there on cue. Tea would already be on the table for our family: Dad at one end, Mum at the other, my older brother Stan and sister Mary across from my younger brother Brian and me. I used to think it was such a big table, but Mum (who's now ninety-one) still lives in the same house, and it's only four by three feet.

In fact, I thought the whole house was enormous, as it had three bedrooms. When Brian came along, my older brother—Big Mac, we called him—moved into a sleep-out extension, and Brian was in a twin bed in my room. It stayed that way for my entire childhood, and even when Mary got married and moved out Brian and I chose to share our little bedroom. We were only two years apart, shared a love of sport and were very good mates—and I'm proud to say we have remained so. And our backyard had a brick wall, perfect for a hit on the odd occasion when I couldn't drag my siblings, all good players, out for a hit.

Dad was born and raised in a little goldmining town called Tarnagulla, about forty-five kilometres from Bendigo. His father, Frank (my middle name), was the town blacksmith. Grandad and Dad were storytellers—they could both peel off a ripping yarn. When Grandad passed away in 1961, aged eighty-five, Dad inherited the family home and this became the scene for our weekends until I was twelve.

We all loved the old house, built circa 1857, which remains in our family. How could you not, with its open

In the backyard with my younger brother, Brian, circa 1963. Note the matching Essendon jumpers.

fireplace and big kitchen table, its quaint billiards room and little bedrooms? It could get plurry cold in winter, though, and it shocked me to find out later that my dad, along with his three brothers, spent many years sleeping on the veranda, as there was only enough room inside for the three girls.

We'd roam the magnificent bush at Tarna, helping Dad chop firewood. We'd play cricket or kick the footy in open spaces, or explore the nearby pine plantation, build cubby houses and enjoy the company of kangaroos at dusk. Two sports were mandatory: tennis and golf.

Tarnagulla Golf Club has a typical layout for a small country town—nine holes with variable tees to make an eighteen-hole course, and sand-scrape greens. That's where I learnt to play, and it didn't take long to get the hang of it. Just like Dad, I suppose. He held the club record (67) there for many years, and I loved to caddy for him on tournament days. We were addicted to the sport, and we spent a lot of days playing together.

One day we set off early and managed to play thirty-six holes before lunch. Not fully satisfied, we played another eighteen—and decided to keep going. Once we'd finished another nine there was still some light left, so we pressed on. By the time we got to the dogleg (eighth/seventeenth hole) it was getting really dark, so Dad sent me off to hide behind a tree and listen for his ball landing, and I'd run out and locate it. We got to finish that last nine, which meant we played seventy-two holes in a single day! It was great fun, and I've never forgotten it.

For some reason I was left-handed at golf. All I had was a spoon (3-wood), putter, 4-iron and mashie (7-iron). That was enough for me, and I'd say it's enough for anyone to take up the sport.

Then there was tennis. The courts at Tarna were only a hundred metres or so from the house, but I can't say they were ever as well kept as the golf course. There were two old asphalt courts, with plentiful weeds and gatherings of sand, where bull ants roamed. The net wasn't exactly pristine, either, but all you need is seventy-eight by thirty-six feet with a net and it's game on. Those tennis courts, and especially the bull ants, took a hammering from the McNamees—not that I spent anything like the same time on the courts as I did on the golf course.

As cold as the winters were, the summers were

bloody hot—too hot to swelter in a little house. The town reservoir had enough water, but it was not an enticing colour, and full of leeches and yabbies. If you were desperate you'd take a dip, but the absence of locals was a bad omen.

Twenty-five kilometres away was Bridgewater, a lovely town nestled on the Loddon River. Bridgey had a wonderful swimming spot, with amenities, a grass area on the riverbank and gum trees for shade. You couldn't get a better place to escape the searing heat.

The eight weeks of summer holidays went like this on most days. In the morning Mick Riordan, my great-uncle, would walk down for a cup of tea. We'd always play cards, and he taught all of us to play euchre and cribbage. Uncle Mick was a master of crib. In the early afternoon the temperature would be rising, so Mum would make sandwiches, fill the coolers with ice and cordial, and we'd all set off for Bridgey. No stops—a beeline to the swimming area and straight in. There was a generous pier to dive off, a little waterfall to traverse, and a couple of hundred metres upstream a 'springy' where you could stand up on an underwater limb.

By late afternoon, as the sun began to lose its sting, it was time to move camp a kilometre upstream. We didn't water ski, but some of the best exponents going around were often there practising. We enjoyed watching them do the slalom and practising the jumps discipline—it was spectacular.

We weren't there for the water skiing, though. Near the boat ramp was the Bridgewater Tennis Club, with eight grass courts. Enough said! They used a couch grass, which was a touch soft with a lowish bounce. We didn't wear shoes in summer, and those courts were perfect to play on in bare feet.

We spent summer after summer on the Bridgey grass courts, and you can imagine my excitement when at age eight I got to play my first tournament. My partner was Jan Pollock, from a local farming family. She was fourteen or fifteen and, like all the Pollocks and many kids from country families, good at all sports. It was an under-sixteen mixed doubles and I could hardly see over the net. I stuck to my space—something I never did later on—and let Jan do her thing. We ended up winning, and that was my introduction to tournament tennis.

After tennis, when the light was fading, we'd invariably be invited to dinner at the Pollocks' or the Rothakers', who were in the harness-racing industry. I was amazed at the size of their properties, and I couldn't believe it when they'd bring out the ice cream in a container two feet deep, which I'd only seen in large milk bars in Melbourne. I thought that was the ultimate.

Summer after summer went the same way, and we wouldn't have swapped it for the world. We got to experience true country Australia, with its extremes of climate, and I was able to pursue my love of golf and tennis alongside my brothers and sister. You couldn't have a happier upbringing.

My tennis kept improving, so I started entering tournaments in Melbourne. My first victory was at the under-eleven singles at Maribyrnong Park, in Moonee Ponds. In the final I was up 5–2 against Bruce Nunn, and I was enjoying it so much I didn't want the match to end.

I let Bruce win another game. When I tried to put my foot back on the pedal, things had changed. Bruce had gained confidence, and before I knew it the score was 5–5 and I was in trouble.

We were both only nine—from here on it would be a war of attrition. Every rally was thirty or forty shots, as both of us were too scared to take a risk. It must have been awful to watch. I ended up prevailing 7–5, but it taught me a lesson: never let your opponent back into the match.

I must have been eleven when an article appeared in the local paper, the *Essendon Gazette*. It was titled 'Jack of all sports champion', as I was simultaneously doing well at footy, cricket, athletics, golf and, of course, tennis.

Mum sat me down in my room and said we needed to have a talk. She told me how her brother Dick Reynolds, an exceptional sprinter, decided early on to concentrate on Australian Rules football, with outstanding results. 'Paul, Dad and I want you to choose between your sports,' she said.

'But I like them all,' I protested.

'I know, but you need to make a choice.'

'When?'

'Now.'

I was surprised. Here I was, at eleven, being asked to make a huge decision.

'Okay,' I said. 'Tennis and golf are my favourite

sports, so it's between those two…but I love them both.'

'But Paul, if you had to make a choice, which one would you pick?'

'Whoa—that's really tough,' I said. 'I'm quick and like running, so that's an advantage I have in tennis, but it doesn't help my golf at all. I suppose deep down I lean to tennis. So, yes, tennis.'

And that was that. Henceforth other sports would be hobbies. I was all in with tennis.

Mum moved me to Strathmore Tennis Club. Strathy was only a bike ride away, and there was a strong group of eleven- and twelve-year-old boys. It was a step up in standard at exactly the right time. Now I was at Strathy every night after school, sometimes stopping for fish and chips on my way home.

The club president, John Robinson, was a terrific bloke. He hit with me and mentored me, and he suggested I go down to the country tournament in Warrnambool on Labour Day weekend. Mum and Dad couldn't go, so I hopped on the plane, a DC-4, from Essendon Airport. It was my first flight and a little daunting, but I loved that Warrnambool trip. I managed to win the twelve-and-under singles, something my son replicated some forty years later.

The next big tournament was the North Suburban twelve-and-under at the Victorian Rail Institute, in Parkville. Amazingly, I played all of my sparring partners from Strathy. In the quarters it was Paul Clarke, in the semis John Hammond and in the final Peter Brown. I managed to win.

Most of the Strathy boys were being coached by Mervyn Rose, a former French Open and Australian Open singles champion. I was being coached at Maribyrnong Park by John 'Pop' Ryan, an excellent coach but without Merv Rose's playing pedigree.

It was understandable for Mum to ask Merv if he would have a look at me. It didn't take long for him to notice that I had a backhand problem. He had a backhand issue himself in his career, and had revered the stroke of the great Donald Budge, the first person in history to win the single-year Grand Slam. Don Budge's backhand was lethal yet unorthodox, as he placed his thumb along the back of the handle, not around it. Merv believed this was the key, and he forced every one of his pupils, from Kerry Harris, who became a top-ten player, to his new star pupil Ernie Ewert, the same age as I was, to hit their backhand with this unusual grip.

I tried the Budge grip in that trial session, and it felt like I was going to break my thumb in the process. As I finished up I let Mum know the lesson hadn't gone well and that backhand grip was not for me.

Mum and Merv had a chat. He told her I'd never get anywhere with my backhand, to which she replied, 'They said my brother Dick couldn't kick. But he won three Brownlow Medals.' Cop that!

Merv, a little taken aback, pressed on. 'Okay then, send Paul to Glen Iris to play the big boys [meaning Ernie] and you'll soon find out where he's at.'

Mum entered me in the Victorian twelve-and-under championships at Glen Iris. I took the train from

Essendon each day, and when I got home I'd report to Mum and Dad that (although unseeded) so far I was having no real problems. It came to the final and my opponent, naturally, was the number-one seed, Ernie Ewert. He seemed a pro—he was even sponsored. I was a little intimidated, and was promptly down 3–0. Somehow I worked my way into the match, and eventually I came out on top, 10–8, to win my first state title.

Life was never going to be the same again. I was offered discounted racquets by the Slazenger rep, Cedric Mason. The one I used had a little photo of Ken Rosewall (if you used Dunlop it was Lew Hoad, or Pancho Gonzales if you used Spalding). I was also invited to join the Shell Squad, which was like a state squad, on Sunday mornings, which meant the end of Tarnagulla weekends.

In summer there were a couple of tournaments to play, primarily the Victorian Schoolboys' and Schoolgirls' Championships at Kooyong, with 128 draws. I loved those big draws: everyone got a chance to play and you never wanted for mates. Kooyong and the Australian Open were played in December, meaning January was reserved for Tarna and Bridgey, at least for a couple more years.

In all of this there was the influence of my father, Stan. He was a superb athlete who excelled at every sport he took up. Dad was born in 1913, on the cusp of the Great War, and in his teenage years experienced the scourge of the Depression. In 1931, with zero chance of work of any kind, Dad found a seventy-ounce nugget of gold while prospecting at Cleary's Gully—a godsend for a family with seven kids. They used some of the money to buy musical instruments, and formed a band (Dad played the sax).

But he never got a chance to realise his sporting potential. He was a top country footballer and cricketer, bowling out a whole team, taking a hat trick and getting to play against Don Bradman's XI. As a kid, the only way he could play tennis (with his great mate Lennie Ramm) was to break up wooden crates and play with board racquets. It was unimaginable to own a real racquet with strings.

Dad went on to play VFA football for Northcote and sub-district cricket. He took up golf at fifty, and promptly got down to a handicap of 6. He said he'd only play lawn bowls when he was too old or slow for golf or tennis. At eighty-nine he was neither, so he passed away without learning the game.

Dad was also a very capable tennis player, and there was never a shortage of free advice. One day at Tarnagulla I made a derogatory remark about his game.

'Right,' he said. 'Get the racquets—to the courts.' He would not stand for being insulted by his upstart son.

Dad tried his darndest but he was in his mid-fifties, so it wasn't a fair match. I remember winning 6–3, with some guilt at having pushed Dad to such an extreme. I looked up to him so much, and it didn't feel right beating him in those circumstances. Now, older and wiser, I understand that every parent wants their kid to be better.

I don't consider myself the athlete Dad was. He was so light on his feet that he danced, whereas I had more of the Reynolds family make-up. The other defining things about Dad were his simplicity and humility. Like Mum, he was determined to ensure his kids never wanted for opportunities. Having experienced the Depression, he was uncertain about me trying to become a tennis player. He valued the educational opportunities he and Mum were providing. An honest pay for an honest day's work, and don't owe money, was his credo. Mum was a full-time teacher, and Dad was in the fire brigade and always had a second job, and sometimes a third, to help us get a good education. We were lucky.

With my teenage years in full swing, another transition moment occurred when I beat the swashbuckling John Robinson in the final of the Strathmore Club Championships. It was time to move to a bigger club again: Essendon Tennis Club. I was now playing senior tennis, and Essendon provided more strength, so it became my latest second home. At that time the club backed onto Windy Hill, home ground of the Essendon Bombers football team. We used to finish our matches as early as possible on Saturday arvos, jump the fence and go to the game for free. It was a good era for the Bombers, with premierships in '62 (I was there as a seven-year-old, sitting on my Dad's shoulders in the standing-room area) and '65, when Uncle Dick Reynolds helped us get tickets. I was in a D-pennant final for Essendon the day of the '68 Grand Final (which the Bombers narrowly lost), and it would be thirty-seven years before I won another pennant—as a senior, with Ernie Ewert as my partner!

At Essendon one guy, Terry Payton, stood out. He was a couple of years older than me, a likeable bloke and just that bit better. I finally got to beat him in the final of the Essendon Club Championships, which I was chuffed about as I was able to join Dad on the winners' board as club champion.

One day we played a B-pennant away match at Royal South Yarra Tennis Club. Mum, who was ferrying me as usual, was quite taken with RSY. Nestled on the Yarra, its imposing clubhouse and first-class facilities captured her attention. The club even served afternoon tea on Royal Doulton crockery.

It wasn't long before Mum was making discreet enquiries, and I was offered a junior scholarship to become a member. My first pennant season there as a sixteen-year-old saw me ushered into the A-grade team by the captain, Colin Stubs. Stubsy was a fine player who'd done the circuit in Europe and knew his stuff. He went on to become a very successful tournament director of the Australian Open, a role in which I eventually succeeded him.

Those A-pennant years at RSY were a rough ride, good for building character. One day, against MCC at Roy Street, I was in a torrid battle with John 'Doc' Fraser, a former singles semi-finalist at Wimbledon. It was 9–9 in the third set but, being far younger than Doc, I felt the match was swinging my way. Doc went up to the net, grabbed the handle at the post and wound the net down to the ground.

'What are you doing?' I said.

'The street lights just came on,' Doc said, 'so that's it for the day, kid.'

He was technically within his rights: there was a

pennant rule to that effect. I wasn't happy! When it came to A-pennant, there was no quarter asked or given.

My schooling was ticking along at St Bernard's Christian Brothers College in West Essendon. It was an academically focused school but also nurtured footballers. From the years around me, Simon and Justin Madden and Gary Foulds went on to become top players for the Bombers. I asked if tennis could be an option for Wednesday afternoon sport. The school said no, as there wasn't a teacher available.

Then, out of the blue, Mr Johns, an excellent English teacher, offered to supervise us at Maribyrnong Park. Mr Johns was from India and had a good knowledge of tennis, which has a fine tradition there. There were about eight of us, including my brother Brian, and Mr Johns organised some matches against other Christian Brothers schools.

One day he came up to me and said, 'Stick at it, Paul—you'll be playing Davis Cup one day.' That was a kind thing for Mr Johns to say, and I was always grateful that he went out of his way to help us.

My academic bent was towards mathematics and science subjects, so after I matriculated I opted for science at Melbourne University. But my heart was set on tennis.

2.
A RUDE AWAKENING

UNIVERSITY LIFE, for someone who'd attended a Catholic boys' school, was an eye opener. There was nobody on your back to make you go to classes or study. Most of my contact hours were in the mornings, and I spent the afternoons toiling away on the uni courts, desperately trying to improve my backhand.

Early in the year my mother said that her school, St Columba's Convent in Essendon, was short a couple of maths teachers for a month. My mate Denis Fitzgerald and I were given a tryout. Having no formal training and being only seventeen, we were a risk. The curriculum was a breeze—Fitzy and I were on top of that. And the pay was great. But before long the Form Two girls were out of control, and the Form Fives (fifteen- and sixteen-year-olds) had more to say about my clothing than my teaching. One day I wore a plain blue Slazenger jumper and received a round of applause—I'd finally worn something acceptable.

I had terrible trouble bringing the girls into line: they'd turn on their radios and all I could say was, 'You'll get into trouble with a teacher if you keep doing that.' I was the last person who would want to confiscate a radio, especially as I shared their taste in music. It got tougher and tougher, and I'm not sure whether the pin was pulled because the real teachers arrived or because I'd lost control, but I think the latter.

I started missing lectures. I found maths, chemistry and physics (especially quantum physics) were becoming boring, and my marks were tumbling. During the second semester I went to Mum, who was more in charge of these matters than Dad, and made noises about deferring uni and giving tennis a proper go. A few of the guys, including Ernie Ewert, were now playing overseas. I received support from my favourite aunty on mum's side, Gwen, who implored her older sister to let me try my luck.

Mum wasn't happy, and even Dad weighed in: 'I was forced to leave school and work in my dad's blacksmith shop at thirteen, and your mum and I have worked three jobs so you children can have an education. I would have loved to have gone to uni, but I never got the chance.' And the stinger: 'You've never done a hard day's work in your life.'

It was around August, just a couple of months before exams, when I said to Mum, 'I can't pass—I'm too far behind.'

'How is that possible?' she replied. 'Have you been going to lectures?'

'I'm sorry, Mum, but I haven't really gone at all the last two months. I've been playing a lot of tennis.'

Mum was livid, yet she chose her words carefully. 'Paul, you say you can't pass, but I want you to be completely honest with me.' She knew what I was up to. 'If you put your head down right now, and work really hard, surely you'll be able to pass?'

'Gee, I don't know,' I said. 'I think it's too hard now.'

'This is the deal, Paul. If you tough it out and pass first year, your dad and I will support you taking a year off and giving tennis a go. But you have to pass. What do you say?'

'Well, if I study really hard, then I can probably pass. Okay.'

I put tennis on the backburner, got stuck into the books and passed all my subjects, and promptly deferred second year.

My game was rolling along nicely, and it was my last year in juniors. I really wanted to play the Western Australian Juniors, the first big summer tournament, as I'd never been there and didn't want my peers to get the jump on me. So I asked Mum if they'd send me to Perth—not a cheap flight.

Mum pulled fifty dollars out of her wallet and said, 'You're going to the trots tonight. Win enough to fly to Perth.' I followed harness racing closely. The showgrounds weren't far away, and a group of us often went on Saturday nights. I picked some winners that night and won a few hundred dollars, enough to get to Perth.

There, I made it through to the final, where my opponent was another Victorian, Peter McNamara. Everyone was shocked that Macca had made it this far

Keen in my late teens, in the early 1970s— the tongue says it all.

in the tournament, as his tennis was considered a bit of a joke. He never seemed to take it seriously, always going for winners instead of grinding it out. But Macca was on song that week, and in incredible heat he beat me to take the title. Macca barely won another match after that on the Aussie circuit—he could live off that win for a while.

Soon it was the Junior Championships at the Australian Open. I would have been around the eighth seed: it was a strong crop that year. My draw opened up when my Victorian mate John Trickey took out two of the favourites, Mark Edmondson and Chris Kachel. I had the better of Trix in the quarters, and came up against Trevor Allen in the semis.

I was indebted to my coach through juniors, John

'Pop' Ryan, for my service action. He had an amazingly simple technique for mastering arguably the toughest skill in tennis. In my adolescence I saw him every Saturday morning as part of a group, and it was handy to have him around during the Australian Open. I won the first set easily in the semi, then lost the second just as swiftly. There was a rain delay, Pop took the opportunity to give me some good advice, and I duly won the third set.

In the final I was up against Jean-Louis Haillet of France. For some time I had felt my father was too quick to criticise my performances, so I'd not made him too welcome. But this was a major championship, and I wanted Dad there. Jean-Louis was the son of Robert Haillet, a top French player and an Adidas icon. He was tall, charming and good-looking, with a free-flowing arsenal. We were put on the front court on the middle row at Kooyong.

I was up against it, and I knew it. I was quickly down 3–0 but managed to get the break back and it went all the way to 8–8, when Jean-Louis inexplicably served a couple of double faults and the set was mine, 10–8. The second set was similar and I took it 7–5. It was a huge thrill, and it was great that Mum and Dad, and Pop Ryan, were there to see it.

After the match we went to visit Dad's brother Jack McNamee. He'd been a terrific boxer in his day, simultaneously holding the Australian middleweight and welterweight championships. I endured one of his famous vicelike handshakes, and it was just as well it was after the final.

The next week brought the New South Wales Open at White City, where I played Mark Edmondson in the final of the juniors. Edo was intimidating. Our final was the curtain-raiser on Centre Court to the women's and men's singles finals: Margaret Court versus Evonne Goolagong and Ken Rosewall versus Mal Anderson.

Edo and I were toiling away when at 8–8 in the third set the referee, Cliff Sproule senior, suddenly told us we needed to finish the match on an outside court, as we were holding up the scheduled program. Edo said to Cliff, 'No way—I'm not going anywhere,' which was pretty gutsy for a junior. And he didn't go anywhere; he stared the ref down.

He promptly broke my serve in the next game, to the delight of the officials pleading for a quick end to the match, but I ruined the party by breaking back. We went to 12–12, before I finally prevailed 14–12. I'd had a memorable summer.

Having passed my exams, I took Mum up on the offer to head to Europe. As an Australian Open Junior Champion I could get into tournaments. In those days to enter events you wrote a letter outlining your best results, then waited for a reply from the organisers with an offer like 'twenty pounds plus free accommodation and meals'.

Mum and Dad put together the money and allowed their sheltered teenager to head overseas, and I got four hundred dollars from Tennis Australia as the number-one junior, the only grant I ever received in my development. Big money wasn't around in that era, but I wonder whether the hundreds of thousands of dollars spent nowadays on each choice kid isn't counterproductive—our current results don't justify it.

As was the custom for players from Commonwealth countries, we assembled in England in April for events at Cumberland, Norwich, Sutton and Paddington. It was a rude awakening, coming up against so many other strong players from South Africa, Zimbabwe, India and New Zealand, along with all the Aussies, the British contingent and a few Americans.

At Sutton I had my best result, reaching the semi-finals by beating the number-one British junior along the way. This enticed Slazenger to continue supplying free racquets and strings—helpful for the wallet and the confidence. And there was thirty pounds in prize money, enough to cover the ferry trip to Paris to play in qualifying for the French Open.

I'd heard all about European clay. I couldn't wait to set foot on *la terre battue* (literally translated, 'crushed earth'), which was finer and slower than en tout cas, the Melbourne surface I'd grown up on.

My first-round match in qualifying was against Pancho Gorostiaga, a 41-year-old Bolivian who'd seen better playing days—but there wasn't much about clay that he didn't know. To our mutual surprise, we were scheduled on Court Central, the Mecca of clay-court tennis. I couldn't believe its grandeur, and as the stands were nearly empty I felt lost out there—alone and exposed.

There I was, serve-volleying away, adhering to my

Australian upbringing, only to be taunted by deft returns to my feet followed by diagonal lobs to unreachable positions, or angled passes that were utterly foreign to me. When Pancho served, I was confused. I couldn't find a ball to attack him, and as soon as I tried to settle into a baseline exchange he'd throw in a drop shot. He was playing chess and I was playing checkers. I lost 6–2, 6–1, a scoreline flattering me. I'd sat the test in Clay Court Tennis 101 and failed miserably.

As I left the vast expanse of Court Central I contemplated how much I had to learn. I decided not to head back to England, but instead to hang around Paris and observe the greats. Mind you, away from the courts wasn't bad either—spring was turning to summer, and everyone was spilling outdoors to carouse in the bars and cafes. A fresh-eyed youngster, I could watch one of the world's most beautiful cities flaunting its finery.

The energy on court was just as vibrant. I saw our greats, like Rosewall, Roche and Newcombe; the Spaniards Santana, Gisbert and Orantes; plus Kodes, Franulovic and many other exponents of the clay-court art.

But one player stood out in that spring of 1973. He'd won Monte Carlo and Rome, and was on his way to victory at Roland Garros. He had power and touch; flair mixed with a decisive strike; speed tempered by such anticipation that he hardly seemed to be in top gear; a personality and range of facial expressions that seemed to taunt his opponent. Ilie Nastase was a lovable but sometimes volatile Romanian, and I could only marvel at his command of the craft—he had every tool in the kit and always seemed to select the right one at the right time. I sneaked into Court Central to watch him play. It was poetry in motion, the antithesis of my humiliation, and he made it look easy.

Heading back on the ferry from Calais to Dover, I wondered: would I ever be able to play like that on clay? Would I ever gain that special place in the sport, as someone who has mastered the art of clay-court tennis?

I scuttled back for the grass-court lead-in to Wimbledon. The dream of playing there could only be achieved by making it through the minefield of qualifying at the Bank of England club at Roehampton. The standard of courts, and of officiating, was not what it is today. There was only one umpire for each match and each seemed to be an elderly citizen not disposed to backchat from antipodean youths. I made it through the first round of qualifying, then was well beaten by an American, Tom Leonard.

This was the year that Nikolai Pilic, a Yugoslav player, was prevented from playing Wimbledon because he hadn't played a Davis Cup tie, putting him at odds with his federation—and at that time federation approval was a prerequisite for competing. The other professional players were up in arms. A player body, the Association of Tennis Professionals, was formed and a ranking system duly devised in order to allow entry to tournaments based on merit, rather than writing skills or your federation status.

One of the tricks used in letters of application was to claim indirect wins. If Rod Laver at one time lost to Mark

Cox of Great Britain, and a player beat Cox somewhere else, then that player could claim a win over Laver. Or you would say you'd beaten Ken Rosewall, but neglect to note that it was in doubles, when he may well have been playing with a junior.

The ATP was formed so that players could have a collective voice in the game, and to create a merit-based ranking system—the lifeblood of pro tennis to this day. This was readily achieved, and the newly formed association had its sights on redressing the injustice to one of its members, Nikki Pilic. The ATP met on the eve of Wimbledon and decided to boycott the event if Pilic was not placed in the main draw. The committee of the All England Club—egged on by the International Tennis Federation, which administered the Davis Cup—refused to yield.

The players voted to boycott Wimbledon, with only a few ATP members, predominantly those from Eastern Europe, choosing to compete. Ninety-odd places would be filled by those who had lost in qualifying, assuming they were not ATP members—youngsters like me and the up-and-coming Bjorn Borg. That's how I came to play my first Wimbledon, where I lost in the first round to Bobby McKinley, an American. Borg made the quarters, and Jan Kodes of Czechoslovakia beat Alex Metreveli of the USSR in the final.

Nothing of this magnitude had happened to tennis before, and nothing has since.

After Wimbledon I travelled to Europe with my doubles partner, New Zealand's Russell Simpson.

Although we had impressive junior credentials, we were lambs to the slaughter on clay. We had the odd good doubles result, but were cannon fodder for any European who could play. The tennis was tough, the accommodation modest, the food unusual and the language barrier unassailable. Through it all, Russell and I maintained a healthy competitive relationship.

Europe was a wake-up call. My game didn't cut it at third-tier professional level, my weak backhand having been mercilessly exploited on the slower clay, and the prospect of making a living seemed remote. I scurried back to Australia in September, tail between my legs.

My transition from a successful junior in Australia, built around serve-volleying on grass, clearly wasn't going to be easy. I suspected there were hundreds, maybe thousands, of better clay-court players out there.

Then I got a letter from New Zealand. 'Keep your elbow in,' the message read. It was Russell, who had a good backhand, at last giving me some much-needed advice.

3.
CHANGING TACK

MY BROTHER Brian was finishing Year Twelve. He was also a good tennis player, perhaps good enough to have a crack at it overseas, but not particularly dedicated. His attitude to schoolwork was the same. He was bright, but I was shocked at the gaps in his knowledge. Mum encouraged me to help him study. In the last few weeks before his final exams he finally knuckled down.

Shortly after, the Aussie summer circuit began in earnest. Now I was in the Open tournaments—no more of the soft early matches you sometimes get in juniors. The hangover from Europe had dented my confidence, and I found it difficult to win matches.

Brian received his matriculation results: he'd made the cut for medicine at the University of Melbourne. At least one of us knew what was in store for 1975. Everyone assumed I would be heading back to Europe, but I was restless.

Late one night in February I picked up Brian's course handbook. I was still eligible to go back to science at Melbourne University, but that didn't appeal. I perused the options: Architecture—no…Arts—no…Commerce—no…Law—no…Science/Law—hang on a minute.

I'd never thought at all about studying law, yet I suddenly had a gut feeling that it would suit me. Melbourne University was out—I was told I was too late—so I investigated Monash University. Mum was on board with the plan and she mentioned that she knew a chap high up in administration there, Richard Belshaw, who'd taught her at Essendon High School.

He was sympathetic, and getting into science would not be a problem, but the chances of landing an eleventh-hour place in law were slim. The next stop was the Law Faculty sub-dean's office, where my heart began to sink: even though my Year Twelve results would have seen me walk in, my first-year science results didn't look good. And the waiting list for law was enormous.

I reported back to my mum and my sister, who can be persistent if the occasion demands it (Mary is now a barrister). 'Why don't you go and sit in the faculty waiting room,' she said, 'and keep checking if a spot has opened up?'

Each morning I drove from Essendon to Monash, went to the sub-dean's office and touched base. I sat there for a few hours on the first day, and this pattern continued for a couple of weeks. His secretary was quite amused by my determination, I think.

As each day passed, the chances were dwindling—next week classes would be starting. So I decided I would attend law lectures, study hard, even sit the first exam and with luck get high marks. Perhaps I could get in that way.

A couple of days before the start of the semester I got a call from the secretary. I was offered a place—I was too excited for words.

I loved law classes and did well. Monash seemed less formal than Melbourne, and in any case I was grateful just to be there.

I kept my tennis going and was looking forward to Intervarsity Tennis, which that year would be held in Canberra. Brian was in the Melbourne Uni team, and they ended up edging us out for the win. Not happy!

At the time one of the legends of the sport, Charlie Hollis, was living in Canberra. Charlie had coached Rod Laver. Until the 1960s left-handers had been unable to topspin their backhand (something I could relate to, even though I was right-handed). Charlie was a visionary, and he made it his business to give Rocket a lethal topspin backhand. It became Rocket's signature shot.

I'd seen Charlie at the Sydney Indoor tournament at the Hordern Pavilion, near the showgrounds. The Sydney Indoor had a stronger field than the Australian Open in those days. I happened to be in the locker room when Rod Laver came in from another victory. He wasn't the world number one anymore, but he wasn't far from it.

'What the hell were you doing out there?' Charlie said. 'You're only a short-arse, and you weren't throwing the ball high enough on your first serve. How many times have I told you that? I can't believe I've driven all the way from Canberra to watch that rubbish. Get that ball toss up, or I won't be bothering again.'

I was gobsmacked.

'Sorry, Charlie,' Rocket said. 'I won't do it again.'

Now *that's* respect for a coach.

So Charlie's reputation preceded him, but I also knew he liked a drink or two, and had happily retired to live in a modest caravan. I summoned up the courage to knock on the door, introduced myself, and enjoyed the ensuing conversation in the tennis club bar—it was an honour and an inspiration to meet him. Beneath the uncompromising exterior was the wisest of tennis brains.

The other good break for my game was that a tennis-loving benefactor, Albert Mulhauser, sponsored me to play pennant at Grace Park, in Melbourne. Frank Sedgman, the 1952 Wimbledon singles champion, was in the team and asked me to play doubles with him. We went the whole year without losing a match, but more importantly I was getting feedback from one of the greats—at racquet length.

Sedg is a champion, and truly humble. His ease of movement and graceful strokes were illuminating. I've never seen anyone transition so well from the baseline to the net, and he rarely missed a volley.

I was twenty, and Sedg forty-seven, when we played each other in the finals of the Kooyong and Grace Park Club championships. We played a tough three-set final at Kooyong on grass in the morning (which I won, just), then drove to Grace Park to play its final on en tou cas in the afternoon (another tough three-setter, with the same outcome). What a player; what a bloke.

Getting to and from Essendon to Monash every day was a trek, and I was fortunate that Peter McNamara's parents, Bernie and Raz, let me stay a night or two each week at their home in Kew, even though Macca was over in Europe. Macca was a good mate, but at that stage I didn't have an inkling that he and I would share a tennis journey later on.

My first year at Monash came to a close. I'd put in a big effort, and my grades were strong. But the next year brought changes. I was as passionate as ever about law, particularly contract law, but my interest in statistics, my major, was waning.

Intervarsity Tennis was in Adelaide that year and I was captain of the Monash team. Monash had never won it but we had a pretty strong squad. Still, I knew that the University of New South Wales team was probably stronger, and when we played them in the group phase we lost to them nine matches to nil. For the final we'd need to change the order of our players. Under the rules you were allowed to move players up and down one spot, so I hastily moved our weaker players up a spot, given they were likely to lose anyway, and our stronger players down, as it couldn't hurt.

We got smashed in two matches but won four close singles, with three doubles to go. UNSW were livid and ready to protest, then discovered we'd played within the rules.

The doubles had no rules concerning the order of players so UNSW, expecting us to stack them, nominated their pairs in reverse order. I took a punt that they would do this, and put myself with our number-two player, Terry Longton from Warrnambool, in the first doubles.

We won in straight sets: we'd managed to back up a 9–0 loss with a 5–4 win. Most of us earned university blues or half blues for our achievement.

Tennis was coming to the fore again, but I did enough to get my science degree—my grades had dipped sharply, but no matter; I had the piece of paper. Law was different, as I'd continued to put in the effort on those subjects.

Over summer I played the traditional Aussie circuit and in Adelaide beat an established top-fifty player, Raz Reed from the United States. This got me thinking seriously about heading back to the circuit. Compounding my confusion, a letter arrived offering me a place in honours law and requesting I complete a research paper over the break.

I was at the crossroads. I loved studying law, but Europe was calling. Life outside the big league wouldn't be glamorous—but neither would it be so unpleasant.

Law, I eventually decided, could wait. It was time to face the clay courts a second time.

4.
GOING PRO AGAIN

AT TWENTY-ONE I was stronger, more confident and more mature. I was in a far better position to tackle the rough and tumble of the international tour than I'd been three years earlier.

One of my early tournaments was in Valencia—Spanish tournaments were considered weaker than those in France or Italy. How things have changed! I was rooming with Chris Lewis, a New Zealander who'd been a Wimbledon junior champion, and was committed to fitness and healthy habits.

We were staying at a very humble pension, paying a hundred pesetas (or one dollar) each a night. One evening, well after midnight, there was a commotion in the street. It was the annual religious fiesta and a loud procession was marching past our digs. This seemed to go on forever, driving us crazy, so we filled a bucket of water and tipped it over the balcony.

Yes, a very stupid thing to do.

People started yelling, and we could see them pointing in our direction—how could they know? Then Lewi noticed there was water dripping from our balcony...

Next thing we knew, there was a loud banging on our door and angry voices. We'd turned out the lights and stacked furniture against the door, but the situation was tense. Saying sorry in drawled English was not going to cut it.

After a while they headed off, but we knew they'd return. We packed our bags and got the hell out of there—at 3 a.m. or so, luckily unscathed.

That Spanish satellite circuit was tough going, and being in qualifying didn't confer many privileges. One of the events was in Palma, on Majorca (where Carlos Moya and Rafa Nadal hail from), and courts were hard to come by. The only time we could practise was from 5.30 to 6.30 a.m.

The best you could hope for was to win a match or two in qualifying and sometimes sneak into the doubles, where an Aussie who could volley might fare better. I had one ATP point as a result of getting in the Australian Open, which meant I had an ATP ranking on the very lowest rung, but there were hundreds of guys ahead of me and it would be a long journey.

I took to the task with gusto, picking up the odd morale-boosting win along the way, but it was a slog. We went to Asia in the autumn, where we encountered the local players, plus Americans and more Aussies. Hardly any Europeans played that tour, as it was on hard courts.

We went to Hong Kong, the Philippines, India and Japan. I can't remember too much about the tennis, but I recall Halloween in Tokyo. I was mates with the

American Hank Pfister, whose ankles required heavy taping every time he played. We decided that I should cover myself from head to toe with tape, like a mummy.

I got out of the lift on the top floor of the hotel and staggered, groaning, straight into a Japanese wedding. All hell was about to break loose, so I got back in the lift. On the ground floor I could see staff mobilising. With the bellboy just outside the lift, I quickly pressed the button and made sure he couldn't get back in: it was time to escape to the safety of my room. I whipped all the tape off and cleaned up. I got away with it—just!

The tennis was a bit tame after that excitement, but it was all part of the learning process and experiencing new cultures. I'd need to watch the pranks, though.

On returning home I watched an amazing development at the Australian Open. All the hype was around Brad Drewett, who at sixteen had some impressive wins over Mal Anderson and Alan Stone to make the quarters. Brad went on to become president and CEO of the ATP, but regrettably passed away in 2013—a major loss to the sport. The bigger story in 1976 became Mark Edmondson, from my junior year, who went all the way and won the Open, beating Rosewall in the semi and John Newcombe in the final. It was a breakthrough, and it gave all his peers a boost.

In 1977 I joined a team under the tutelage of Barry Phillips-Moore. Barry and his wife, Anne, were part of the furniture on the tour, especially in Europe. Barry had been a heck of a player himself—probably beating everyone at some point in his long career—and was a very accomplished clay-courter, the true rite of passage for a player. Our team included Macca, John Trickey and Stephen Myers: all Victorians, all my age. Barry educated us on the subtleties of clay, while Anne was a huge help when the inevitable defeats occurred.

The French winter satellite in March was particularly gruelling. The weather was freezing and my results on the indoor clay courts were average at best. Only Macca showed glimpses of form. The low point for me was at Tennis Club de la Chataigneraie, in the suburbs of Paris. The referee was the illustrious Jacques Dorfmann, who was also the referee of the French Open at Roland Garros.

In the first round I drew Pierre Cadot, dentist to many of the members. He must have been over forty, had seen better days physically, and judging by his midriff looked like he couldn't run for more than ten minutes. Being a super-fit 22-year-old, I was pleased that finally I had an opponent I could beat up on.

It must have amused my teammates to watch him dismantle me 6–3, 6–3. I did all the running, while he stayed put and dictated proceedings. And the killer was his drop shot, disguised and unpredictable. I was humiliated. I could see Jacques Dorfmann raise his eyebrows as I went past—the curse of Cadot had struck again.

Barry took me aside. 'Paul,' he said. 'I know this seems hard for you to imagine right now, but you're going to end up a good clay-court player. You have two assets—your forehand and your wheels [speed]. If you hang in there, I promise you one day you'll get there.' Thank you, BPM.

The circuit moved outdoors as the weather picked up

in the Mediterranean, which brought with it a defining tennis experience. Bjorn Borg and Guillermo Vilas, two of the greatest clay-court players in history, were playing the final of Nice, in the south of France. They were ripping forehands and backhands high over the net but never seemed to hit them out, putting so much topspin on the ball that it would always, at the last moment, drop like a stone into play.

I was fascinated, as I reckoned my forehand swing looked like theirs. But I'd been brought up to have a 'shake hands' eastern grip, whereas they had western grips on the forehand, with the palm further behind the racquet, creating the ability to hit heavy topspin. I looked at this closely, and decided it was for me. I'd be switching to a western forehand at the first opportunity.

I tried unsuccessfully to qualify for the Italian Open in Rome. Teaming up with another Aussie, Alvin Gardiner from Queensland, I managed to sneak into the doubles. We had a win or two, then a notable victory in a third-set tiebreak over Guillermo Vilas and Ion Tiriac.

There was a rule that if you couldn't make it to qualifying for the next tournament, the two highest-ranked players left in the previous event would get a 'special exempt' entry into the main draw of the following event, with priority given to singles players. Rome being so competitive, there were no eligible guys left in the singles and only one other left in the doubles. I was the second-best ranked, albeit at around 200.

So I was a special exempt for the next week: the French Open at Roland Garros. What an opportunity!

Mum and Dad, who'd been in Rome, caught the overnight train to Paris in time for the first round. I was drawn against a Swede, Kjell Johansson, and managed to win in five sets. Then I played an Aussie, Kim Warwick, chalking up another win. In the third round I played the great Adriano Panatta, who had won the French the previous year, beating Bjorn Borg along the way.

Before the match the referee, Jacques Dorfmann, came in to the locker room to send us off to a show court. He took one look at me and, gesturing with a hand out, uttered 'Pierre Cadot,' then gestured with the other hand and said 'Adriano Panatta?' He had a point. I lost in straight sets to Adriano, but played well—I took many more games than I did against the dentist who had embarrassed me at the suburban club.

This lifted my ranking inside the top 150, and I knew if I could improve a little and play the right schedule a top 100 ranking was within reach. That magic number ensures direct entry into the four Grand Slams—in essence, a place on the tour.

I made the difficult call to bypass the grass-court season, including qualifying for Wimbledon (a tough miss for any Aussie), and go to the States to play the Pacific Northwest satellite circuit. This offered humble prize money but, more importantly, a swag of ATP points if you did well. I also felt that dropping down a level would help me transition to my new forehand, as a grip change is no small matter.

My first week was in Eugene, Oregon, followed by Tacoma, Washington. I wasn't exactly flying, but the new forehand seemed to have potential. The third week was in Victoria, in British Columbia, a small city on a lovely island only a ferry ride from Vancouver. I was staying with a terrific family whose house overlooked the ocean. I'd watch the seals playing on the rocks every evening.

My forehand suddenly clicked, and I went all the way and won the tournament, beating the American Dick Bohrnstedt in the final. My grip change was locked in—I would never be hitting flatter eastern forehands again.

I ended up coming second in that satellite circuit. It took my ranking close to the precious 100 mark, allowing me direct entry into some ATP (then called Grand Prix) tournaments.

Around this time there was another career-altering moment. Chris Lewis, my best mate, had been to the Harry Hopman International Tennis Academy in Tampa, Florida, a few times and implored me to go there to train. Lewi was intelligent, strong in his views and extremely disciplined. He treated his body like a temple, and went on to have an extraordinary tennis career.

We both loved running as a hobby—not a bad thing for a tennis player—and had been helped by a Melbourne trainer, Barry Riordan, who'd been a professional runner. At the peak of our playing careers we thought nothing of running demanding road races. One in Tampa was 10.5 miles (almost seventeen kilometres) and we finished side by side in sixty-five minutes, averaging under four minutes per kilometre. We both wanted to be the quickest and fittest on the tour. On a normal match day we thought nothing of warming down with an eight-

The western forehand, on my beloved clay.

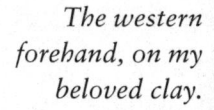

kilometre run. Then along came Bjorn Borg with his Amazonian physique—way too good.

That American summer, Lewi dragged me to Hopman's for the first time, but that was the last time I needed persuading. The visit changed the course of my life.

Mr Hopman had captained Australia to sixteen Davis Cup wins in twenty-one years, and was an Aussie at his core. He was always there before 8.45 in the morning, when courts where assigned, and if you were going to arrive late you didn't bother to arrive at all.

Although there were many hard courts at Hopman's, nearly all of the training was done on Har-Tru, or green clay. Although Har-Tru is a different colour, its playing characteristics are very similar to European clay—slow, perfect bounce, and offering the chance to slide effortlessly. Not only is clay ideal, even imperative, for game development, it is also less demanding physically, perfect for a couple of fanatics like Lewi and me.

At Hopman's, to be assigned Court Thirty-two meant you were a beginner or too modest about your standard. Court Twenty, you're more advanced; court eight, you're pretty good. The pros got the top two or three courts. Court One was a real honour, as there were always tour players there. And the top courts had the best coaches on them—what better incentive than to reward players with a better court and coach? It was an inbuilt player-development system.

The great man had another ingredient in getting a player to raise his level: arriving on the court himself. First, there'd be a rumour that Mr Hopman was going to feed a few balls that afternoon. Then everyone would be on golf-cart alert, as that was his mode of transport, and you'd dive around the court hoping Mr Hopman would be so impressed that he'd park his cart alongside, grab the basket and start feeding balls.

Now, this wasn't just any ball feeding—this was the Hopman way. You hadn't completed your follow-through when the next ball was on you. The intensity had to be seen to be believed. Once, I witnessed a Japanese player being fed an entire basket of more than a hundred balls by Mr Hopman, and he didn't touch a single one. At the end of the basket Mr Hopman congratulated him: 'You've improved—you nearly got a racquet on a ball today.' He was brutal on the basket, but it made you lift your intensity, and it set the tone for the camp.

Lewi and I loved Hopman's so much that we scraped together a deposit and bought a condominium there. That little hacienda was a beauty—only half a kilometre from the assembly point at the camp. Hopman's became my base for life on the circuit, as Tampa is easier to commute to and from tournaments than Melbourne, and there couldn't have been a better environment in which to improve.

That year's US Open, on Har-Tru at Forest Hills in New York, duly arrived. This was the first Grand Slam for which I earned direct entry on my ranking. I went out in the first round, but it was a different story for one of my mates, the American journeyman Mike Fishbach, a real character who was struggling financially like most of us. He travelled the States each summer with a tent, pitching it in tournament grounds. He'd picked up a new invention, the 'spaghetti' racquet—double strung, and with tape and rope wound around each string, resulting in even more topspin than Nadal creates these days—and with it he qualified for the Open.

In the second round he drew Stan Smith, legendary All-American, former world number one, and former Wimbledon and US Open champion. Fish did the unthinkable, beating Smith and riling tennis lawmakers around the world into the bargain.

The week after the US Open there was a Grand Prix tournament at the Racing Club de Paris, where each court is separate, surrounded by flowers and gardens. The cafe is akin to a horticulture exhibit and the dressing rooms are fit for aristocracy. But amid all the glamour the doubles was won by Christophe Roger-Vasselin and Jacques Thamin using spaghetti racquets. These weren't ideal for volleying, so the two Frenchmen sat on the baseline and used the double-strung mega-spin to hit lobs over hapless opponents, a point at a time. It was cruel.

Next was Aix-en-Provence, in the south of France. The hype around spaghetti racquets was reaching fever pitch. We all were starting to experiment with them (paying top dollar and waiting in line to get one strung). I played Gene Mayer, a top-ten player, in the first round. We both used conventional racquets, and I had the unforgettable experience of being 5–3, 40–love down, and 5–4, love–40 on serve, then winning the match. That doesn't happen too often.

The clown prince of tennis, Ilie Nastase, now past his sublime best, decided to use the spaghetti racquet in Aix. He swept to the final, where he met Guillermo Vilas, who'd won the French Open and the recent US Open. Vilas was on a 46-match winning streak but was undone by the newfangled racquet. He retired mid-match in disgust, his streak over.

It wasn't long before the International Tennis Federation rules committee forbade any appendages to strings on racquets. The threat to the essence of the sport was over, but at a price. Vilas deserved but never attained the number-one ranking.

I had a top 100 ranking, a western forehand, a place in Florida—what more was there to life for a young player? Well, my backhand was still letting me down. All the pros knew that was my Achilles heel, and it was preyed on. Gene

Mayer aside, I hadn't beaten a top player—not even close.

This pattern continued on the Aussie summer circuit and into 1978, but suddenly doubles offered hope, courtesy of Peter McNamara. Macca and I had always been mates and had always been different. I was north of the Yarra and he was south; I was dedicated and he wasn't; I didn't mind academia and he...you get the picture.

But that's the point of doubles, in a way—generally, the more disparate the two players, the better. Put a good backhand (Peter) with a good forehand (Paul), a good server (Paul) with a good returner (Peter), a good backhand volley (Peter) with a good forehand volley (Paul), add in varying levels of optimism: you could have a winning combination.

In doubles, diversity is your friend—you can build a package that eliminates weaknesses and plays to your strengths. Ensure the better server serves first in each set, take pressure off the weaker returner by both playing back, and play on sides where both can poach with their pet volley (most players have one).

Picking the right partner for your game is the priority. You don't need to get along that well: three-time Wimbledon winners Bob Hewitt and Frew McMillan are the most popular example, but they may disagree... again. And there's an exception to every rule—the Bryan brothers are mirror images of each other. Which means that one, Mike, is right-handed and the other, Bob, is a leftie, as is the norm for identical twins. Just don't ask me to tell you who's who off the court!

It was certainly worth Macca and me giving it a shot. We had gone our own way for a few years, until we were both twenty-three. I think we both felt that it would be fun to play together, but up to then hadn't had a chance.

At Wimbledon in 1978 Macca mentioned he was looking for a doubles partner, as he and Terry Rocavert were going their separate ways. Macca and I thought we'd try that American summer together. Our first match was at night in Cincinnati against Gene Mayer and Raul Ramirez, top-ten singles and doubles players. It was a terrific match that we ended up losing in a close third set. We seemed to click right away. We decided to play whenever we could.

Macca could see the positive effect Hopman's was having on Lewi and me, and he figured using the camp as a base was a good idea for him too. I think it worked wonders: a sometimes unmotivated but undeniably talented player now had an environment where he was forced to work hard on and off the court, and his body quickly became that of an elite athlete.

I headed back to Australia for the summer tournaments. After having spent years striving to make the top 100, reaching the goal wasn't as fulfilling as I'd hoped. I'd just spent a full year stuck in the nineties. I was an efficient and fit professional, but also getting that sinking feeling that maybe I'd peaked and would be unlikely to make any waves in the sport. I was an upgraded model of the same player—but at least I had the western forehand. Thank goodness I'd taken the plunge on that. Now I just had to figure out everything else.

5.
THE MAN IN THE MIRROR

IN EARLY 1979 I returned to the States, playing indoor events and popping in to Hopman's camp. A mate, Dave 'Space' Carter from Queensland, came over to the hacienda one night for a drink. Space was a thoughtful character who summed up situations well, and a good player too.

Space, Lewi and I were talking about regrets. After the usual focus on women, we switched to tennis. 'Everyone knows I can't hit a topspin backhand,' I said. 'It's driven me crazy over the years, and I regret not having a two-handed backhand.'

'Why don't you switch?' Space asked.

Lewi saw my expression change and, knowing me well, said, 'Don't be crazy; don't even think about it.'

But I did think about it, a lot, on my next trip to Europe and Africa, even though I could never remember hitting one before. I had a recollection of a photo of me as an eight-year-old with two hands on the grip, but it must have been because the racquet was too heavy.

I was left-handed at golf, so the idea seemed plausible.

The only problem was that no one in the history of tennis had changed mid-career from a single- to a double-handed backhand—they'd gone the other way, from double-handed to one-handed, with Peter Sampras the standout, but he did it when he was a teenager.

Europe in the northern spring of 1979 brought the doubles breakthrough that had been beckoning—in Nice, Macca and I won our first ATP doubles title, then backed up the next week in Cairo, where we beat the Amritraj brothers in the final. Next came Johannesburg, where we lost to the great pairing of Hewitt and McMillan in a high-standard match. We were now a team to be reckoned with.

On Anzac Day, during the long flight back to Hopman's from South Africa, I made the decision to leap into the unknown, to leave the tour to switch to a double-handed backhand—and there would be no turning back. I felt I was as fast, and fit, and competitive as I could be. Game-wise, my serve and western forehand were right up there. But my ranking had stalled. The way I was going I would never be better than eightieth in the world, always losing to anyone who could exploit my backhand.

Knocking on the front door to the great man's apartment took gumption. 'Mr Hopman,' I said, 'I'm switching to a two-handed backhand.' I didn't want to ask him if I should switch, as he might have talked me out of it.

He asked my reasons, then said that it would take some doing and offered me all the help he could. He dedicated a coach to me for five hours a day. His name was Pete Stecker, and at the academy he was known as Captain Video. Mr Hopman asked me what sort of double-handed backhand I preferred.

'Just like Borg,' I replied. He was number one, and I'd already copied his forehand—I might as well copy his backhand.

But this was something else entirely, and the reaction of my peers said it all. Lewi, speaking on behalf of almost everyone, repeatedly said, 'You're crazy.' Only Space gave quiet approval.

Once the dust had settled Lewi was supportive. For Macca, though, this 'crazy idea' was understandably annoying and, in his defence, it wasn't ideal timing. We'd just won our first ATP titles, and now I was walking out on him and he'd have to team up with someone else.

I was sent out to court fifteen with Pete Stecker. We'd spend the normal training time, 9 to 11.30 and 1 to 3.30, hitting only double-handed backhands. But for me that was only half a day's work. I'd join in sets late in the day, take a break for tea, then go back at 8.30 p.m. for two hours of returning serve. Ten hours a day (never fewer than eight), day in, day out.

Before long my left hand was covered in blisters, as I'd never used it to hold the racquet, so I started wearing a golf glove to protect it. After a month or so, perhaps a little brain dead, I knew I needed one day off a week.

I was fanatical about the job at hand, fuelled by my pact with myself that under no circumstances would I revert to a one-handed backhand. This was not an

The two-handed backhand.

experiment. If I never got back to the standard I'd been at, or even my past satellite level, so be it.

There were two reasons. I was not daunted by leaving the tour and returning to Monash University, where I could complete a law degree. And I had a strong sense that leaving the door open to reverting my backhand was not the right mindset if I was to pull off such a major switch mid-career, at age twenty-four.

It might take months, even years to get a decent—a topspin—backhand and return to the tour. I was aware of the risks to my tennis career and accepted them.

I wasn't alone in fanatical, sometimes odd, behaviour at Hopman's. My friend Abilio, who was Portuguese, served hundreds of balls to me every night for two hours. It was so good of him. And for some time it was pretty much the only time he set foot on court. Abilio was in his early twenties, a late starter in tennis. He believed his best chance at making it was to hit millions of forehands and backhands, and the best way to do this was on a backboard, a tennis wall. For five hours each day, when the rest of us were on court, Abilio would be hitting by himself on the backboard.

I decided we needed to honour this effort in some way. I went to a shopping mall, had a plaque engraved 'Dedicated to Abilio' and nailed it on the backboard. We all crowded around the next morning to watch his reaction. He noticed something was different right away, as he knew every square centimetre of that wall. Unfortunately, he confused 'dedicated' with 'commemorated'! Otherwise, he seemed amused.

I visited his house once and was surprised to see the huge living room had no furniture. Then I noticed one wall had a mark at the height of a tennis net: Abilio used it as a backboard after hours. Such was his dedication. I'd love to be able to tell you that Abilio discovered a new way to make it in pro tennis, but I'm afraid I can't.

After a few months of rigorous training I figured it was time to give the backhand a try in tournament play. I went to a satellite circuit in the Midwest. I'd played that circuit before, winning in Sioux City and making the final in Kansas City. This time I didn't win a match in four weeks, so I scurried back to Hopman's to regroup.

When I began to feel better again I decided to return to ATP events. At the start of the warm-up for my opening match, in Boston, my first backhand landed on the service line at my end and the second one went over the fence. I was embarrassed: I knew fans had paid money to watch the match. Worse, I had a continual fear of 'air swings', especially on the return of serve.

My mind was a mess. I bombed out match after match. My new backhand was the object of amusement among players and plenty of them came along to have a look, which piled more pressure on.

But that was part of the deal and I just had to tough it out. If you can hit a shot okay in practice, you'll eventually be able to do it in a match, right? That's what I'd always believed.

The events in the States ended with the US Open, now on hard courts, where I drew John Lloyd, a Brit, in the first round. It was torture. Flossy himself had been in a form slump, and I was terrible. He led 5–2 in the first, but I won it 7–5. He led 5–3 in the second, and I came back and won it 7–6. I led 5–3 in the third, but lost it 7–5. I led 5–2 in the fourth, and lost that 7–6.

The fifth set was just as bad. I think he led, then I did, and it went to a tiebreak. Eventually Flossy won 7–6, which is still the record for the most number of games played in a US Open match since the tiebreak was introduced.

Flossy went to the media first, and all the British press could talk about was that his form slump was over. 'If you saw the match, you wouldn't be saying that.

I can't honestly say I played well at all,' he told them.

I was asked to comment. 'He's one hundred per cent right—yes, it was close, but the standard was really bad.'

It was back to Hopman's to do more work on my backhand. Then it was time for the autumn clay-court events in Europe, starting with Palermo, Sicily.

I'd never found anything in my life as confronting as I did that one day in September 1979. A simple brick wall at the back of the tennis club in Palermo stared me in the face. I dared not be seen by anyone; I was too vulnerable to handle that. If everyone has a moment of truth once in their life, this was mine—and I didn't have the tools to deal with it.

Palermo Tennis Club is a typically affluent Italian institution, with beautiful clay courts and a generous clubhouse with cuisine to match. I had an excellent draw, as my initial opponent had withdrawn. I was playing a lucky loser, a player who'd lost in the last round of qualifying and had got in through the back door.

The lucky loser was Ernie Ewert, the player I'd grown up with, the boy I'd beaten in the twelve-and-under Victorian titles. Post-juniors, we'd gone in different directions. Ernie was ranked around three hundred. Sure, he knew my game and he was as good a competitor as you could find, yet rankings don't lie. I had my new backhand but was feeling better about it after five months of pain, and Ernie had his own challenge: he'd just switched to an odd-looking pearl-drop-shaped racquet that no one thought would help much—including Ernie, I suspect.

We went out to Court Two and it didn't take long

for me to start feeling the pressure. I lost the first set and started thinking: Okay, but I can't lose to Ernie. The harder I tried, the worse the backhand became, and I started to freak out. I lost in straight sets.

This wasn't an ordinary loss—this would travel to the other side of the world, to everyone who'd played in our age group. The other losses I'd had since switching backhand were expected, no big deal. But now I'd lost to a guy I'd grown up with in juniors, to someone who—with respect—was now not in my league.

I knew I'd hit rock bottom, and I had trouble talking to the other guys. Onny Parun, a New Zealander who'd been in the top ten, was a straight shooter. 'Paul,' he asked. 'Do you think you would have beaten Ernie with a one-hand backhand?'

'Yes,' I muttered.

'Then why the hell didn't you play with the one-hander? You're a pro, this isn't some charity event, and you've got a duty to give your best—to the event, but more importantly, to yourself. Leave the two-hander on the practice court till it's ready.'

I didn't challenge him—it made sense. He offered to have a hit with me if I wanted, but I said maybe later.

I was in a real state, and I knew if I asked any player they'd tell me I should stop this farce and go figure things out.

So I slunk away to the outer reaches of the club, alone in my depression, racquet and ball in tow, and came face to face with a brick wall. In tennis terms, this is facing the man in the mirror.

I did the unthinkable—I started hitting my old single-handed backhand. With each swing, it was like I was trading my goal for another piece of silver. I felt sick.

I started wandering aimlessly around the club when I ran into a Brazilian, Carlos Kirmayr. Carlos was a very good player, an excellent musician and a super bloke. He went on to coach Gaby Sabatini to Grand Slam glory. When Carlos saw me, he could tell right away something was wrong—I must have looked like I'd seen a ghost.

'What's up?' he said. 'You look awful.'

'Carlos, you know about the Bible—I feel like Judas,' I replied.

'What do you mean?'

'You know my new backhand—well, when I switched I made a pact that I'd never go back to a one-hander, that if it didn't work I'd leave the circuit and go back to university. And today I lost to Ernie Ewert'—Carlos raised his eyebrows—'and I reckon I'm not going to make it back to the tour. All the guys are telling me to take the two-hander and ditch it. So, I just went out to the back of the club and hit some one-handers on a wall. I've broken my pact. I don't know what to do.'

He looked into my eyes, grabbed me by the shoulders and said quietly but firmly, 'You forget what the boys are saying. You stick with the two-hander. I know it'll be incredibly tough, but you must press on.'

'Really, Carlos?'

'Yes. And if you ever feel you're starting to weaken, you call me up right away and I'll give you the strength, I'll be there for you.'

A weight lifted from my shoulders—I felt liberated and reinvigorated. I couldn't thank him enough.

Macca had a burden of his own to carry around this time, a heavy one. He was returning from his dad's funeral in Melbourne. He put in a great effort, making the final of the singles. We reformed our combination, and we managed to win the doubles in Palermo. Here it was: the first positive sign.

The next week we went to Barcelona, and in the first round I drew a powerful American clay-courter, Terry Moor. He was a better player than I was, ranked higher at around sixty, but I beat him in two sets. Then I came up against Jose Luis Clerc, number four in the world, a great clay-courter who was runner-up at the French Open. I took a set off him.

In my wildest dreams, I'd never have taken a set off Clerc on clay with my one-hander. This was a revelation: the moment I knew I was a better player than before.

I was using the wooden Jack Kramer Wilson racquet, the best going round, but the technology was moving fast. A lot of the guys were switching to metal racquets, and there was another change afoot. Prince was making an oversize racquet and Ion Tiriac, followed by Gene Mayer, had switched to it. I liked the stiff graphite Prince, and the clincher was that I knew, no matter how bad a swing I took on return of serve, I couldn't help but make contact with the ball—overcoming my fear of humiliating 'air swings'. It didn't hurt that the oversize racquet made half-volleys and overheads easier.

Now I had some steam up—in January I reached the last sixteen of the Australian Open in singles. In doubles, Macca and I won the New South Wales Open, then went to the Australian Open at Kooyong Tennis Club. We reached the final, where we were up against another two Hopman-trained Aussies, Paul Kronk and Cliff Letcher. Macca and I prevailed, winning our first Grand Slam title in our home town. And at the place where we'd both been club champion, and which had been so instrumental in our formative years that to this day we call it 'headquarters'.

In April 1980, almost a year after the backhand switch, I won my first ATP singles title, symbolically in Tampa, against Stan Smith. After the match, Stan said that his opponent had 'put on a Superman cape and changed his game'.

I was soon ranked in the top thirty. In Palermo I'd faced my moment of truth and had come through.

6.
McENROE AND ME, MACCA AND ME

AT THE French Open in 1980, shortly after I'd won that ATP singles title, I had my first significant encounter with John McEnroe. What a player—and what a character!

He was number two in the world, the heir apparent to Bjorn Borg, and other than our Irish ancestry we didn't have much in common, save for one huge influence on both our careers. John received his tennis education in the early 1970s at Mr Hopman's academy in Port Washington, New York. Apparently John was a handful, but Mr Hopman knew he needed to handle such a prodigious talent with kid gloves—he could spot a potential tennis genius a mile away.

The third-round match with McEnroe on Court Central was the best of five sets. I'd played on many arenas around the world as I made my way up the rankings, but this was the first time I'd been back on that court since my ill-fated qualifying match against the veteran Pancho Gorostiaga. Now I was up against a master. But I was armed with a western forehand and a two-hand topspin backhand, and I was no longer a raw teenager.

John and I were honoured that Mr Hopman was in the stands. He'd flown across from Florida as a tournament guest, and to support John in his quest to win the French Open. I was nervous to start with, and knew I probably needed to win the first set to have any chance. I went all the way to a tiebreak before John prevailed. But I wasn't fazed: I hadn't been blown away.

The second set followed a similar pattern, and my strategy was to hit high bouncing balls to John's backhand, forcing him to back up. The instant he committed to retreat I would storm the net, knowing he was out of position. The second set went to a tiebreak as well, but this time I won it. Game on!

From there it was one of those matches where both players are going hard and hoping to see a moment where the other weakens. But neither of us would blink. The third set went game for game to a tiebreak, and once again I prevailed. Two sets to one up, but I knew it was far from over.

Halfway through the fourth I noticed Mr Hopman re-entering the stadium, which by this time was packed with fourteen thousand spectators sniffing a huge upset. John, facing a shock defeat in front of a crowd baying for blood, seemed to go up another gear. I tried to stay with him, but it was getting tough. John broke me to go to 5–3, and he was serving for the set.

I'll never forget that game, as John had four set points on his serve. On each occasion he approached the net, and somehow I found the inspiration to hit a topspin lob over his head into the far corner. Every lob went to an unplayable spot (Pancho Gorostiaga would have been impressed).

I broke back and we went to 6–6, the fourth consecutive tiebreak. It was a balmy Parisian evening and I was in the zone.

When I was 4–3 up in the tiebreak John hit a huge serve to my forehand. I can see it now: I whistled a winning return past him as he followed his serve in. And then I saw him flinch. It was probably only a blink of an eye, but for me it was the instant when an almost imperceptible change in body language exposes a lot, a player's revelation that he's going to lose.

It took four hours for that moment to arrive. Two points later and the match was mine.

I'll always remember the cathartic feeling as I left Court Central to a standing ovation. It was the antithesis of the feelings of a humiliated teenager seven years earlier: now I knew how to play on clay, and the other players would know it too. The sense of fulfilment was truly special.

Life can bring a quick reality check. I lost to Wojtek Fibak in a tough four-setter in the last sixteen.

The next week I ran into Johnny Mac at Queen's Club and he said, 'Tell me, how can you play like that against me? It's insane!'

He admitted that it had taken him days to recover from the match—which is some concession, coming from John.

I think that match was the defining moment in our friendship. I'd beaten him fair and square, and he admitted it, so there was mutual respect. Over the years I saw him treat far better players than me with disdain, but never me.

In doubles, that European stretch was problematic. Macca and I were zooming up the singles rankings, but we were getting on each other's nerves on court. We played a shocker at the German Open, and at the end of the French (where we lost in the semis) we decided we'd part company for a while. Macca arranged to play Wimbledon with the American Bruce Manson.

Entries were closing soon for the Wimbledon doubles, but I was having second thoughts about the split (a doubles pairing is like a relationship, after all). I decided to go to Macca's hotel room for a heart-to-heart.

'I know we need a break,' I said, 'but it's kind of a pity as Wimbledon's only two weeks away.'

'So?'

'Well, I think we've got a shot at winning it and it might be the best shot we ever get, so why don't we play Wimbledon and split after that?'

'There's no way we'll win it and I don't think much of delaying a split,' Macca said. 'And what about Manson?'

'I'll speak to Bruce.' He'd be cool, as we were mates, and he'd find someone else.

'Okay,' Macca replied, 'let's play.'

He drew our fellow Victorian Warren Maher in the first round of the Wimbledon singles. During the match Macca fell and badly sprained his ankle. Warren was a good player, though not at his opponent's level. Macca tried to soldier on, but went down in the fourth set.

66 | GAME CHANGER

*The moment I beat John McEnroe
at Roland Garros, 1980.*

I knew that put paid to our chances in doubles—we'd be forced to withdraw.

I didn't see Macca for a couple of days after that. He'd gone underground, feeling down about his injury. We were scheduled for our first-round doubles match and, being seeded, we were on a decent court. I asked around the locker room, but nobody had seen or heard from him.

We were being called on court for the match, and there was still no sign of my partner. The referee, Fred Hoyles, came into the locker room and asked if we were ready. 'I'm really sorry, Fred,' I said. 'I'm not sure if you know Macca sprained his ankle really badly in the singles and obviously can't play doubles.' I added sheepishly, 'Has he not withdrawn yet?' in a manner that suggested it was an oversight, though I knew that taking care of formalities wasn't high on Macca's agenda.

'No, he hasn't.'

'Very sorry about that—he must have forgotten,' I said awkwardly.

'It's rather late to organise a lucky loser,' Fred replied, 'but I guess I've got no choice.'

At that, Macca walked through the door, hobbling on one leg and in obvious discomfort.

'There's no way I can play,' Macca said. 'I haven't been able to put any weight on it at all. I need to see the doc.'

My mind started ticking over, and I asked Fred if he'd give us a couple of minutes to consult.

'Have you cleaned out your locker, Macca? Are your racquets and kit still there?'

'All my stuff's still in my locker, but so what?'

'I've got a crazy idea. The ref isn't happy that he has to find a lucky loser pair at such short notice, so how about we go out there and you just stand in the corner?' If a ball comes, give it a whack.'

'You're not serious?'

'Yeah, if you can't reach it, it doesn't matter. I'll take

care of the rest of the court. Just for one set. These guys'—Byron Bertram and Bernie Mitton, an accomplished South African pair—'are good. We'll just play one set and then default. At least we can say we tried.'

I was really taking the mickey, Macca thought. He kept saying, 'No way,' but I wouldn't take no for an answer.

Finally, he relented. 'Okay, one set and that's it.'

'It's a deal,' I said.

Out we went—I served first, as usual, and held. They held serve too. The problem would be holding Macca's serve, as he couldn't serve-volley—not ideal for Wimbledon doubles. I crossed after every serve and knocked off some volleys, and we held. Macca eventually made a couple of stinging returns and we managed to break, hold his serve again, and I served out the set, 6–3 to us.

Macca headed to the net to shake hands and default.

'Hold on,' I said. 'Let's just think about it.'

'No way—I'm really hurting and I can't run for a ball.'

'I can see that. Just keep not running, no problem. Macca, here's the deal: one more set and then we default. One set all, that's it, I promise!'

Wimbledon is the last bastion of best-of-five-sets doubles, so that didn't help my cause. But Macca relented. We played the second set and it went like the first—one break to us, 6–4. I got in first this time: 'Macca, I know you're in bad shape, but two sets to love—I reckon we play one more.'

So we did, and the third set went exactly as the other

two had. (I must confess I enjoyed running here, there and everywhere in a doubles match.) We'd won in straight sets, but we both knew we hadn't done Macca's ankle any favours—he'd be in worse shape come tomorrow.

But tomorrow didn't matter, as it was raining, as it did for two more days after that. Macca had treatment day and night for three days straight, without having to hit a ball. By the end of that his ankle was feeling pretty good.

We moved through the draw to the quarters, when Macca said a strange thing: 'I always figure that once you're in the quarters, you've got a chance to win.' Coming from Macca, who was prone to pessimism, that was extraordinary.

In the quarters we played Brian Gottfried and Raul Ramirez, who'd been Wimbledon doubles champions a couple of years before. This was our first major test, and we passed with flying colours, winning in straight sets. Then we played defending champions John McEnroe and Peter Fleming in the semis. John was nearly always on, but Peter had his good days and his not-so-good ones. We caught him on a dodgy one, and beat them too in straight sets.

A Wimbledon final, especially your first, is an occasion. It was also Macca's birthday. The singles final was Bjorn Borg against McEnroe: a well-chronicled epic in which, after John won the fourth-set tiebreak 20–18, Bjorn prevailed in five sets. We were playing Stan Smith and Bob Lutz, who won the US Open three times but never Wimbledon.

I got a message in my locker left by Bob Brett, a good friend from junior days and a coach on the tour who was to play an important role in my career in the years to come. It was from Mr Hopman, and it said, 'Bob Lutz cocks his wrist on his volleys so he can only volley cross-court.' Little pieces of information can be vital in a tight final; this meant I could cross without fear of him volleying behind me—and it meant a lot to me that Mr Hopman was taking a keen interest in the match.

When the singles went to the fifth set, we were sent out to Court One. Macca was on his game, we went up a break and I served for the set. I dumped my serve for the first time in the tournament, but fortunately we prevailed in the tiebreak.

During the second set we noticed Lady Diana Spencer watching from the stands. This got us excited: if we won, Lady Di would present the trophy. As in the first set, birthday boy dominated the second and we were up two sets to love.

If we won in straight sets, we'd have gone the whole tournament without losing a set, a rare achievement. Macca was still on fire, we were up a break, and then out of nowhere we lost Macca's serve and then the third set in a tiebreak. I thought to myself: Macca's played by himself for nearly three sets and we should have won by now. It's about time I did something.

I needed to step up. So I tried to switch to a mode like that in the first round, and got active and aggressive.

We snatched a break in the middle of the fourth, and we both needed to hold serve once more to win. On

Macca's serve, I remember one point when we had two smashes and didn't middle them, and when the third came I said, 'Mine,' and promptly buried it forty-odd rows up in the stands.

Macca held. It was my turn to serve, to serve out a Wimbledon final. I held to 15—we'd won, and as a team. It meant an awful lot: for both of us, growing up in the 1960s, Wimbledon was the pinnacle of the sport.

Then, out for the presentation came...the Duchess of Kent. There we were holding the trophy—I reckon Macca's perm had put off Lady Di! It was still a very special ceremony, of course.

After that, Macca and I decided not to split up.

Later that year we made our Davis Cup debuts. Our opponents were Italy, at the Foro Italico in Rome, an amphitheatre surrounded by Roman statues. It was an imposing venue, and Italy had a strong team, headed by Adriano Panatta. Our captain was the wily and experienced Neale Fraser, who'd taken the baton from Mr Hopman. Frase assembled us at the Palermo tour event the week before. There I got through to the semis to play Panatta—which shows how much things had changed in the twelve months since I lost to Ernie in the first round.

Frase didn't want me to show all my cards in the match. So I didn't play my traditional game of net-rushing off heavy forehands, but still managed to win a close three-setter. Adriano was not the player he used to be. In the final I played Guillermo Vilas, who was way too strong.

Our Davis Cup team in Rome was Macca, Phil Dent, Rod Frawley and me, with John Alexander there as a mentor. JA was a great Davis Cup player in a period when the boys played for little money. He had a wonderful sense of humour and his advice was always genuine. I wasn't surprised when in 2010 he reclaimed John Howard's federal seat of Bennelong for the Liberal Party.

I drew Panatta in the opening match, but this was a different player. Clearly his defeat a week earlier had stung him into action. His experience in Davis Cup tilted the match his way and he beat me in four sets.

Macca played Corrado Barazzutti in the second singles. Corrado was like a brick wall. He was also fit and a shrewd tactician. Macca started getting on top, and when Macca and Frase rightly took exception to a line call the crowd started throwing coins onto Campo Centrale. It all got a bit messy, and JA was hit above the eye by one. But peace was restored, and Macca went on to win in four.

The doubles would be pivotal. As reigning Wimbledon champions, Macca and I went in favourites against Panatta and Paolo Bertolucci. Paolo was one of the only guys on the tour who I'd witnessed in the early days have a splash of red wine for lunch, even on the day of a match. (By the way, the lines people sometimes did as well.) Paolo might've been a touch unfit, but he could play—he had power and flair, and was the perfect foil for Adriano. They'd beaten Newcombe and Roche on that same court, in the same situation, four years earlier.

It was a classic doubles encounter, and they'd done their homework on me. When I crossed on Macca's serve, Paolo would invariably sideline me. We made it to the fifth, and you'd expect the younger guys with the Wimbledon title to prevail. We broke twice, but I was broken twice too. They were up 8–7 and, on the change of ends, I said to Frase, 'Don't worry—I can't lose my serve three times in a set.'

Wrong. I got broken again, and the match was lost.

That swung the tie in Italy's favour, and in front of rowdy support the next day Adriano rode the emotion to beat Macca, who tried valiantly, in four. In a searching Davis Cup debut we'd come up short.

I'd been told it was the ultimate test, and now I'd experienced it. Never again would I take anything for granted in Davis Cup competition.

7.
LONDON LIFE

I WAS starting to pick up decent prize money, and by this stage I had endorsements from Prince for racquets, Ellesse for clothing and Nike for shoes. Now that I could save money I was keen to get a European base, as most of my tennis was there, given my preference for clay. London was the natural choice and the Barons Court area appealed. It was next to Queen's Club, site of the Wimbledon lead-in tournament, and possessing the gamut of grass, hard, clay and, sensibly given the climate, indoor courts.

I found a nice two-bedroom apartment in Queen's Club Gardens overlooking the courts. I was being managed by Mark McCormack's International Management Group and the London office crew were very helpful. IMG had seen a lot of athletes over the years and my astute advisor, Neil Grainger, warned me not to overstretch on the purchase, but winning the Stockholm doubles with Switzerland's Heinz Gunthardt got me over the line. Furnishing the apartment was more hit and miss, and I can remember stopping my cab on the way to Heathrow to order carpet in under fifteen minutes.

Sebastian Coe lived down the street. Often we'd bump into each other and stop for a chat. One day he asked me if I wanted to join him for a run. I was fit, but not like that—thank goodness it didn't pan out!

I returned home for the summer. First up, Macca and I defended our New South Wales doubles title. At the Australian Open I got to the quarter-finals of the singles, where I lost to the American Brian Teacher 7–6 in the fourth set. Macca got edged out by him in the semis with a similar score.

In doubles we were stopped in the final by another Aussie pair, Mark Edmondson and Kim Warwick from New South Wales. Being Sydney–Melbourne rivals, we weren't thrilled with the loss. But they were excellent players and each went on to win the Open doubles three times.

Our doubles successes had earned us a spot in the four-team Masters Tournament of the tour in early 1981. The Masters was notable for being played at Madison Square Garden in New York City. It was early January and bitterly cold outside, but what an honour it was to play in one of the most famous sporting arenas in the world, where so many greats have performed: Michael Jordan, Wayne Gretzky, Muhammad Ali...We beat Smith and Lutz, but lost in the final to McEnroe and Fleming.

It was back to London for the newly created Braniff World Doubles Championships, at Earls Court arena. Macca and I won through to the final, where we were up against Hank Pfister and Victor Amaya from the

United States. We were down two sets to one, and I said to Macca, 'About time we won a five-set doubles.'

Our Wimbledon win meant we had a following in England. Once the match started turning our way, it felt like a home crowd for us, and the momentum carried us through to win the fifth. The presentation was made by the wife of Lamar Hunt, the Texan oil billionaire who had bankrolled the championship. I politely kissed her after receiving our trophy. I heard some murmurs in the crowd—I suppose you can't do that in London. Macca and I each received our biggest cheques yet, a trophy and a set of Queen Anne Waterford crystal glasses, which we still use on special occasions.

We returned to Australia to prepare for Davis Cup, but I had a tough period with a back problem. I had started burning the candle at both ends, out clubbing a fair bit, and perhaps I was paying the price. Recurring back spasms stalled my momentum, especially in singles.

Not so for Macca. He was flying, and after beating Jimmy Connors in the final of the German Open he broke into the top ten in singles. We reached the doubles final too—a fine week all round.

By the time Wimbledon came around, my doubles results over the previous year had shot my individual doubles world ranking to number one. That was a milestone, and nice for the CV to have been number one in the world at something.

We lost in the semis to Smith and Lutz in five sets after I messed up a backhand overhead that would have won us the match. I tried to bounce it over the fence but it hit the tape…I'm not sure whether Macca has ever forgiven me.

Just after Wimbledon came the Davis Cup quarter-final in Malmo, Sweden. It didn't start well: I arrived at Heathrow and realised I'd forgotten my racquets! Sweden's team was blooding a young teenager in singles, Mats Wilander. I played him in the fourth match, and it took all of my clay-court knowhow to break him down. He was like a backboard. I took the match in four sets, so we were into the semis, but not a year later Wilander would win the French Open.

I'd started seeing an excellent British osteopath, Terry Moule. He was a wizard with his hands, and whenever I had a back spasm he ensured my recovery time was days rather than weeks. He had a lovely wife, Patsy, and four gorgeous kids. They were living in a huge mansion adjacent to the parklands of the magnificent abbey in St Albans, where I was warmly welcomed.

I brought Terry and Patsy out for the Davis Cup semi in Perth, where we went down to a McEnroe-led United States. We moved on to Melbourne, and I was able to return their hospitality and give them a taste of the Australian bush. They stayed at Dad's old family home in Tarnagulla—we had a memorable time exploring the hills and caves in the surrounding countryside.

At the Australian Open I couldn't play singles due to my back. We lost the quarter-final of the doubles to Pfister and John Sadri.

At the start of 1982 I'd had more than two years with the double-handed backhand, and with Terry on board I was getting in shape. As always, I looked forward to the

European clay-court season leading into Roland Garros, particularly Monaco. The Monte Carlo Country Club is set on a hill with views across the Cote d'Azur. I think it's the most picturesque setting for tennis in the world, with the brilliant blue Mediterranean as the backdrop to the rich red clay arena. Having lunch on the terrace at the club, which overlooks Centre Court and the sea below, is one of life's joys for a tennis connoisseur.

It's also one of the best stops on the tour, a town you can have a lot of fun in, and the casino party for the players is a highlight. That year, there was a lucky-dip draw for an expensive watch, and Ilie Nastase was asked to do the draw. He picked out a ticket and, seeming not even to glance at it, named his mate Vitas Gerulaitis the winner. That was Nastase for you!

In that week there are always lots of parties, with many attractive single women. It's a bit of a scene, and this year one party stood out. It was at the Rizzoli mansion, owned by the Milan publishing family, on a cliff top at Cap Ferrat. Macca and I were in the final of the doubles the next day, and he and his wife passed on the party. It was shaping to be a big night, and fortunately our opponents, the Texan Steve 'the Bull' Denton and South Africa's Kevin Curren, were up for it too. I remember being dropped off in the early hours by a budding race-car driver, who did donuts outside my hotel.

The next day three of the four finalists were sluggish. Macca was all systems go and I was reasonable, but poor Curren and Denton were out of sorts. The Bull could party with the best of them, but it probably wasn't the norm for Kevin. We were up 6–0, 3–0 in half an hour, and ended up winning 6–0, 6–3.

Winners have their names engraved on a marble plaque at the club. The singles winners get individual plaques, and the years 1911–14 bear the name Anthony Wilding of New Zealand. He was largely responsible for the Australasian Championships being formed. In 1905 Australia and New Zealand got together to nominate a team to compete in the Davis Cup. We had the great Sir Norman Brookes (known for taking a nip of brandy before a fifth set, a custom he'd have picked up at his club, Royal South Yarra), while New Zealand had Wilding. To celebrate this accord the two tennis associations decided to hold a joint tournament, the first Australasian Championships and the forerunner to the Australian Open.

It was a smart move: Australasia won the Davis Cup for the first time in 1907, over the British Isles at the All England Club in Wimbledon, with Brookes and Wilding playing both singles and doubles. However, tragedy struck. The plaque at the Monte Carlo Country Club for 1915 states: 'Anthony Wilding, killed in action.' The great Kiwi would never be forgotten in a place where his skills had been admired.

It was soon time to shift to grass and return to Wimbledon. I was playing well and beat Kevin Curren in five sets in the third round of the singles, before Jimmy Connors gave me a lesson on Court One. This championship was very wet, even by Wimbledon standards. It was so inclement that the committee decided to reduce the men's doubles to the best of three sets.

Macca and I got through to the quarters, where we met Edmondson (who made the semis of the singles that year) and Warwick. As the pair had got the better of us in the final of the Australian Open, Macca and I were feeling protective of our Wimbledon record, which made it something of a grudge match.

I got overzealous in the warm-up on my side with Edo—it was tense out there. 'I'm too fired up,' I said to Macca. 'I need to settle down!' But I think saying it helped me, as we played a good match and won in straight sets.

In the semis we faced the American duo of Sherwood Stewart and Ferdi Taygan. We fancied our chances and were happy that the committee restored the format to the best of five sets. We were going well, at a set all and up a service break in the third, when I noticed my racquet had a string that was about to break.

I was fussy about my racquets and had decided this was my favourite. And I didn't want to break a string in the middle of the set, as I felt I would need this racquet when it was likely to be my chance to serve for the set in a few games. So I changed racquets, and it went with serve until 5–4, with my serve to come. My plan had worked—I happily switched back to my favourite racquet.

You can guess what happened next. I got broken. I was so scared of breaking the string that I backed off my first serve—that weapon was rendered impotent; I'd been too smart by half. When it went to the tiebreak and we lost it, I was filthy.

Luckily, it was deemed too dark to play another full set, so the match was suspended with us down two sets to one.

I went back to my flat and saw Lewi, who was staying there. I was in a foul mood: Macca and I should've been in a winning position, perhaps even have won already. Lewi had befriended a well-known actress, Kelly LeBrock, who went on to star in the movie *Woman in Red*. She'd generously offered to pop by and cook dinner for the boys, and it was an excellent pasta dish. But I was still not a happy chappy.

Lewi and Kelly were heading off to meet some of her friends at Tramps, a cool nightclub in the West End, and Kelly asked if I wanted to join them.

'Thanks,' I said, 'but I can't. Tomorrow I've got the semis to finish and, if we win, the final after that.'

'You can't just stay here and go to bed—you're way too aggro to sleep well.'

Kelly was right—I needed to chill out for a while and get that stupid now-ex-favourite racquet out of my head. I knew it wasn't textbook preparation, but my hunch was that my state of mind was more important than anything else and I needed a lift. So we headed off to Tramps around 11 p.m. and after that time slipped away from me a bit.

Macca and I needed to be on court to finish the match at noon. When I joined him for our warm-up he wasn't speaking to me. I asked him what was up.

'I've had two people tell me they saw you at Tramps at 3 a.m.'

Macca had gone home and had an early night. I tried

to explain that Lewi and Kelly had convinced me to join them in an attempt to help my bad mood.

'Yeah, sure, good one,' Macca said, reflecting the side of his personality that didn't like missing out on a party. Clearly there'd be no more conversation.

Out we went for the fourth set, with Macca serving the first game. We lost it to love. He'd put in a shocker, but I wasn't about to say anything. We went to 3–1 down with Macca to serve again. I knew if we lost this game we were finished—we couldn't come back from two breaks down. Macca was still in a foul mood, and went down 15–40 on his serve.

Ferdi got a lob over my head and I just got it back to Sherwood, who had an easy put-away smash. Macca was a statue in the middle of the court, a bear with a sore head. Sherwood smashed it at him, thinking that he would move. But he didn't, and the overhead hit the throat of Macca's Prince Woodie racquet, freakishly going back over Sherwood for a winner.

Ridiculously lucky. So now it was 30–40, and I knew how big this point was. I decided to cross, wherever Macca served, and he went to Sherwood's forehand. Sherwood was a big Texan with an even bigger game, and his forehand was huge yet risky. I crossed, leaving him the line, and he smashed the return down there but the ball hit the tape. It popped up and went…agonising wait…back onto his side. Fate. Deuce.

We scrambled out of that game and were 2–3, not 1–4 and cactus. It went to 30–40 on Ferdi's serve when he faced me, a huge moment. This was the one chance to right the mess on our side. I was in the dogbox: Macca was still not talking to me. Well, I took the chance and smoked a return past Sherwood for a winner—break back. It went with serve to the tiebreak, which we won. The match had turned, they were shattered and the fifth set was a one-sided 6–2 in our favour.

Tramps was now a distant memory. We were into the Wimbledon final, to meet McEnroe and Fleming, right after John completed the singles final against Jimmy Connors.

Connors by now was well over thirty and the underdog, but he produced something special that afternoon and beat McEnroe in four sets. Now it was Johnny Mac's turn to be in a foul mood. He was saying the doubles final had better be the best of three sets to guarantee it would finish that day, as come what may he was taking the Concorde back to New York in the morning. (I was lucky enough to experience that journey once myself: seeing the curvature of the Earth from seventy thousand feet was awe-inspiring. But in this case John just wanted to get home pronto.)

The committee was meeting to discuss the matter and summoned us to canvass our view. Macca nominated me as our spokesperson. In I went to the Wimbledon Committee room and stated our case: 'This is not any ordinary final, it's the Wimbledon final, and as is tradition it ought to be the best of five sets. Secondly, surely the committee will not bow to the sentiment of John McEnroe?'

Macca asked me how it went. 'No problem,' I said. 'There's no way they'll cave in to McEnroe.'

*The Maccas' second Wimbledon win, 1982.
(My turn to have a dodgy haircut!)*

We waited in the locker room until a committee man came in and said, 'Mr McNamee, the committee would like you to know that was one of the finest and most sincere speeches given to the committee, but the final shall be best of three sets.' I'd been told where to go in a most polite British way.

In fairness, there was probably only enough light for a three-set match, and the prospect of bringing everyone back on the Monday to finish one match did not appeal. We went out to play and, to be honest, it was ordinary tennis. Fleming was struggling, as were Macca and I, and McEnroe was inconsolable after his loss to Connors.

Macca and I got to 6–3, 5–3 and match point on their serve. Then came an incredible point where, at one stage, I fell over, Fleming smashed it straight at me, and I played the ball back while on the ground, then jumped up and ripped a backhand. The point kept going and going, and finally Macca ripped a forehand winner between them and we'd won the match—our second Wimbledon title.

Recently the BBC compiled a video of the top twenty points played at Wimbledon and called for the British public to vote for the top three. I was gobsmacked to find that our 1982 doubles final match point was number one, voted the greatest point in the history of Wimbledon. And in what was actually an average match—but no one remembers that!

8.
MATCH POINT

WE WERE buzzing after winning another Wimbledon title, but we needed urgently to get to Brisbane for a Davis Cup match against Chile. By the time we got our act together it was late. We figured we had a shot at getting out that night, so we called ahead en route to Heathrow and explained our predicament. No promises were made, but we were encouraged to come.

A message was sent to the pilot, who held the Qantas flight for us. The captain told the passengers that the delay was due to our Wimbledon win. No one seemed upset—we even got a round of applause when we boarded. (Well, Qantas is the Australian airline.) It was a special feeling.

We took care of the Chileans in Brisbane, then headed back to Hopman's to get ready for summer in the States.

By this stage Lewi, Macca and I were all driving Mercedes Sports. I wanted to take mine home to Australia at some stage, so it had a right-hand drive. This was turning a few heads around the backblocks of Largo, Florida. I was even advised by a well-meaning fellow motorist to return the car to get the steering wheel put in the correct position.

On one occasion Lewi was in the front passenger seat and he suddenly stood up—the car was a convertible—turned around and waved to the people in the vehicle behind. They freaked out, assuming Lewi was in the driver's seat and the car was no longer being steered.

It's not that funny, but we thought it was hilarious at the time. We were young and single, life was an adventure, and I suppose we had a bit too much money for our own good.

By this stage World Championship Tennis, funded by Lamar Hunt, had effectively become a breakaway tour. There were about a dozen events on the WCT calendar, with prize money rivalling the big tournaments on the ATP (still known as Grand Prix) tour. Almost all players were criss-crossing between the two tours, and there were two ranking systems running concurrently.

Macca and I played in Asia in the autumn. There was a Super Series (the highest-level Grand Prix event) in Sydney, followed by one in Tokyo, where I lost early to Robert Van't Hof in singles, badly damaging my ankle mid-match. Macca had a terrific win over Vitas Gerulaitis in the semis, before going down to McEnroe in the final.

The next week there was a WCT event in Baltimore, Maryland. The indoor WCT tournaments had big prize money and small draws. Out came the draw and who should I be playing? Peter McNamara. I thought, It's not a big deal if I lose to Macca—he was now firmly ensconced in the top ten—and he knows I'm injured, so he'll take the foot off the pedal if needed. I decided to ignore the doctor's advice about my dodgy ankle and play.

Facing your doubles partner and long-time buddy is never easy—a lot of feelings are stirred up. I was just hoping I could finish the match and not be humiliated. The first set did not go according to plan: I hardly won a point, and 6–0 to Macca wasn't pleasant. He cruised to 3–0 in the second set, and as we changed ends I thought about asking him to give me a game. He could see I was hobbling, right? Only pride stopped me from asking him to throw me a bone.

I finally managed to hold my serve in the next game—at least the score would not be the dreaded double bagel. Out of the blue Macca served two double faults and lost his serve. I knew what that meant. He was getting tight. Suddenly there was a glimmer of hope. My ankle was bad, heavily taped, but I was otherwise feeling loose and hitting the ball freely. I held again in the next game and noticed Macca was agitated. He knew he should be steamrolling me, heading for the finish line.

There's an old sporting adage: beware the injured player. The uninjured player, who everyone assumes will win, feels more pressure when the result appears to be a foregone conclusion. Conversely, the injured player has nothing to lose and hits the ball without inhibition.

Macca played another bad service game. Then I held and it was a set each. Macca was gone after that—he couldn't get it back, no matter how hard he tried, and I won the third set comfortably. Macca was beside himself. I've never seen him so filthy, and he left town that day.

I played John Sadri, a big-serving American, the following day and I figured I'd better win or Macca was going to be even more aggro for me stuffing up his week. The medical team were doing a terrific job on my ankle, getting the taping down pat. I took the match in three sets. Phew.

The semi was against Kevin Curren, never an easy assignment, but now I was the Macca on a roll and again I won in three. I was into the final. This would be different, as I was playing world number three Guillermo Vilas over the longer journey, the best of five sets.

This would be a tall order even if I was totally fit. Nevertheless, I was hitting the ball better than ever. The match was live on ESPN, and I was interviewed beforehand about my chances. 'There's only one certainty,' I said. 'If it goes to five sets, Vilas will win.' That wasn't a bold prediction, as he was one of the fittest and strongest men in tennis, second only to Borg, and I was carrying an injury.

Away we went, and the one advantage I had from the get-go was my stronger serve. We split the first two sets, and Guillermo won the third. Then, surprising myself, I came back strongly and won the fourth, evening the ledger. We got to 3–3 in the fifth, break point on Vilas's serve. He came in to my backhand, and I smashed a two-handed winner cross-court (with topspin!) right on to the line. As we changed ends I saw Ion Tiriac, Vilas's coach, shaking his head in exasperation.

My job now was to hold serve two more times and, for the first time all week, I was feeling the pressure. In the WCT set-up the runner-up would receive $32,000, but the winner stood to get a whopping $100,000, the biggest cheque on either tour aside from the majors. Somehow, and I'm honestly not sure how, I completed the task—a more improbable victory I could not have imagined.

According to his wife at the time, Macca was watching the match in Florida and throwing things at the TV. To this day, the ultimate swear word in Macca's presence is 'Baltimore'.

On a high, I headed back to Europe for a couple more tournaments. I caught up with my younger brother at the London flat. Although he'd graduated as a doctor, Brian wasn't enamoured with the prospect of life as a general practitioner and years of specialist study were not for him. He'd been giving tennis a go, battling away for a year on the satellite circuits. He had some decent wins in qualifying, and we'd played a couple of doubles tournaments together, getting to match point against Curren and Denton when they were reigning US Open champions.

Brian had a modest ATP doubles ranking, yet the prospects were grim. Married to Virginia—whom he'd met at medical school—he needed to make ends meet, but was close to broke. Trying to make it in tennis is brutal, and his game fell short. I never dared tell him— far better to be supportive and let him figure it out. Now he had made a decision: he was done.

Quitting is emotional for any athlete at any level, so I was feeling raw about it too. I gently protested but no, he was firm. He grabbed a nail and hammered it into the wall of my flat, then ceremonially hung up his racquet. I gulped.

Not long after, a pharmaceutical company in Cologne was seeking someone to handle its English-speaking markets. Brian took to business like a duck to water, and after a couple of years he set up an office in Melbourne. His career progressed with various companies before he became CEO of Commonwealth Serum Laboratories, which was about to become a public company.

CSL floated with a share price of $2.40 and Brian helped build it into one of the biggest pharmaceutical companies in the world. Recently he was named the Ernst & Young Entrepreneur of the Year and Chartered Accountants Australian Business Leader of the Year. This year he retired from CSL with the share price (factoring in a one-time three-way split) sitting over $150. And he's still got a great forehand volley.

I went in to the Australian Open with my confidence high and in fine form. In an early round I beat Lewi—it was one of only two occasions when we met in a tournament (he'd won the other time). I got through to the quarters, where I was to play a seventeen-year-old, Pat Cash.

Pat had been our orange boy at the Davis Cup in Perth, and I'd spent a fair bit of time hitting with him there. I noticed Macca, our number-one player, wasn't hitting with him at all. I asked Frase why and he explained, 'Macca played a set with Pat and only just won the tiebreak, then told me to get that kid away from him as it wasn't doing his confidence any good.'

So Pat was dangerous, and this was grass—history would show he wasn't too bad a player on that surface. I was relieved to beat him in a tough four-setter. I figured it might be the last time I would (and this almost turned out to be true—but there was always clay).

My opponent in the semi-final was Johan Kriek from South Africa. Johan was very talented, had won the Australian Open the previous year and was a top-ten player. I was the underdog and putting a lot of effort into my preparation. Stan Nicholes, a Melbourne sporting legend and our Davis Cup trainer, helped me get my body in shape. He was an outstanding trainer, having worked with Frank Sedgman, Margaret Court and many Olympic gold medallists. Stan never missed a trick—except the day he worked on Tony Roche's right arm, forgetting that he was a leftie, and Rochie and the boys kept mum!

I started out all right against Kriek but the match soon became a dogfight. The first two sets went to a tiebreak and I lost them both. I decided to change my return-of-serve position. The courts had been slow all tournament due to rain, so I'd had plenty of time to hit my returns with full grips and full swings. But by the semis the courts were quicker, and I felt rushed.

I reasoned that I'd stand in and chip the return off his first serve, to cut down on the error count. This brought swift success, and before long I'd won the third set, then the fourth. Now I was feeling good. I made a crucial break of serve in the middle of the fifth set, and went to a 5–3 lead with Kriek to serve. It got to 30–40 and match point. A place in the final of the Australian Open beckoned.

A match point is a moment suspended in time, because the occasion will never be repeated. You may be only half watching a contest, and there can be a lot of noise and distraction, but on match point you can hear a pin drop, that eerie silence paying homage to the gravity of the moment.

Countless match points are won and lost by luck or lack of it, but when it's a net cord on match point there's a rare poignancy. It can even make or break a career—and it happened to me at that very moment.

Kriek stayed back on his serve and we got into a baseline exchange. Both of us seemed afraid of making a mistake. I thought about going to the net a couple of times, and could have, but I held back. Finally, Johan made a move towards the net. I could see daylight up the line and ripped my forehand for the target. It was going for a winner when suddenly the ball caught the net cord and jumped straight up.

This suspended moment, when the ball is airborne above the net and only fate will determine its outcome, feels timeless. There's no way of knowing whether it will fall just over, winning the point and match, or fall agonisingly shy onto the same side of the court.

The ball hovered and, to my horror, fell back on my side of the net. Kriek went on to hold his serve, but at least I was still to serve for the match.

I remember every point of that game, especially the forehand return winner he hooked past me at 15–30, which I dared him to do again at 30–40—and he obliged. I had break point again in the next game but didn't break, and then he broke me for 7–5. My dream had been snatched away after I'd had match point.

In the final the next day Kriek played Steve Denton, but the Bull was sick. Kriek won 6–2, 6–2, 6–2. That I had beaten Denton before is also of little consequence—other than my forever suspecting that I might well have gone on to win the Open.

Outside the top ten, you often only get one chance for glory. The last Australian man to win our Open did it way back in 1976: that was Mark Edmondson. I was never in such a position again in singles at a Grand Slam—frankly, I wasn't good enough.

If I took one positive thing away from that 1982 Open experience, it was that it's imperative to take the initiative on a big point, especially match point: to be bold. Who knows what direction my life would have taken if I'd been a Grand Slam singles winner?

Perhaps not so different. In sport the knocks are as important as the wins, possibly more so, in formulating who you are. I've never been one for regrets. Ups and downs were part of the tapestry of my playing career, and that particular heartbreak on match point has helped me whenever I've coached players, or when I've felt I've caught the rub of the green in my post-tennis career.

I know the vagaries that come up in a match. And I'm in illustrious company—I'm one of many players who had something big in their grasp and saw it snatched away. That's the nature of sport, and its enduring attraction.

9.
JUMPING JACK

OUR FIRST Davis Cup tie in 1983 was in Adelaide against Great Britain. They had a good all-round team, with Buster Mottram (a top-twenty player) and John Lloyd (a former Australian Open runner-up) in singles, and the highly proficient doubles pair of Andrew Jarrett (these days the referee at Wimbledon) and Jonathan Smith.

Macca was unavailable for the tie; Edo was starting to struggle in singles; John Fitzgerald was coming into his own; and Pat Cash had just won his first tour title, the Victorian Open on grass at Kooyong. Taking Mr Hopman's lead of blooding future champions, Frase threw Cashy into the singles alongside me, while Edo and I were selected in doubles.

My opening match with Buster shaped as being difficult, as he was a renowned Davis Cup player, having once led his team to the final. Yet I jumped quickly out of the blocks, he never seemed to find his rhythm, and I won easily in three straight sets. Cashy's encounter with Lloyd was a ripper, with our youngster responding to the challenge. He notched a notable four-set victory in his cup debut. This put the British on the back foot for the doubles, and Edo and I, playing together for the first time, teamed up well and won in four sets.

Shortly after that tie Macca and I caught up in Memphis, where we won the US indoor doubles title against the Gullikson twins, Tim and Tom. Macca headed to Europe, where he made the final of a Super Series in Brussels. His opponent was Ivan Lendl. Macca had finished the year in the top ten in singles and doubles for the second time in a row, confounding observers who'd predicted he'd never make it, as he hadn't even been a top junior in Victoria. It was some career he was setting up for himself—and it wasn't doing me any harm either. By all accounts, that final in Brussels was exceptional tennis, with Macca winning 7–6 in the third set. When the rankings came out the next day he was number seven in the world.

Macca was superbly fit, at the top of his game, and even he must have been starting to believe that a Grand Slam singles victory might be attainable. But the next week, in Rotterdam, he twisted his leg in the joins of the indoor carpet during a first-round match, doing substantial damage to his knee. Conjecture over whether it was the court or his shoes that had failed him muddied any claim, and he ended up with no compensation.

This took a heavy toll on Macca professionally and personally, and understandably he lost his way a bit. It would be two years before he made it back to the tour, and he was never the same player again.

With Macca sidelined, a sober reminder to us all of

the fickleness of international sport, I pressed on. But my doubles tennis had changed irrevocably. We'd been paired up for not even four years, yet already had three Grand Slams and fourteen titles. I missed playing with my mate.

The WCT tournaments were in full swing. In Houston, on clay, I beat Curren and Denton in singles, making the final, where I lost to Lendl—no shame in that. It had been an excellent twelve months, raising my combined ATP and WCT singles ranking to fifteen in the world.

For Wimbledon 1983 I teamed with Brian Gottfried of the United States. He'd been a top-ten singles and doubles player, and in our first outing we won my local event, Queen's Club, beating Curren and Denton in the final. In the weeks leading up to Wimbledon there was a familiar figure out on the practice courts at Queen's Club from 7 a.m. every day: Lewi.

Gottfried and I were bullish about our chances at Wimbledon, and cruised through to the quarters. Our opponents were two relative unknowns at the time, the Swedes Anders Jarryd and Hans Simmonsson. We figured grass would not be their best surface. We duly led the match two sets to love, but the wheels started to fall off and we ended up losing in five.

I had lost in the third round of the singles, but Lewi beat the Bull in five in the first round, then went all the way to the quarters. He was up against the American Mel Purcell, who in the previous round had beaten Gottfried. Lewi and Mel were both quick, but Lewi always seemed to have the edge and won in four sets.

In the semis Lewi played Kevin Curren, who'd beaten Tim Mayotte in five sets in the quarters. Curren had a wicked serve and flashing ground shots, but was prone to streaky play. You needed to sit out his good stuff and, over five sets, there'd be a window.

That semi-final was a cracker, with Lewi scraping and scurrying his way around the court. As fearsome as Curren's rapier shots were, Lewi would run them down. It was a competitive and entertaining match, and the longer it went the more it suited Lewi's athletic prowess. By the end of the fifth my mate was into the Wimbledon final, the first Kiwi to do so since Anthony Wilding.

Waiting there was John McEnroe, still smarting from his loss to Connors the year before. There would be no upset this time. But Chris Lewis was still a Wimbledon finalist, a testament to commitment and athleticism and the Hopman way. We were all very proud of him.

My next assignment was the Davis Cup tie against Romania. Our preference was to play on grass, and the best option was at Milton in Brisbane. Romania were a one-man band, led by the ageing but wily Ilie Nastase. We were too strong and ran out the tie comfortably, with Edo again playing the doubles with me in Macca's absence.

From Brisbane it was straight to the States for the summer. Lewi and I decided to rent an apartment in New York City, a brownstone on the Upper East Side between Park and Madison. It was in a great spot, near the reservoir in Central Park, perfectly situated for us to get our running fix. Lewi and I lapped up life in New York, not least because an antipodean friend of many Aussie tennis players, Gene Barakat, was the number two at the Ford modelling agency. Gene went out of his way to introduce Lewi and me to the Ford stars, and we didn't raise any objections.

We enjoyed NYC so much that we thought we'd try to buy an apartment. One real-estate agent was a classic. We asked her to show us places on the Upper East Side. She was sometimes a little reluctant, depending on the address, but we insisted. Each building, she told us, had a body corporate with the right to approve purchasers. And being male and single and jocks, we were far from ideal. We wanted to inspect a particular apartment on Fifth Avenue. 'Forget about it,' she said. 'They won't accept new money.' Wow. So we left New York after the Open with great memories, but without an address.

We were now in the semis of Davis Cup, to be held at White City, Sydney, against a formidable French team that included Yannick Noah and Henri Leconte. Fitzy went down to Yannick on the first day, but Cashy's win over Leconte sent us into the doubles at level pegging.

Edo and I were Frase's choice for doubles. Edo always found an extra yard in pace when playing for his country. We played a torrid first set against Noah and Leconte, which we finally won 14–12. I think that dented their spirit, and we ran the match out in three straight sets.

That night *Australia II*, skippered by John Bertrand, was on the water at Newport, Rhode Island, in the deciding race for the America's Cup. There was hardly an Aussie not glued to the TV. It was on at an ungodly hour, especially for us Davis Cup players preparing to do battle, but we had to watch. I was speaking to my brother, Brian, who was living in Germany, so he could listen over the phone to the TV coverage. That victory is arguably the greatest moment in Australian sports history, but for me Rod Laver's Grand Slam as a pro in 1969 and Cadel Evans' Tour de France win in 2011 edge it out.

It didn't matter that we were sleep deprived—I've never seen a tide of euphoria sweep across Australia like that. It was surreal, magical and blatantly patriotic. Fitzy was up against Leconte and went in as the slight underdog. It was a fabulous contest, enlivened by a sea of boxing-kangaroo flags waving in the crowd. I think it's fair to say that Leconte would have beaten Fitzy on most occasions, but that day Fitzy rode the euphoria and toughed him out.

We'd made it to the final of the Davis Cup, to be played against Sweden at Kooyong on Boxing (Kangaroo) Day. Frase didn't want to leave anything to chance, and he suggested to Edo and me that we play the Australian Open together at Kooyong beforehand.

The 1983 Australian Open was important to Edo, as he was high up in the Grand Prix bonus pool, which rewarded your overall standings in singles and doubles for the calendar year. Edo had a chance to get to third place in the doubles bonus pool, which would yield a big cheque. But he needed to win the Australian Open.

Edo had a soft heart underneath his gruff exterior, but was not known for parting easily with his hard-earned. 'If we win,' he said, 'I'll buy you a bottle of French champagne.' I was impressed, and readily accepted his offer.

We made it to the final, against the American pair of Sherwood Stewart and Steve Denton. Malcolm Fraser, until recently the prime minister, watched from the stands. It was a gruelling fight in which we managed to prevail.

About an hour later I was part of a crew assembled in the bar at Kooyong, the best place to celebrate a win. Edo came and tapped me on the shoulder. 'Hey, mate—they didn't have any French at the bar, so I bought you a glass of Great Western.' He handed me the flute and bolted. I couldn't believe it—a bottle of French champagne had become a glass of cheap sparkling! I enjoyed it anyway, as I was happy to win the Open. Edo had been a terrific partner and it's the gesture that counts.

By this stage we were in the lead-up to the Davis Cup final, and it brought with it the launch of a tennis charity, the Victorian Tennis Foundation (now called the Kids Tennis Foundation). The idea had come from a Melbourne man about town, Don Gibb, a journalist. He had approached me after I'd beaten McEnroe at the French Open saying I should think about starting a charity for underprivileged children. I remember another journalist telling me, 'Paul, you really should think carefully about doing this, as you'll need to do more than just put your name to it.'

He had a point. But I really liked the idea—I'd been impressed by Vitas Gerulaitis's efforts in raising money for racquets to give to poor (mainly black) kids in New York City. I was reminded of the perception in the States that all Aussie kids find it easy to take up tennis, which I knew was not the case, especially in the densely populated inner suburbs of Sydney and Melbourne.

All my Davis Cup teammates attended the launch, so the charity got off to a flying start. The program introduces tennis to children in socially disadvantaged primary schools, providing a coach for weekly lessons. I was the organisation's inaugural president and remain its chairman. Thirty years on, it's helped more than one hundred thousand kids, from every state and territory, to take up the sport. It's still going strong, driven by its indomitable CEO, Susie Norton, with whom I'd taught at St Columba's all those years ago.

As usual in a Davis Cup tie, Frase put us through the Hopmanesque ordeal of earning our singles places, and I was challenging Fitzy pretty hard for the second spot—Cashy was by now formidable. Making players beat each other in practice is sound strategy. It not only ensured that the ones who miss out are less aggrieved, but that those who do play are match-tough, as the lead-in sessions are fierce. Who wouldn't want to play for their country in a Davis Cup final?

Frase went with Cashy and Fitzy in singles, and Edo and me in doubles. Fitzy deserved that second singles spot, especially after the Leconte win, but at least I'd kept him honest.

The first day saw a mature Mats Wilander see off a valiant Pat Cash. The second rubber was now do or die.

Playing Davis Cup with Edo—Mark 'the Rock' Edmondson—in 1983.

Joakim Nystrom, who'd won Sydney, was a handful for Fitzy. Both were totally committed, but Fitzy was a touch more resilient, with perhaps more grass-court nous under pressure. In near-darkness he took it in four.

The doubles again would be pivotal. Our opponents were Anders Jarryd and Stefan Simonsson, the same pair who'd beaten Brian Gottfried and me at Wimbledon. They'd be tough to overcome, but Edo and I were fired up. I knew Edo was going to be the rock. My job was to be the flamboyant front man—he sometimes called me Jumping Jack, a nickname I'd been given by the Channel Seven commentator Peter Landy.

I remember the first forehand volley that came my way. I swung as hard as I could...and missed, but it helped get out some stress. Edo hardly missed a return,

I was having a field day at the net, and we were soon up two sets to love. I couldn't forget that Gottfried and I had lost to that pair after having the same lead. It was not going to happen again, I was sure of that—we won decisively in three straight sets.

The third day arrived, and none of us could really be confident of Fitzy beating Wilander if it went to the fifth match. So Cashy, who was only eighteen, was playing in his home town in what was effectively the deciding match of a Davis Cup final. And his great serve might be nullified by arguably the best returner in the world, Nystrom.

It was a torrid match, and with Pat leading two sets to one the tension was palpable. Cashy, ably guided by Frase in the chair, held his nerve, and when he hit a topspin lob over Nystrom on match point the release of energy was extraordinary. Cashy leapt metres into Frase's arms—one of the most iconic victory gestures in Australian sporting history, though he later outdid it in a certain Grand Slam victory. It set off wild scenes.

Prime minister Bob Hawke joined us in the locker room for the impromptu celebrations. It was a special moment for us all, and I can honestly say that this was the highlight of my tennis career—we were all unsung, ranked outside the top thirty, and the four of us had each won a match and contributed to the victory.

The Davis Cup dinner was a night I'll never forget (made more memorable when Cashy grabbed the microphone at the after party at a nightclub and put out a challenge to the women present!). We all wrote a note to each other on our dinner menus, as we knew there was no guarantee it would happen again, and that even if it did it was unlikely it would be the same four guys. The replicas we all received were stunning, so I paid a visit to a now-elderly retired teacher in Parkville to show him the trophy. Mr Johns was chuffed.

A month later Frase had a terrific celebratory barbecue at his house, and we each had a little swig from the upper bowl of the cup trophy. He organised a unique display of the America's Cup and Davis Cup standing side by side. What a year 1983 was for sport in Australia.

I'd reached the pinnacle of my playing career, and Father Time was sounding a warning. A month earlier I'd turned twenty-nine. For any athlete, the r-word begins to loom large once you hit thirty. And it's a shock the first time you see 'veteran' before your name in the news. You feel like calling up and saying, 'I'm at my peak…I've got plenty of good years left before I retire!'

Now the reality was hitting me: I was in the last phase of my playing career. I started questioning everything from my dress sense to my taste in music, but the real denial was when I started colouring my hair to hide the greys that were appearing.

Next year my coach, the legendary Fred Stolle, made a quip about boot polish. He'd rib me now and then about it. Some years later a good friend, Sandy Taylor, who was terminally ill, said to me: 'Why don't you let your hair go, just be yourself?' This jolted me, and when she passed away I did let it go, and I've been grey ever since and comfortable with it.

I had a terrific time in 1984 under Fred's tutelage—he was good at calling my bluff. I was fixated on the tension of the strings in the racquet. As soon as it rained I'd get all of my racquets restrung. Then, if the next day was warmer, I'd get them restrung again. The logic is that you need tighter strings in fast (warmer) conditions and looser strings in heavier conditions: looser strings provide more of a trampoline effect. In the first week of the French Open I had a record thirty-one restrings. But I also had one of my better wins that tournament, beating Henri Leconte on my old favourite, Court Central.

When we arrived at Queen's Club the next week for the first grass-court event, Fred had had enough. After all, he'd played in an era where racquets and strings were precious, and I needed reminding that, like most players, I'd sold Klipspringer strings during my first year in Europe to earn money on the side.

Sure enough, I told Fred I needed all six racquets one pound tighter. Fred took them to Pat Menon, an excellent stringer in Shepherd's Bush, and said: 'Pat, can you do me a favour? Paul's paranoid about string tensions. Can you just rub some lacquer on the strings, and I'll tell him they're all done.'

I received the racquets and started checking them, putting them up to my ear and bouncing the strings on the left hand between the palm and the wrist. You can tell the tension by the subtle difference in pitch. 'Oh, that sounds good,' I'd say, and Fred would reply, 'Yes, Pat's a spot-on stringer.' Fred only told me years later…

I should have twigged that the racquets smelt different.

Macca was still out of action, so Cashy and I, who'd become good mates, teamed up for doubles. We won Queen's, and would give Wimbledon a crack. It was a good idea for me to focus on the doubles because I was facing the defending champ, John McEnroe, in the first round of singles.

Fred organised lefties to practise against in preparation for the match, and I didn't win a single set, even against guys ranked well below me. I knew I was facing a shocker, so I channelled all my energy into thinking about how I could avoid humiliation.

The anointed hour arrived. As is the unique custom at Wimbledon, Johnny Mac and I were huddled in the little Centre Court waiting room. I noticed John was wearing blue shorts and was just about to ask him if he'd forgotten the dress code—predominantly white—when I realised this was my best chance to win the match. If John went out in those shorts, he might be defaulted, or at least blow his fuse. At the least he'd be asked to leave the court and return properly attired.

As we walked onto Centre Court and bowed to the Royal Box (another unique tradition, especially for an Australian and an American, both with Irish roots) I could hear the quiet murmurings and chuckling among the crowd. I knew what the chatter was about, but John was oblivious. We met the umpire, tossed the coin, went to our respective ends and started warming up.

I couldn't believe it—was he actually going to get away with it? Then little Leo, the locker-room attendant, came sprinting onto the court yelling, 'Mr McEnroe, Mr McEnroe, your trousers! Your trousers!'

Johnny Mac looked down and, to my great disappointment, said, 'Sorry, I forgot,' and ducked back to the locker room to change.

He hadn't made a fuss at all, and I was back to square one. Bugger.

I was relieved to be the first to break serve, though I lost a close first set. Then I went on to win a set, and the match ended up a close one—I lost in four tight sets. I was rapt. I'd played much better than expected, and hadn't embarrassed myself in front of a global TV audience.

Pat Cash was waiting in the locker room. 'What were you doing out there?' he asked.

'What do you mean, Cashy? I thought I played well.'

'Exactly—well enough to win the match!'

'No—well,' I said. 'I was just trying not to be humiliated.'

'Great. You know you broke his serve in every set?'

'Yeah, I guess that's right.'

'On grass that's normally enough to win the match, right? You just blew knocking McEnroe out of the tournament!'

I'd played the script before the match had started. I hadn't played the match on the day, on its merits. *Carpe diem*. Cashy was a kid, but he knew more than a—okay, I'll cop it—veteran like me.

There was a sting to Cashy's gentle rebuke: still a teenager, he got to the semis, where it took a sublime McEnroe to beat him. Johnny Mac was at the peak of his powers, and destroyed Jimmy Connors in the final. The defeat of 1982 was avenged. McEnroe finished the tournament having lost only a single set—to me.

Cashy and I continued our good doubles form from Queen's, and in the semis had a narrow escape against two fellow Aussies, Michael Fancutt and Peter Doohan. The final brought us face to face with McEnroe and Fleming.

It was a tough match from the beginning, and it went to the fifth set. I was serving at 4–4, and we were down break point. I hit the biggest serve wide out to the ad court to Johnny Mac, and made it. Ace?

Miraculously, he zinged a forehand at a thousand miles an hour past Cashy and on the line. Chalk flew everywhere—break to McEnroe and Fleming. They served it out in the next game.

Some years later I had John over to my apartment in Melbourne. We were reminiscing, and I asked: 'How the hell did you make that forehand on break point in the Wimbledon doubles final in '84—it had to be a fluke?'

He just grinned and said in that sharp New York accent of his: 'I knew you were goin' there.'

Too bloody good, mate!

The year was rounded out with a Davis Cup semi-final against the States in Portland, Oregon. They sent in McEnroe and Connors in singles, and McEnroe and Fleming in doubles. Connors was too much for Fitzy, and Johnny Mac beat Cashy in a high-quality but volatile match. They were both of Irish descent, uber-competitive and a touch too temperamental, frustrated rock 'n' rollers.

When they played it was a bit like a rock gig that had got out of control: exciting, and a shade dangerous.

The next day McEnroe and Fleming handed Edo and me our first Davis Cup doubles defeat, and the tie was over. The reverse singles were irrelevant, but Cashy played Connors in a match you'd never know was a dead rubber and duly won the battle—never an easy thing to do. (Especially since his beloved Hawthorn Hawks had gone down to my footy team, the Essendon Bombers, in the AFL grand final the night before. He wasn't too delighted, I can tell you.) We hadn't retained the Davis Cup, but a semi-final appearance wasn't too shabby.

Then the day I'd been dreading for twelve months finally arrived. I turned thirty. I was playing an exhibition event called the Gold Coast Classic, organised by a tennis mate, Charlie Fancutt, who'd been retired for a while. He had the novel idea (later copied by the Madrid Masters) to hire models as ball persons and lines people.

Unsurprisingly, the lines people were invited to my thirtieth, and it got a little out of control. A blue birthday cake got splattered in my face, and the dye got onto the cushions, which ended up on the beach at Surfers. Let's just say we had a bill to pay and were not welcome to return to that establishment in the future.

Hijinks aside, I couldn't for the life of me figure out why I'd been so stressed about turning the big three-o—what a waste of energy.

10.
MIXING IT WITH MARTINA

THERE WERE signs that Macca was going to attempt a comeback. He'd played some of the Aussie summer events, causing a stir when he turned out for his match at the Western Australian Open in long strides to hide the dicky knee—a look that hadn't been seen since Jack Crawford in the 1930s.

Cashy and I, though we'd lost the Wimbledon final to McEnroe and Fleming in five sets, had also won three tournaments. So, should I stay with Cashy or go back to Macca? I was good friends with both, which didn't make things any easier, and I knew Macca's pride meant he wouldn't ask me directly.

I didn't have a choice—I needed to be loyal to Macca, end of story. Our first tournament back together would be Wimbledon. Macca had the long trousers to hide his injury. He could still produce exquisite backhands. And we still had our SuperMacs reputation, courtesy of a poster Prince had produced after we won Wimbledon— the first Prince male players to do so. Perhaps we had enough game to bluff some opponents.

In the meantime I was out on the regular tour. I'd become friends with Switzerland's Heinz Gunthardt, and we played the French Open together that year. When he lost early in the singles, he said he had a niggle and wanted to leave. I said no way, and told him I thought we could win it (heard that before?). Heinz didn't really buy that, but I'd convinced him enough to stay and try.

In the third round we played the Aussies Darren Cahill and Mark Kratzmann, who were coached by the legendary Bob 'Nails' Carmichael, a fine player and a former singles quarter-finalist at Wimbledon. The young bucks were confident of taking us out, but we played well and did the job.

Nails was upset, shaking his head and gesticulating silently, save for maybe a grunt. Many a waitress experienced Nails' silent gesturing if the food wasn't right. He was a wonderful storyteller, though, and his jokes became legendary. When he died too young he left a legacy to Australian tennis that ranks with those of the better-known heroes.

His funeral service was as celebratory as it could be, and I'll never forget the Nine Network presenter Charles Slade's eulogy to Bob, which captured his persona to a tee. Charles said, in essence: 'We all know Bob was tough to play golf with at times. He was very slow over the ball, and you were never allowed to stand directly behind him when he teed off. But there were two things about Bob we loved. Firstly, it didn't matter where or when you were playing, he made you feel like this was the most important game of golf you would ever play. Secondly, that Bob's next shot was the most important shot he'd ever played.' A great philosophy, a great friend, a great man.

I think Heinz realised I was serious after that win, and we went all the way to the semis, where we played Fitzy and the Czech Tomas Smid. It was a strange match—Fitzy and I are serial crossers at the net and knew each other's game backwards. We must have tubed (hit the opponent's body hard) each other at least five times, which never bothered us. We got to match point in the final set on Smid's serve, with me returning.

I knew Fitzy would cross, and he knew that I knew, and so on…it would be a lottery. I decided to return down his line—after all, he's a serial crosser! I think he did decide to cross, but had managed to hedge his bets enough to get his outstretched racquet to my return, spooning the ball up to Heinz. Uncharacteristically, Heinz dumped the high backhand volley and we didn't get to match point again. *C'est la vie*.

Wimbledon finally arrived—I was back with Macca, and Heinz was playing with his old partner, the Hungarian Balazs Taroczy. 'You guys have a good chance to win it this year,' I said to Heinz. His take on it was that he and Balazs, though they'd won the French Open, had never focused on Wimbledon. They'd never played well on grass, and he said they'd be heading home as soon as they were out of the singles.

'You're kidding,' I said. 'If you win Wimbledon, it's the biggest thing you'll ever do, and it can help set you up for the rest of your life. Take it seriously!'

On the other hand, I had pretty low expectations

for Macca and me. We'd never lost before the semis at Wimbledon, but surely that would be a bridge too far this time. Cashy was teaming up with Fitzy, and when Pat lost early in the singles he made a big call: 'It's okay, as I think Fitzy and I will win the doubles.'

Macca and I ground away—he'd admit he was struggling. Yet we were scraping through. We made it all the way to the semis where—you guessed it—Gunthardt and Taroczy were waiting. This time our bluff would not cut it, and they were up two sets to one, 5–4, 40–love on Balazs' serve when rain stopped play for the night. Macca was grumpy about the way he'd played; we both thought it was curtains.

We came out the next day expecting to play only one point, but Macca was a different person. With the pressure off, he was his old self—and on fire. We saved the three match points on their serve to get back to deuce, and I could see they were choking a bit. Macca hit another winner return at deuce and we had break point. But I blew it—I hit a lob return that was knocked off, then they won the next two points and it was all over. Talk about lost momentum.

Gunthardt and Taroczy were in their first Wimbledon final, up against Cashy and Fitzy, the favourites. Yet the Aussie duo were undone by inspired tennis, and Gunthardt and Taroczy won in four sets. They were Wimbledon champions, a life-changing achievement for any player.

The mixed doubles that year was something else, as my partner was a legend of the sport—and outside it too.

She's a character, a political and gay activist, an animal-rights advocate and an all-round fine person, someone who makes a difference.

Martina Navratilova was the dominant player of her era, at one point winning five Grand Slam singles titles in a row. She won eighteen Grand Slam singles, including Wimbledon nine times; thirty-one Grand Slam doubles titles; and ten Grand Slam mixed-doubles titles. And it didn't come easy. Aged eighteen she defected from Czechoslovakia, thinking she might never see her family again, and endured the difficulties of integrating into American society, given her openness about her sexuality. Martina had an incredible work ethic; she was the consummate professional.

Martina and I were in the IMG stable, both represented by Peter Johnson, an agent in Cleveland. He called me and said that Martina was looking for a mixed-doubles partner at Wimbledon, but was 'sick of playing with men who choke'.

'I can't promise I won't choke,' I said. 'But tell Martina I think we've got an excellent chance of winning it. See how that flies.'

Martina was happy to give it a shot—a big opportunity for me to win another Wimbledon title, my first in the mixed, and the first for her too. We were seeded second but had a couple of early round three-setters. Martina had a heavier workload than I did (I lost in the third round of singles), and one day as we sat down in the chairs before a match she said, 'I've got singles and doubles tomorrow, so I need this to be quick.'

Meanwhile, I'd just come from the men's locker room, where the guys were ribbing me about how unfair it was to the opponents to be playing mixed with Martina.

It went to three sets. I was relieved that we went two breaks up. I said to Martina on the change of ends, 'We're fine now,' and she shot back, 'Yes, but what happened on your serve in the first set?' Trust me, Martina meant business.

As is often the case at Wimbledon, it rained a lot. On the final Saturday, Martina played the finals of the singles and doubles events. She won the first, beating Chris Evert in a great match, and went with Pam Shriver into the doubles on a streak of 106 consecutive matches. But they were defeated by Kathy Jordan from the United States and Liz Smylie from Western Australia—Martina's bid to win all three events in one year was kaput.

On the Sunday, given the backlog of matches, we were only up to the quarter-final stage of mixed doubles. Capturing the title now meant three matches on the same day.

My mother and father had come over to support me, and I was hoping today would be the day they saw their son win a Wimbledon title. Then disaster struck at my flat: as we were heading down to the courtesy car Mum tripped and fell down a flight of stairs with the carpet up and exposed nails on every step. To hospital? She wouldn't hear of it. By this stage in her mid-sixties, she dressed the wounds and dusted herself off, refusing to shed a tear. Mum would let nothing distract me that day—she was fine, and there'd be no further discussion.

Our quarter-final was against Steve Denton and Jo Durie, and we prevailed in two tough sets, 7–6, 7–6. We were sent back on court for the semi-final against Scott Davis and Betsy Nagelsen of the United States. This became an epic that stayed in the Wimbledon record books for years. We split the first two sets, 7–6 and 5–7, then the third set just kept going.

We served for the match a couple of times, each on Martina's serve. I must admit I assisted in the loss of serves, especially when I fluffed an unmissable smash on one match point. On another match point I crossed and volleyed what I thought was a winner, but Scotty D. did a running full-length dive and hit a swing volley off a ball one centimetre from the ground and a few centimetres inside the baseline. It went like a rocket between us for a winner, and the match was slipping away.

We were playing on a packed Court Two, and I could see that in the player's box for our opposition was the doyen of agents, the founder of IMG, Mark McCormack, who was dating Betsy. Mark was one of the most incredible people I've ever met. He was the pioneer of athlete and event management, which he kick-started with his first three clients, Arnold Palmer, Jack Nicklaus and Gary Player.

IMG became involved with many international athletes and sporting events—including, later, the Australian Open when I was CEO. Mark would host an annual Australian Open meeting during the French Open at the Hotel de Crillon in Paris, one of the finest hotels in the world, in the Salon Marie Antoinette, an ornate room with a balcony overlooking Place de la Concorde. This hotel became Roger Federer's base during the tournament, and the Swiss flag is flown in a show of support, duly rewarded when Roger brought the 2010 Coupe de Mousquetaires trophy to the Crillon after his career-defining French Open victory.

In dinners with Mark there'd always be a moment when one of his personal assistants would sign off and another would sign on. I was told that he had three full-time PAs, one for each eight-hour segment of the day! He was a great man, in his field unquestionably one of the most influential characters of the twentieth century, and he left a legacy without equal.

That epic semi-final went to 22–21 in the third set before we prevailed—it was a record number of games played in a mixed doubles at Wimbledon. I was delighted, and not a little relieved too: we were through to the final and thus far I'd held up my end of the bargain with Martina.

The final would be played on Centre Court following the men's singles. Boris Becker and Kevin Curren were in the fourth set, with Boris up two sets to one. He was only seventeen, and Curren had beaten McEnroe and Connors along the way, so the South African had gone in as strong favourite. But Boris was special.

I'd run into him at the Milan tournament a couple of years earlier. Bob Brett organised a young German to play a practice set with me—Bretty said he was pretty good. I served first, directing my first two serves to Boris's backhand. He ripped them both back for winners.

I figured he must have a dodgy forehand, and directed the next two serves there. They also were dispatched with venom—the fifteen-year-old had broken me to love.

We changed ends. No kid has it all, I thought, so his serve must be weak. Boris sent down a 200-kilometre thunderbolt for an ace. Pretty impressive, but I figured he must have a weak second serve. At 15–0 he missed his first serve—here was my chance to show him my stuff. I'd step around and rip a forehand. I leaned to the left to take a forehand and he hit a huge second serve down the middle, on the line, for a clean ace. I looked at Bretty with my mouth open—this kid was something else.

Two years later Boris prevailed in the fourth set against Curren to become the first German, and the youngest male (at seventeen), to win Wimbledon.

Martina and I would've preferred that the match had gone a little longer, as we only had a thirty-minute break after that long semi-final and this was our third consecutive match that day. Our opponents were the Aussies John Fitzgerald and Liz Smylie, a very good pair. Again we went to three sets—and again Martina and I succeeded. We held the trophy aloft in the Royal Box as I waved and pointed it towards Mum and Dad. Spectators for life, as parents so often are, they'd earned it too.

When it was time to enter Wimbledon again a year later, I realised I hadn't heard from Martina or her management. I put in a call to the agent and received a message back: 'Martina wants to let you know that you didn't choke, but she felt you didn't win it easily enough, so she's playing with Heinz Gunthardt.'

The Wimbledon mixed-doubles win with Martina, 1985. I'm looking towards Mum and Dad in the player box.

Although they'd won the US Open together, I was gobsmacked, and the news soon got around the locker room. 'Not defending a Wimbledon title!' Nails spluttered. 'If she ever asks you to play mixed again, on behalf of the boys, you tell her where to go.'

So Martina played that year with Heinz and I played with Hana Mandlikova. Hana and I lost in the first round. Martina and Heinz, meanwhile, swept to the final against Ken Flach and Kathy Jordan. I had only a passing interest (a negative one, I suppose), but I couldn't help but take a peek at BBC when the match was deep in the second set, with victory in Martina and Heinz's grasp.

I knew Heinz well. He'd sometimes get nervous on court. Suddenly, he lost his serve. Was it a choke? Suffice to say, the wheels came off, and they lost that set and the third as well.

Another year went by and the mixed doubles at Wimbledon went to the back of my mind—until I answered the phone one day in June. It was Martina: 'Paul, I was wondering if you'd like to play the mixed at Wimbledon again?'

Nails's words were ringing in my head. 'If you get the chance…' I hesitated. 'Of course, Martina,' I said. 'I'd love to play.' I really was a choker!

No. I liked the idea of winning another Wimbledon—and I wasn't going to let pride stand in the way. I figured that the offer, made directly, was Martina's way of making up, and I respected her enormously.

As it turned out, we didn't get to play. The Steffi Graf juggernaut was starting to roll and Martina felt that taking on all three events would be too much, which I understood. (Incidentally, Heinz Gunthardt went on to coach Steffi, with incredible success.)

Nothing, though, could stand in the way of Martina creating record after record. And her lifelong activism was rewarded with Barack Obama's recent proclamation in support of marriage equality.

11.
COMEBACK

WHILE THE highlight of 1985 was the Wimbledon triumph in the mixed doubles, we were in the midst of another long Davis Cup campaign.

Earlier that year we had a challenging tie on clay in Yugoslavia (as it was then known), in Split. As is customary, as visitors we had local hosts who attended to our needs: language, dining and laundry, those kinds of things. Our driver was a most hospitable chap, and it turned out his son was a ball boy. His name was Srdjan Ivanisevic and his ball-boy son, Goran, later won Wimbledon.

In the opening match I was down two sets to love, 8–7 and 40–15 on Marko Ostoja's serve. I survived those two match points, won the third set, then the fourth, but went down 3–0 with two breaks in the fifth. I managed to pull it out 9–7, my biggest comeback in Davis Cup, which was just as well as Cashy lost the second match to 'Bobo' Zivojinovic in four sets.

The doubles would be pivotal, and Cashy and Fitzy faced a match point themselves before squeaking through.

Cashy was too good for Ostoja, so ultimately the tie went our way.

After Wimbledon storm clouds were gathering. I was again getting severe lower-back pain, but it was a different sort of pain. I came back to Melbourne and had an MRI. The results showed that my right kidney was functioning at only 10 per cent, as there was a kink in the urinary tract. I required an operation as soon as possible, preferably within weeks, as there was a risk of further deterioration and infection.

But I had other pressing concerns: foremost, the upcoming Davis Cup semi-final against Sweden in Malmo, on clay. I'd had my sights set on that tie for some time, as I believed I needed to be there if we were to have a chance of winning.

Macca, a genuine clay-courter, had played very little singles tennis after his knee surgery. Cashy was out injured, and the young guys—led by Wally Masur—were not ready and were afflicted by the widespread Aussie antipathy to clay. (Macca and I were highly unusual in our love of clay.)

The Swedes would be led by Mats Wilander, arguably the best clay-court player in the world in the 1980s and the winner of three Roland Garros crowns. Though I'd lost to him on other surfaces, both times I'd played him on clay I'd won.

Swedes loved taking the ball early on the backhand but tended to retreat diagonally when forced to the forehand. My tactic was to get them out of position with the forehand, then attack the net on the next ball, making them run hard and stretch to the two handed-backhand. Naturally, I was relishing the prospect of another pressure-cooker Davis Cup semi.

I asked the medicos if I could manage the kidney pain. The condition was congenital, they said, and although it was not advisable to play there might be a little while until the kidney gave out.

'How will I know when it has?' I asked.

'You'll be in so much pain, you'll know, all right. It's the closest men get to a woman's pain during childbirth.'

I decided to press on. Before I did anything else I informed our captain, Neale Fraser, of the situation, so it would not be a complete surprise if something happened.

I played the US Open first, beating Guillermo Vilas in five sets before bowing out to America's Tim Wilkinson, who was such a grinder his nickname was Doctor Dirt. Frase then assembled us all in Barcelona to train for a week prior to heading to Malmo. It was a great camp, with the right conditions and atmosphere. None of us had any illusions about the difficult assignment that lay ahead, and I was looking forward to the challenge.

Then it struck. My last night in Barcelona was absolute torture. I've never experienced anything else like it, thankfully. I was in agony, and called Frase's room at first light. Not relishing the prospect of an operation in Spain, I only had one thing on my mind: get to London.

Frase helped me pack and took me to the airport. We knew my Davis Cup dream for that year was over. The boys would need to do it without me, and I wished Frase and them all the very best.

I was in so much pain that I feared it would be noticed and I wouldn't be allowed on board. But I bluffed as best I could. The flight was horrendous—I couldn't sit, and kept moving and trying to alleviate the pain.

In London my personal manager at IMG, Annie Adam, drove me straight to emergency. I don't remember which hospital, but Annie had teed it up. I was given painkillers, which helped a bit. They took a scan and the doctor said I needed an operation immediately—but I wanted to make it home to Australia, where recovery would be far easier with the help of family and friends. He tried a super-strong painkiller that he said wasn't always effective; but if it was it would give me a day of relief, enough to get home.

Luckily, the drug worked. I headed back to Heathrow, then for home. In Melbourne a splint was placed in my urinary tract. I ended up with a twelve-centimetre scar, but got my kidney function back—a huge relief.

Over in Malmo the boys did it tough. Macca was selected for singles with Wally Masur. They battled hard but went down without winning a set. It was always going to be a tough assignment.

For me, the question was whether I'd be able to get back to full fitness. I wondered if my career had reached an anticlimax. But I soon resolved to try to claw my way back. I needed some help, so I got in touch with Bob Brett.

Bretty was a Frankston boy (an outer-Melbourne seaside suburb) and a decent junior player. His goal had always been to become a career tennis coach. At only nineteen he followed Mr Hopman to the United States to be one of his founding coaches. He set about learning everything he could from the master, and they soon became close. I think he was the son Mr Hopman never had. Boris Becker, Goran Ivanisevic, Mario Ancic and Marin Cilic are just a few of the excellent players Bretty's coached over the years.

Naturally, he shared Mr Hopman's training philosophy, which had yielded the world's most successful Davis Cup era. Perhaps it wasn't surprising when Bretty said to me, when I approached him for help, 'After you've done a month in the gym we'll talk again.'

It was cruel but necessary. Bretty felt I'd slackened off over the past couple of years on the tour, and he wouldn't take me on unless he was convinced I was serious. And he was a firm believer in actions speaking louder than words. After all, I was thirty-one and had just had invasive surgery—realistically, what were the chances of me coming back better than before? Bretty wanted me to understand, through day after boring day in the gym (not my favourite place, which he knew), the size of the challenge I faced.

I took it on. By the end of 1985, after a lot of hard graft, I was starting to get in reasonable physical shape. Match fitness was still a way off. I got the all-clear from the docs to resume playing in January, too late for the Australian Open.

I started gently with some doubles at the Australia Day tournament at Maryborough in central Victoria, not far from Tarnagulla. I played with my older brother, Stan. Unfortunately, we were edged out in the semis of the men's doubles, but I won the mixed with Miranda Yates, a very good partner whom I was dating at the time.

It was hard to sustain relationships on the circuit—in one city for a week, another city the next. Sure, you'd meet women, but it was a big call for them to drop their careers, and life, to go on the road, where sightseeing and shopping was usually all there was to do. Generally, the girls we met casually were looking for a distraction, and a visiting tennis player fitted the bill. It didn't go much deeper than that.

Over the years I had only travelled with two genuine girlfriends. I just wasn't ready to settle down. It was probably selfish, yet I figured one day the right girl would come along.

My mission now was to be ready for the March Davis Cup tie against New Zealand in Auckland, the first round of the 1986 World Group competition. My old training partner, fellow fitness fanatic and best mate, Chris Lewis, would be in the Kiwi team. I was dreading a match-up, and I suspect Lewi was too. His best days were behind him, while I was attempting my comeback.

Lewi and I were drawn to play in the fifth and possibly deciding match. Of course—fate had made it come to this, an endgame for two friendly rivals.

In the opening match I played Kelly Evernden, whom I rated but felt I should be able to defeat. I led two sets to love, then lost a drawn-out third set in the tiebreak. During the break I sat grumpily in the locker room. I knew that Kelly now had some momentum, and the crowd to egg him on.

Kelly was fired up in the fourth set and I was in trouble. I wasn't sure how much gas I had in the tank after my absence from the tour. Yes, I'd got fit, but was I match-fit yet?

Frase was giving me advice and, unusually in our captain–player relationship, I kept disagreeing. He'd want me to come in to Kelly's backhand, and I'd shoot back: 'No, I need to stick to his forehand.' I lost in five sets. Not pretty—and Kelly's fightback gave the Kiwis an enormous boost.

Next up was Macca against Lewi. This was my doubles partner's first big singles test after nearly three years away from the game. Macca and Lewi had a fair bit of history too. I wasn't sure how that dynamic would play out.

Of the three of us who frequented Hopman's, Macca had clearly been the best player. He wasn't about to lose to Lewi, and I have to say it was one of the gutsiest matches I saw him play. Macca won in a drag-em-out four-set match to my—and the Aussie team's—great relief.

The doubles was our trump card. Cashy and Fitzy won in three straight sets. We went to the reverse singles leading two matches to one.

The dreaded day had arrived. First up would be Macca versus Kelly Evernden, followed by me against Lewi. I knew Lewi, fit as he always was, would have taken heart from my capitulation to Kelly. I sensed I was slightly the better player these days, but that didn't mean too much.

With everything we'd done together—trained, shared a coach, shared a house, gone clubbing, had the odd argument—it was probably inevitable that we'd have to put everything on the line against each other. There wouldn't be a winner, only a massive loser.

Then Macca coolly dispatched Evernden in four sets, and just like that the tie was over. Lewi and I went out to play the 'dead' match, but neither of us had much motivation. It was lame and irrelevant—the antithesis of what it would have been.

I don't know who would have won if the tie had been up for grabs, and I've never asked Lewi what he thought. I reckon we were about even, overall. And in a way I'm happy it never transpired, as it wouldn't have been right that one of us got to have the last word. Sport is cruel, but on this occasion the sporting gods (and Macca) gave us a reprieve.

Having survived the Davis Cup tie relatively unscathed, I felt ready to tackle the rigours of the tour again. It didn't take me long to hit my stride—by the time the clay-court season had hotted up I was playing well. In Rome I knocked out the world number six, Aaron Krickstein. I played him again in the French Open, but this time lost in five sets. My ranking was on the upswing and suddenly I was at twenty-four, my highest ATP ranking.

My singles ranking was peaking, and I was fit again, happy, and with a supportive coach. With Bob Brett's help I'd stared down retirement, and my rehabilitation as a player was complete.

Davis Cup was humming along. We were playing a home semi-final against the United States in Brisbane, on grass. For more than a decade Australia had made at least the semis of the Davis Cup each year. Thankfully, 2013 is the last of six straight years in which we'd failed to be one of the sixteen nations that make up the World Group—how far we had fallen.

In the opening match I drew Brad Gilbert, the world number twelve at the time. Although grass was not BG's best surface, I found myself down two sets to one and struggling. But Frase and the boys in the locker room thought that I was still well in the match.

We came out from the break and I played like a man possessed, winning the fourth set 6–0, then the fifth 6–1. BG wasn't injured and can't explain what happened. Nor can I. All I know is that I got into the zone and didn't miss a ball. If only you could bottle that formula!

Cashy beat Tim Mayotte in the second match, then lost the doubles in five sets with Fitzy, after leading two sets to love. Cashy was too good on grass for BG in the fourth match, and we were through to the final.

The tie would be at home at Kooyong, against Sweden, spearheaded by Stefan Edberg. Their number two was Mikael Pernfors, who earlier in the year reached the singles final at Roland Garros, and Edberg with Anders Jarryd was a top doubles pairing.

Our practice leading into the tie was, as always, arguably more competitive than the tie itself. Macca was

The boy with his one-handed backhand and bucket hat, 1967.

Deep in post-match contemplation, 1981.

BELOW: *Our first Wimbledon win, 1980. (Note Macca's perm!)* © News Ltd / Newspix.

Before the 1982 Wimbledon final, with a grumpy Johnny Mac.

Overlooking Queen's Club, London, from the balcony of my flat in the early 1980s.

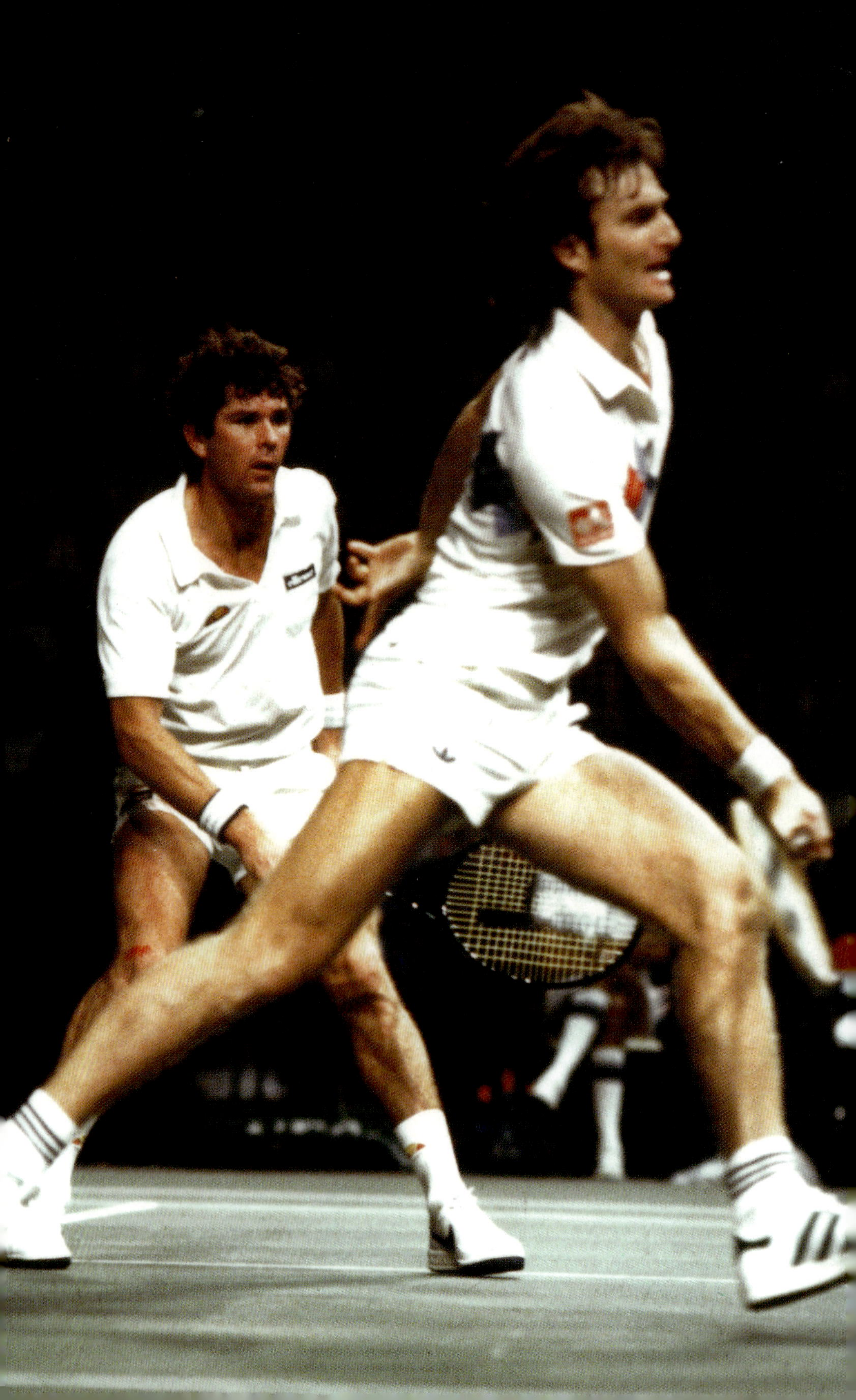

MENU

FRESH SEAFOOD SALAD
IN LIGHT LIME MAYONNAISE

•

FILLET OF BEEF WITH FRESH HERBS
AND MUSHROOMS IN PUFF PASTRY

•

COUPE MOZART

•

COFFEE AND MINTS

•

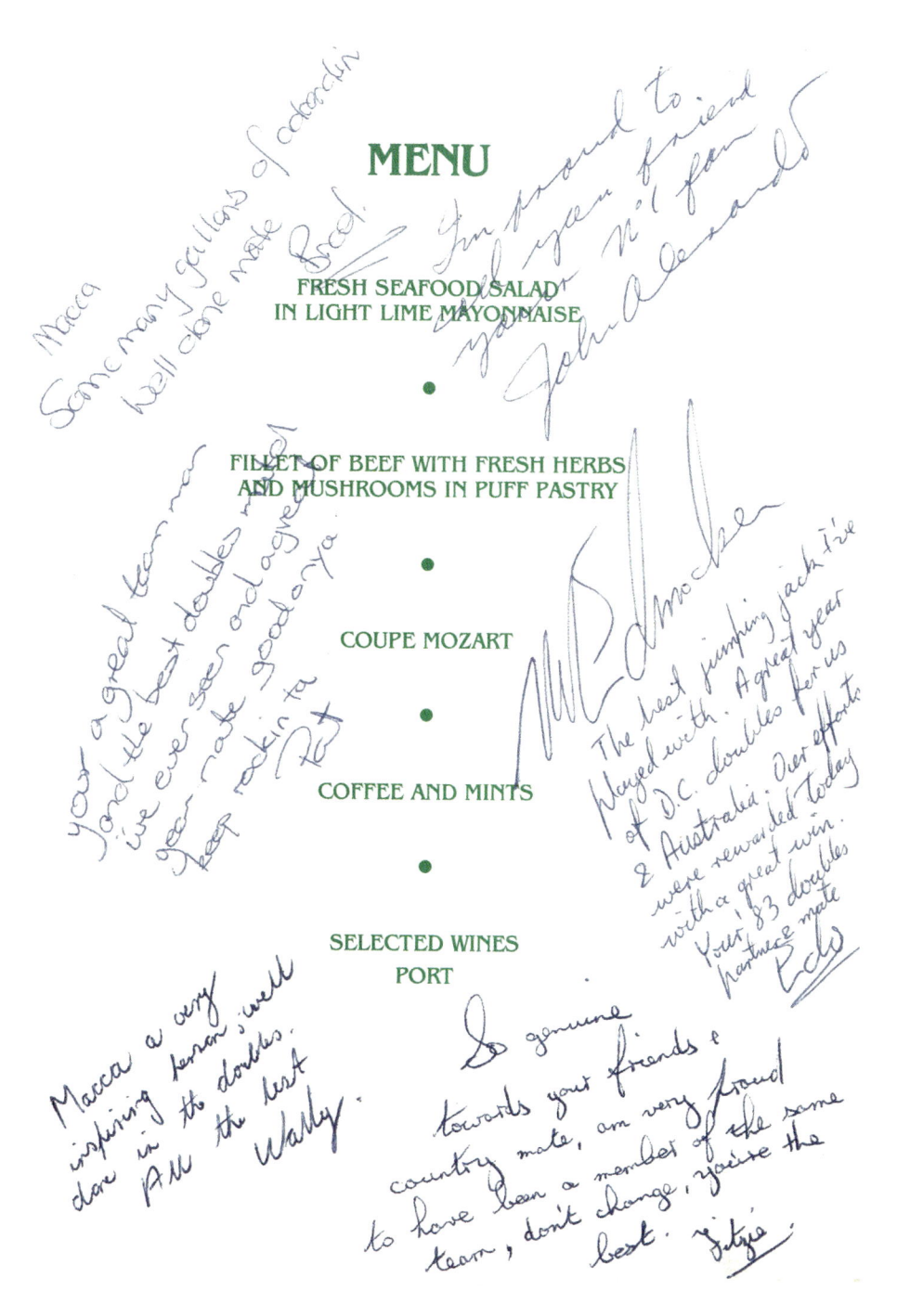

SELECTED WINES
PORT

The guys on the team penned notes to each other at the 1983 Davis Cup Final Dinner.

OPPOSITE: *SuperMacs in full flight, early 1980s.*

King of the kids: at a Kids Tennis Foundation clinic in 1984.

With my sister, Mary, and Mum and Dad at the 1986 Order of Australia ceremony.

A golden day—Mum and Dad's fiftieth wedding anniversary. Brian is on the left; Mary and Stanley are on the right.

A second Davis Cup win, 1986.

King of Moomba, 1987, with Prince Macca and Prince Cashy.

in the team, Fitzy and I again were fighting for a singles spot, Cashy was aggro, and Frase had to stop practice one day when our emotions boiled over. This time I got the nod.

I was playing Pernfors in the opening match. It felt like there was doubt in the team's collective mind about my commitment to serve-volleying, and I suspect if I'd stayed back at all in practice I would have been overlooked for singles. On the day of the final the president of Tennis Australia, Brian Tobin, popped in to the locker room to wish me luck, and innocently added: 'You are going to serve-volley, aren't you?'

It was as if I was expected to represent the brand of Australian tennis. How could an Aussie worth his salt play like a European? Imagine if I stayed back and lost—it would be humiliating for all concerned.

I felt I had no choice. I would serve-volley every ball, come what may. When I'd played Pernfors only weeks before at the Paris Indoors I'd played him from the back of the court and, although I lost, it was one heck of a match. But this was on grass, in Australia, so get those silly ideas out of your head!

Pernfors took me to the cleaners. He dined out on my second serve and broke me seemingly at will. Deep in the third set, when the match was all but over, I finally stayed back on my second serve for a game—and held, easily. As I approached the chair I said to Frase, 'I'm sorry, I don't know why I did that. I won't do it again,' to which he replied, 'Actually you played better that game.' Too late.

It took a mighty effort by Cashy to topple Edberg, one of his best matches ever against one of the great grass-courters. Then, in the doubles, Cashy and Fitzy were superb, beating Edberg and Jarryd in a world-class performance.

We were a match ahead going into the third day. Cashy was first up against Pernfors, and I was taking on Edberg in the last match. And you don't need to be Einstein to work out that Cashy needed to beat Pernfors, as there wasn't a single person in Australia who believed I could beat Edberg.

Except me. I'd learned my lesson from that Wimbledon encounter with McEnroe in 1984, when I'd played to the script and didn't play the match on its merits.

And I'd played Edberg in practice before Wimbledon that year. I'd employed a strategy of chip-charging his serve—first and second serves. He had a high-kicking serve, which gave him extra time to take up a good net position. Taking it early and chip-charging prevented the serve kicking high, where it was difficult to return from outside the singles court. Edberg didn't like this tactic, and I'd beaten him in the practice match. I had my strategy and, this time, no one was going to sway my thinking.

Cashy's match with Pernfors was a Davis Cup epic. Pat was completely outplayed for the first two sets, so I was preparing myself for what would likely be the decider. But he dragged himself off the mat and into the match, and his five-set comeback victory became part of Davis Cup lore. Australia had won the cup for the second time in my career—and Macca's first, which he deserved—and I'd played singles in every tie.

Would I have beaten Edberg if it had come down to it? Logically not, but we'll never know. I do know as a coach that indecision on strategy is the father of failure. In the end we'd won the Davis Cup and, in a team event, that's all that matters.

12.
WHERE TO NOW?

AFTER THAT Davis Cup win, late in 1986, I knew that at thirty-two it was time for me to make the transition to the next stage of my tennis life. The younger guys, like Wally Masur and Peter Doohan, needed blooding. I told Frase to leave me out of the Davis Cup equation: 1987 would be my last year on the tour. Macca and Lewi were hanging up their racquets too.

I was accorded a huge honour by being crowned Melbourne's King of Moomba, a fun festival on the Labour Day weekend. Unfortunately around that time a bomb went off in the South Yarra apartment block I was living in—regrettably, with a fatality. I was in the building at the time, so that shook me up for a few days. Luckily I had rescued my car before the fire got to the garage area, as I was attached to my Mercedes 500 SEC coupe, a model not sold in Australia. I shouldn't have been focusing on something material, but you know how it is with boys and their cars.

Rumblings to try my hand at something other than playing tennis had got louder a couple of years earlier.

One night Cashy and Charlie Fancutt came over to that Melbourne apartment for a drink. Charlie had been focusing on the Gold Coast Classic, which had struggled a bit, but at least he'd gained some valuable event experience.

Cashy was still on the way up—he'd already been to the semis of Wimbledon and the US Open in singles, was a two-time finalist in the Wimbledon doubles, and had been part of our winning Davis Cup team in 1983.

At that stage I still felt I had some tennis left in me. However, having hit thirty, I needed to start contemplating the future. The three of us were shooting the breeze when Charlie said, 'It's amazing there's not a team event for men and women.'

'That's right,' I replied, 'considering the Davis Cup is so big, and there's Fed Cup for women.'

Charlie turned to me. 'Why don't we do one?'

'It's a good idea,' I said. 'I really want to keep playing if I can, at least for another year or two. But when I retire, I'm happy to look at it.'

'If you guys do it, I'd be happy to play,' Cashy chipped in, which was unusual. Generally he'd not embraced women's tennis with enthusiasm.

I didn't think too much about it over the next couple of years. Charlie was scratching around trying to enlist some backing, but these kinds of projects aren't easy to get off the ground.

Now that I was retiring at the time of my choosing, thankfully not because of injury, I started exploring a few career options. One was to join Sfida, the sportswear and racquet company that I was endorsing; another was to try athlete representation; yet another was to go into commentary. But the one that held my interest was starting up the mixed teams competition we'd discussed over drinks.

I decided to spend 1987 going back to my favourite stops on the circuit: Rome, Paris and the mountain villages in the European summer, like Gstaad, Kitzbuhel and St Vincent. These days I was travelling with my golf clubs, and at one stop I asked Bill Ryan from IMG if he'd be so kind as to take my clubs back to London for me. I knew this was a big ask, so I said, 'Go ahead and use them in London if you want. They're a good set.'

'That's nice of you,' he replied. He didn't think so kindly of me when he took off the cover of the clubs on the first tee at Wentworth—they were left-handed, and like most people Bill was right-handed! Next time he saw me he said (among various expletives), 'Too good—you got me.'

Wimbledon that year was truly special—I lost to Cashy in the third round of singles and stayed to see him beat Wilander, then Connors, then Lendl, all in straight sets, to become the Wimbledon champion, the first Aussie man to achieve it since John Newcombe in 1971.

The Champions' Dinner that night was great, as I shared the table with Pat; his coach, Ian Barclay, who'd taken him from a young adolescent to the Holy Grail; his fitness trainer, Ann Quinn; and his family, including his father. Pat senior was a sportsman, an opera lover and a staunch defender of his son, and was immensely deserving of sharing first-hand his boy's greatest triumph.

Coincidentally, a French film producer, Michel Mattei, was making a documentary about Cashy—that Wimbledon win sure was timely. Michel needed a hand, so I took on the role of executive producer for *The Pat Cash Story: No Second Prize*. This challenged my time-management skills, as between singles matches I had to commute from the edit suite in London to the Stuttgart ATP event.

This was also the year that the new Flinders (now Melbourne) Park complex neared completion. To fulfil the requirements of an indoor entertainment arena for Melbourne, as well as a Centre Court for an outdoor Grand Slam, it needed a retractable roof.

Realistically, this necessitated a change of surface, as a grass court in a year-round entertainment arena was highly impractical. It really needed to be an artificial surface—but the Australian players were doing everything possible to try to keep the grass-court cause alive, and I was chosen as their representative in the process.

Tennis Australia and its president, Brian Tobin, seemed keen to see synthetic grass laid. This was an understandable link to grass. But it didn't sit well with the Australian men, who—in the end resigned to a change from grass—strongly preferred a hard court. Various options were considered, and Tennis Australia had sample courts laid so that we could try them out.

We played on them all, and soon came to a unified position that the Australian Open should be played on Rebound Ace, a rubberised hard court with the advantage that it was 100 per cent Australian owned and developed. By early 1987, not twelve months out from the change of venue from Kooyong to Flinders Park, the decision was still pending. I could tell the numbers were against the Aussie male players, so at the Tennis Australia subcommittee meeting I suggested that there should also be a representative of the women players. Another vote for Rebound Ace, I figured—not to mention fairer.

The players' concern with synthetic grass was that, despite its aesthetic advantages, it did not replicate the response to spin that other surfaces provided. Slice seemed to be accentuated, and topspin didn't kick on commensurate with the effort expended by the player. We didn't think that synthetic grass had been developed to the point where it was acceptable as a tournament surface, and certainly not for a Grand Slam. (To this day, synthetic grass has never been used at an ATP tour or WTA tour event.)

In the meeting to make a decision I vehemently campaigned that the Australian players needed to be happy, they wanted Rebound Ace, and I believed overseas players felt the same way. It was obvious, though, that the numbers were not favourable and, if a vote was taken then and there, a clear majority would opt for synthetic grass.

Desperate action needed to be taken. 'Look,' I said. 'We can't make the decision today, as there will be a player poll on the options next week in Miami and all the players will be there. We have to hold off on the vote.'

I got a few looks from around the table. 'Is that right?' I was asked. 'I haven't heard anything about that.'

Now going further than I would have liked, I said, 'I'm sure there'll be a vote next week. The players would be really upset if we didn't allow them input.'

Reluctantly, I suspect, the subcommittee agreed to adjourn until the results of the player poll were in.

I left the meeting and got straight on the phone to Weller Evans, a senior player representative on the ATP tour. 'Weller,' I said, 'You know how there's this big push for the Australian Open to be on synthetic grass? I swear it's really going to happen.'

'You're kidding,' he replied. 'They can't do that... How can I help?'

'I told the meeting that there'll be a player poll happening next week at Miami and we have to wait for the result. It's important.'

'Sure, but what exactly are we polling again?'

'It's a straight choice, Rebound Ace or synthetic grass. We need the players to choose one or the other. And I'll go to the WTA to do exactly the same, so we get the women's vote as well.'

'Done,' he said.

Phew! Things would have got a little sticky if the ATP hadn't been prepared to play ball.

In Miami seventy-seven male players voted: a landslide, all but one in favour of Rebound Ace. Then I heard the results of the WTA poll. Thirty-three votes for Rebound Ace, thirty-four for synthetic grass. I couldn't believe it. Wendy Turnbull, the female players' representative for the subcommittee, was now obliged to vote for synthetic grass, nullifying my vote.

The most outspoken opponent of synthetic grass was the world number one, Ivan Lendl, who intimated that he would boycott the Australian Open if it used the surface. This and one other factor swung things back in favour of Rebound Ace. On the morning of the formal vote Bruce Matthews, a *Herald Sun* journalist not prone to hype, penned an opinion piece saying that surely Tennis Australia could not go against the unwavering view of the top male players, led by the world number one and our own Pat Cash.

In a close vote Rebound Ace was given the nod and became the surface of the Australian Open for two decades. Little did I realise then that the surface would be a hot topic for most of its life at Melbourne Park.

The 1987 tour wound its way through the summer in Europe and the States. In the first round of the US Open I was drawn against a fifteen-year-old Chinese-American. Michael Chang could hardly see over the net, but already his legs were like tree trunks.

This fellow gave me no end of difficulty—it seemed he could run all day. He beat me in four sets and, somewhat in justification, I ventured to the media later that he'd go 'top ten, for sure'. It was clear that my retirement timing was spot on.

I felt less embarrassed when quizzed by CBS twenty-five years later, on the anniversary of the day the youngest player in history won a men's match at the US Open. After all, Michael Chang won the French Open at seventeen, reached the finals of the US Open and Australian Open, and was ranked as high as number

'Macca's last stand.' My final professional match, with my mate Cashy, 1988. © Tony Phelan / Newspix.

two in an era that included Pete Sampras, Jim Courier and Andre Agassi.

The 1990s was the golden era of American tennis, a long run that finally petered out with Andy Roddick's retirement at the US Open in 2012. The United States too is struggling on the men's side, following in the footsteps of the other great nation that used to dominate the game, Australia.

Finally, the tour arrived at the sparkling new Flinders Park for the Australian Open. I had no reason to second-guess my decision that this would be my swansong. I was looking forward to the next stage of my life—after, I hoped, playing on the new Centre Court with a Rebound Ace surface.

The draw didn't do me any favours. My first two rounds were tough, but the third-round potential match-up on the big stage loomed large: Cashy, the reigning Wimbledon champion.

I was dreading my first-round match, where I was pitted against Bill Scanlon, an American who'd been top ten and was playing better tennis than I was. I knew I was facing a likely first-round exit with a 'he's better off retired' chorus in the background.

Then the forecast came: forty degrees. It'd be a killer out there. This would be a one-set match, as the loser of the first would be demoralised. I had to play that set as if I was incredibly fit, immune to the heat. A bluff, if you like, but I figured that's all I had. I went out and ran for every ball, and took it 6–3. Following the script, the score was 6–3, 6–3, 6–3—and it wasn't much chop as a tennis match, but I'd passed the first stage of my mission.

The second round was against another American, Sammy Giammalva, on another hot day. It was a torrid match and it took all of my resolve to win the tiebreak in the second set, to get into the match. Cashy's uncle, Brian Cash, was particularly supportive in the stands. When I won the third and went a break up in the fourth, Sammy was done. I would get my last wish: meeting Cashy in the third round of our home Open on Centre Court.

We were scheduled for the Friday evening. The build-up in press and TV was impressive, with my imminent retirement adding to the occasion. But in the match itself Cashy was way too strong, and out I went in straight sets. He was most respectful, stopping for photos together as we left the court. I felt privileged to finish my career on the magnificent new Centre Court, and to have my curtain call alongside a teammate and friend.

All went well in the inaugural year at Flinders Park, and with an ounce of luck we'd have crowned Cashy as the Aussie Open winner—sadly, he lost an epic final to Mats Wilander. Rebound Ace proved to be a fair surface for players of all styles, and nearly all of the Australian Open winners since have been either world number one or on the verge of it, which confirms its fairness.

My old life was over—but I didn't take time to reflect. I was up for a new challenge: establishing an international tennis event. Charlie Fancutt and I caught up for a drink the night I lost to Cashy. We already had a potential HQ in the frame.

'Let's check out the office tomorrow,' I told him. I was raring to go.

Behind the scenes: settling in to office life in 1988.

PART II

13.
ON THE HOP

I STARTED work the next day—my first in an office. Charlie had never worked in one either, and we needed guidance. Luckily we had help setting up in St Kilda Road, Melbourne, from the staff of USP Needham. (It later became DDB Needham, and is now part of DDB Worldwide Communications Group, a leading company in marketing communication.) The company's CEO, Paul Leeds, was generously mentoring me.

His staff reacted with a mixture of bemusement and cheerful support. A new tennis event with no name, no sponsors, no TV coverage, one player—Cashy—and no city to play in, let alone a venue? Good luck, boys.

When you're starting something like this, you need to address things in the right order. My hunch was that we couldn't get sponsors without TV, but we couldn't get TV without players—so we'd go with our strong suit and focus on players first. As for the city, well, that was something to work out later.

It was a great start to have Pat Cash's commitment, as he was now the Wimbledon champion. But it was a team event for men *and* women. We needed a top female player. Charlie had met Steffi Graf a couple of times, and had a hit with her once—that was a connection. We touched base with Steffi's agent, Phil de Picciotto of Octagon.

Phil is one of the best in the business, and he could recognise inexperience a mile away. He was very fair—supportive of a couple of newly retired players having a go. Steffi would play if she received her normal fee, but if the Hopman Cup didn't go ahead there'd be no financial obligation. We were much obliged to Phil.

This was all we needed. We had the reigning Wimbledon men's champion, and the reigning Australian Open champion and new women's world number one. And that year Steffi went on to win the Grand Slam *and* the Olympic gold medal.

Armed with our field of two I went to Channel Seven, which covered the Australian Open, and asked if they'd televise this new event. They were a little nervous initially—no sponsor, no host city, and IMG had approached them with another proposed tennis event for the same week ours was scheduled.

Charlie and I had agreed that we'd dedicate the event to our mentor, Mr Hopman, who'd recently passed away. Coincidentally, IMG had approached Mrs Lucy Hopman, as we had, to seek her blessing for their new event. She didn't hesitate to approve ours, as she knew how close Charlie and I were to Mr Hopman, and that he would have wanted to support us. So we had the okay to call our tournament the Hopman Cup, but from the TV network's perspective the commitment from Cash and Graf was the clincher.

Once we had free-to-air TV we were in a position to talk to sponsors, but naturally they wanted to know where the tournament would be staged. There were already tournaments in the major markets of Melbourne, Sydney, Adelaide and Brisbane.

I liked the idea of Perth, and started asking people in Melbourne what they thought about staging the tournament there. I got the same answer every time: 'Don't do it. It's too far away.' That got me thinking. If everyone thinks Perth's so remote, imagine the welcome we'd get there. Plus, Perth had just hosted and lost the America's Cup, so I figured there was a chance we could fill the void.

Charlie was friends with Michael Edgley, a gifted entrepreneur aligned—as the name suggests—with Perth's Edgley Entertainment Centre, where we'd played the United States in Davis Cup in 1982, and where the West Coast Classic tennis tournament had been held with Edgley as the promoter. Michael suggested that we check out a new resort under construction in Perth, as it included a sports stadium.

This was the Burswood Island Resort. I contacted an entertainment manager there, Andrew Firman (who became general manager of the Hopman Cup some twenty years later), and asked how we'd get spectators out to the island. I figured Burswood Island must be somewhere near Rottnest Island. 'Would they need to catch a ferry,' I asked, adding wishfully, 'or is there a bridge?'

There was a fit of laughter at the other end. 'Burswood is in the centre of Perth,' Andrew said.

I felt silly, but this was all new to me and there was no Google Maps back then...

After a few conversations it was clear that Andrew was supportive. Burswood would give our project serious consideration.

Charlie went to Perth for reconnaissance, especially of the Dome, the stadium on site. He came back positive about the resort, but less so about the Dome. It was huge, far too big for tennis, so a fitout would need to be done almost from scratch. And there was no air conditioning—a major issue for a tennis event in the middle of the searing Perth summer. Still, we didn't have many options for a host city.

I went to Western Australia to meet the state's minister for sport, Graham Edwards, and the two most senior executives at EventsCorp, a government organisation set up to maintain Perth's position on the major sporting events roster post-America's Cup. Terry Penn and Bill Eastman were affable and willing to help. They seemed to recognise the potential of the Hopman Cup, and were supportive of an alliance with Burswood. EventsCorp was an offshoot of the Western Australian Development Corporation. Its chairman, John Osborne, was also favourably disposed, so in a short time we'd made a good start with the relevant authorities.

They'd made us feel welcome, as did everyone in Perth. There was definitely the right vibe—the remoteness of the city allowed a cavalier entrepreneurialism to flourish. We seemed to fit in and the timing seemed to be right. The air conditioning was still a major impediment, so when the Burswood resort's owner, Dallas Dempster, said that if the Hopman Cup came he would air-condition the Dome—a million-dollar upgrade—the stars were aligned.

I feared blowing the nest egg from my playing days. I'd heard many stories of former tennis pros who'd lost everything quickly on a project like ours. So far the fledgling Paul McNamee Enterprises—or PME, as we always referred to it—hadn't spent too much cash, but the bills were starting to mount: the office, trips to Perth, hotels, and trips to London and New York to touch base with players. (While in New York I attended a gathering in the car park at the US Open for the historic announcement of the new ATP tour. As I had retired and was moving in a different direction, I passed on my ATP board position to my fellow player and good friend Russell Barlow.) EventsCorp was sympathetic and looked to find a way for the state government to provide financial security.

I was fortunate that Paul Leeds had not only set us up in the DDB Needham building, but had recommended we work with Needham Consulting, an offshoot company, and its CEO, Brian Bacon, and manager, Julie Fernandez (who became the longstanding sponsorship manager for the tournament). Brian was invaluable in the first year. Early on, he sat Charlie and me down in front of a large whiteboard and said two things. First, you never get a second chance to make a first impression. And, second, you must have a clear vision.

His priority was not who would be playing, but what the event would look like: the grandstands, the court, the signage and colours, where the public and corporate patrons would be sitting, the type of entertainment, the sights and sounds, the story. Brian believed we needed to visualise our event as if it was actually happening. Then we needed to channel our energy into replicating on paper the image in our minds. And that image needed to impart a positive and enduring first impression on those who attended. What pearls of wisdom these were.

Charlie and I were adamant that the Davis Cup, run by the International Tennis Federation, was the best annual team competition in world sport. We wanted to replicate the look of this iconic event, with its understated commercial overlay in the 'tennis green' colour of the court signage, the flags of the competing nations, the national anthems played before each match. And our event must be a fitting tribute to the greatest Davis Cup captain in history, Mr Harry Hopman.

We could visualise the court and surrounds without difficulty. Brian was happy with our clarity, as it helped define our story—the Hopman Cup, an international team event where men and women represent their countries head to head in singles and side by side in mixed doubles, which we hoped one day would stand alongside the Davis Cup and the Federation Cup in the ITF family. Brian, without us realising it, helped us to sketch a blueprint that would remain intact a quarter of a century later.

We were making great progress, but there was still one missing element: sponsorship. I had a meeting with

Nissan Motors, as I knew a senior manager there, Graeme Nichols, through family ties. Charlie and I met Graeme and an associate, and they suggested we come back with a formal proposal—with the rider that the Nissan brand was sacrosanct, its corporate look critical. They'd be interested in secondary (associate) sponsorship.

Charlie and I were pumped. This would be a healthy six-figure deal that would leave the major sponsorship—arguably easier to sell—available. So we worked with the Needham crew to prepare a mock-up of the court, with the Nissan signage in its off-centre backcourt position and in blue corporate colours—despite our vision being uniform tennis green, a la the Davis Cup presented by NEC. The colour issue could always be dealt with later if it became a problem, we thought. We had to fire our best shot at getting Nissan on board.

We met with Graeme again and discussed the sponsorship sum, subject to all the boxes being ticked. We were pretty confident we had landed our first big sponsor.

After that highly promising meeting, Charlie and I debated the previously unspoken matter of the Nissan corporate colour being blue, not our green. We came to the only conclusion we felt comfortable with—we must remain faithful to our vision of the colour scheme. Nissan was keen to be involved, we reasoned, so they'd come around to accepting non-corporate colours behind the court. We'd put their corporate colours in the grandstands and on other venue signage. And if they were disappointed we could always discount the price a little.

Off we went to the follow-up meeting, where we expected the deal would be consummated. We seemed to be in agreement on everything, when I ventured, 'Everything's fine, but you may remember we talked about replicating the Davis Cup...The only thing is that the mock-up we showed you last time was a little inaccurate.'

'How so?' Graeme asked.

'Well,' I said, 'the colour around the Nissan letters is blue in the picture, but it needs to be green just there. But we will keep it blue everywhere else.'

Graeme's expression changed. 'The blue represents our brand, and I think I told you that's central to our thinking.'

'Yes,' I said, 'you did say that, but—'

'Paul and Charlie, I like you guys a lot, and I think you've got a great concept. And I know you're just starting out, but let me give you some advice. When you approach a sponsor again, never offer them something you can't deliver. I wish you well with the project, but Nissan won't be involved.'

Ouch. There's nothing like learning a lesson the hard way. He was absolutely right. We'd misrepresented the selling proposition, and it backfired. It was a lesson delivered early in my post-playing life, and I've always heeded it.

We scoped a number of Perth and national institutions in our search for a major sponsor, and the one with the most traction was the Swan Brewery, part of the Bond Brewing empire owned by Alan Bond. An iconic West

Australian company, it was a good fit—especially as the brand that would be aligned to our event was a reduced-alcohol beverage and, importantly, green signage wasn't an issue.

It all fell into place in the west. The inaugural event would be sponsored by Swan Gold, hosted by Burswood Island Resort, underwritten by EventsCorp, televised live on the Seven Network, dedicated to Mr Hopman, and feature Steffi Graf and Pat Cash as the marquee acts. And all of that had been lined up in reverse order.

The Hopman Cup by Swan Gold came together between February and July 1988. I had no idea there was so much work involved. Charlie headed to Perth, soon followed by a woman named Lesley Hateley, who worked with us in Melbourne and who could help Charlie get organised. She was pleased to go, as she was originally from Perth and knew how much was at stake.

Soon after I realised I should relocate too. Off I went to the west—not for three months, as I expected, but for more than seven years.

It was madness getting ready for that first Hopman Cup. Though we'd been players, there was no way of knowing the enormousness of running a tournament. The amount of detail is incredible—fixing ticket prices, putting together a program, selling corporate boxes, organising sub-sponsors, arranging umpires and officials, servicing the sponsors and players, creating a TV village for Seven and the international networks, media liaison and PR, hosting launches, and marketing all that you're doing. It was the A to Z of event management.

We were babes in the woods. I had to beg our media expert, Alan East, not to resign. He ended up doing a mighty job in various roles for twenty-odd years. A friend, Jenny Della Vedova, took on marketing with aplomb. I also drew on tennis friendships I had in the west. Rob Casey, who I'd travelled with as a player in the UK, became the deputy tournament director. Jeff King took charge of the ball kids. The president of Tennis West, Harry Spilsbury, was highly supportive, as were his successors, Alan Hicks and Dean Williams, even though the state association was not running the event.

We figured we needed a major social function, especially with the New Year falling during the tournament and being at a casino. As a player, I'd been blown away by the Alan King Tennis Classic at Caesars Palace in Las Vegas. They had an over-the-top pool party with live animals, including lions, in cages. Everything was on the house—making for an unbelievable tournament. (Caesars also introduced me to craps, a game I have quite a fondness for!)

The resulting Hopman Cup New Year's Eve Ball, which included a charity auction benefiting the Variety Club and the Kids Tennis Foundation, got off to a flier—Cliff Richard, a tennis lover whom I'd met in the UK, was visiting Australia and agreed to be the headliner. He then won the inaugural pro-am with Steffi Graf, hitting a topspin backhand winner (not a shot in his repertoire) on match point. Cliff generously waived his appearance fee, and a decade later returned to celebrate the Hopman Cup's tenth anniversary.

But inevitably things slipped through the cracks that first year, especially when the players hit town. One of the staff came up to me and said the Japanese player Shuzo Matsuoka had a problem with his racquet. We hadn't organised a stringer. Another little thing I'd taken for granted when I'd arrived at tournaments in the past.

With extreme nervousness we greeted day one of our first event—I could only imagine what might go wrong. The opening match was Australia versus Great Britain, Pat Cash playing Jeremy Bates. It was a sell-out, eight thousand people, and I was petrified. Would the court and net and everything stand up okay? Would the fans demand their money back? Cashy served that first point...and nothing bad happened. We were on our way.

During the event I asked a staff member to quickly find out the score. She seemed unsettled by the request, but I insisted. She came back and informed me, 'The top line says 3, 6, 2 and the bottom line says 6, 4, 5.' Tennis knowledge was definitely not a prerequisite to employment!

Cashy was partnered by Hana Mandlikova, a Grand Slam singles winner who'd recently become an Australian. The Aussies took on Germany in the semi-final, which pitted Cashy against Steffi in the mixed doubles. Pat was ruthless in the quick net exchanges, and the tie went in the Aussies' favour.

Their opponents in the final were Miloslav Mecir (the Big Cat) and Helena Sukova of Czechoslovakia, who defeated the Aussies in a tough encounter. The first Hopman Cup had played out in front of large and enthusiastic crowds, a deeply satisfying result.

When you're starting out in business you're entering the great unknown. Athletes can have fascinating second careers, but they're green about how things work in the real world. The nomadic life of hotels, parties and a new city every week—whether hard work or glamorous, or both—has to be left behind. I found the adjustment hard but energising.

And Lesley Hateley, who moved back to Perth, doing an unbelievable job of keeping the whole thing together? We started dating, and twelve months later we married.

14.
HOW THE WEST WAS WON

FOR THE crew at PME that first Hopman Cup had a learning curve as steep as they come. But the best way to learn about a business is to start from scratch and get immersed in every aspect of it. The apprenticeship is quick and ruthless—and this is the experience of countless just-retired athletes. You get one good go at your new project and you'd better not blow it.

So it was a relief that the first Hopman had gone well, turning a modest profit. The state government could now look at a longer arrangement, securing the event's future, and reassuring sponsors, media and the public.

Heading back to Melbourne to live was no longer an option—there was too much in Perth that needed to be attended to. I did, however, go back to receive an Order of Australia at Government House, for services to tennis and disadvantaged children through the Kids Tennis Foundation. It was certainly an honour, but I didn't feel comfortable wearing the little medals. In fact, I've never worn one since that day, but perhaps I will find the right occasion.

When I was playing pro tennis the question I was most often asked was: 'What's John McEnroe really like?' When you're involved in the events industry the most common question is: 'What do you do the rest of the year?' It's unfathomable to people that you could spend a whole year on an event that only lasts a week. But the amount of detail involved is mind-boggling, and if you're asking for the sort of money required to attract elite international athletes to the most remote city in the world, your sponsors will need more than one week of kudos.

For a start, they'll need to receive a seasonal marketing campaign to justify their involvement. This can range from exposure at a launch three months out from the start of the event to promotions for the tournament, especially money-can't-buy experiences such as playing in the pro-am, or a meet-and-greet with Boris Becker or Ana Ivanovic, or an exclusive hit on Centre Court. You need to meet constantly with sponsors, making sure their needs are being catered for and that they're across what you're doing.

Charlie and I were perhaps too enthusiastic to make the arrangement with Swan Brewery, our major sponsor, successful for the company. In the second year we badgered them into a co-promotion featuring Swan Gold beer. At our urging the brewery reluctantly invested in an event competition that encouraged people to purchase cartons of Swan Gold. It went for weeks, at considerable expense to Swan, and it did promote the tournament—but ultimately there were only a handful of entries in the competition.

While we might have gleaned a reasonable amount of knowledge about marketing a tennis event, we clearly knew nothing about marketing beer. Nissan was lesson one in sponsor relations; this was lesson two—don't teach your sponsor how to suck eggs. They know their product and how to market it.

To their credit, the crew at Swan remained supportive. It helped that Alan Bond was interested in the Hopman Cup. He came to the first event, took one look at the Swan Gold signage and said the narrow spacing between the parallel lines in the logo was causing them to 'bleed' on TV. We made the slight adjustment, as I figured that another lesson in event marketing was 'ignore the major sponsor at your peril'. And this wasn't an idle observation from a meddling executive—pre-empire, Bondy was a sign writer by trade.

He was also responsible for importing a brand of Korean cars new to Australia, Hyundai, through Australia's western gateway, Fremantle. Hyundai was the official car for Hopman in year one, and in year eight it became the title sponsor—as it remains today. This is one of the longest-running major sponsorships in Australian sport.

In its second year the Hopman Cup had a super field that included Cashy, Yannick Noah, Pam Shriver, Emilio Sanchez, Arantxa Sanchez-Vicario and Mikael Pernfors. But the biggest attraction that year undoubtedly was John McEnroe, who partnered Pam.

I found out John was playing when I was at the US Open that year and stopped by the Grandstand court to watch him practise. I was sitting in the crowd, minding my own business, when he stopped hitting and yelled, 'Hey, I'm comin' down for your tournament!'

Everyone around me was looking at me quizzically: who's this guy?

'That's great, John,' I called back.

That is often how I found out if a player was coming. I'd make contact directly with them, sounding them out. If they were interested, I sent a formal invitation to their manager, which included any business matters to be discussed. (I never spoke to players about money.) I wouldn't necessarily get a final answer from their management, but body language is always a giveaway. I could tell by the way a player looked at me when I bumped into them whether they were in or not.

Johnny Mac went out of his way to come over, and he certainly made his presence felt, not just on the court. The big auction item at the New Year's Eve Ball was a bright yellow jacket once worn by Stevie Wonder. John entered the bidding, as did Mikael Pernfors. Things escalated quickly, and I think Mikael had a hunch John didn't want to lose, so he kept bidding. Ultimately, it was knocked down to John for $10,000.

The next morning I received word from the hotel that there'd been a ruckus on John McEnroe's floor in the early hours of New Year's Day. John was said to have been yelling at his then wife, the actress Tatum O'Neal, 'Why didn't you stop me buying that jacket? It's gotta be the ugliest jacket I've ever seen. It's disgusting.' It might not be a verbatim account, but it sure sounds like John!

There's one catch with the ball: who will play the next morning at 10 a.m. It was quickly developing a reputation for showroom entertainment, risqué dancers, guests dancing on tables, that sort of thing. One year the Swedes got the short straw for New Year's Day and Pernfors was scheduled. He sent a mannequin in black tie (with his trademark headband) to sit in his seat at the ball as a protest. The other players kept putting the mannequin's hand up to bid during the auction, and one item was knocked down to Pernfors' stand-in for $5,000. It was pretty funny at the time, but I'm not sure how Mikael felt about honouring that.

Johnny Mac had ruffled feathers the night of the ball, and unsurprisingly there were on-court antics as well. In one tie the United States were playing Italy. John's singles match against Paolo Cane was last, a dead rubber, as the US had already won.

John was cruising along, winning the first set, when Paolo started playing out of his skin and the match looked headed for a third set. John began complaining about line calls and everything else, muttering, 'What am I even doing playing this BS match? It's meaningless.' And the real reason for his frustration: 'This jerk is trying like it's the most important match of his life.' Paolo had really got under his skin, and Johnny Mac lost the plot. He started cursing and, after being warned, received a point penalty.

At that moment the match referee, Peter Bellenger, a fair-minded man who was also the Australian Open referee, came to me and said, 'There are new rules in place under the Code of Conduct for 1990.'

I'd heard something about them being tougher.

'Under the new rules,' Peter continued, 'it's a default on the third infraction, so if John does anything more'—which looked inevitable—'technically we must default him. However, given the Hopman Cup started before 1 January 1989, I suppose we could say last year's rules apply...'

I didn't let him finish. 'Yes, definitely last year's rules.'

Then John broke a racquet and refused to play on. I asked Charlie if he would go over and have a word with him.

Charlie went courtside and appeared to have a brief conversation with John, who after a short time got up and started playing again. There were no more dramas and he won the match.

We were all fascinated: what had Charlie said to the simmering Johnny Mac?

'I didn't know what to say at all,' Charlie explained. 'So I asked him if he wanted a drink.'

'What did John say to that?' I asked.

'He didn't say anything at all. He just looked at me like I was a complete idiot.'

Disaster averted, the United States were now favourites to take the title, and in the final were up against the brother-and-sister pair of Emilio Sanchez and Arantxa Sanchez-Vicario of Spain, one of many great sibling combinations that would play in Perth. Emilio had a shock win over John in the opening match. The Americans duly won the mixed, so it came come down to Pam Shriver against Arantxa.

Emilio was scheduled to play an ATP event in Auckland. After wishing his sister well, he jumped on the overnight flight from Perth. Arantxa, in her prime, was too strong for Pam, who was entering the twilight of her career. It completed a surprise win for Spain. We got a message to Qantas, who informed the pilot en route to Auckland—and that's how Emilio found out that they'd won. The official photo of the siblings with the cup had to be taken the following year.

These were a big few days for Lesley and me. The New Year's Eve Ball was on the Friday, the final and end-of-tournament party on the Saturday, the buck's and hen's night on Sunday. Thank goodness Monday was free, as we were married the next day.

A Perth girl with five sisters, Lesley has a wonderful group of family and friends. She graduated in Phys. Ed. from UWA; basketball was her game, and one year she played for Western Australia's highest representative team nationally. Her being an athlete helped put us on the same wavelength. The only regret she had in sport was losing all her grand finals, and recently tennis redressed that when she won a doubles event at Warrnambool.

Lesley has a good sense of humour and is very popular. She's more low-key than me, and fortunately many of her personality traits have flowed on to our son.

It might seem odd to get married straight after the Hopman Cup, but it meant many of my friends from the tour could be there, as well as family. At the buck's party the crowd included Johnny Mac (say no more), his manager Sergio Palmieri (likes a drop of red), Yannick

Noah (familiar with sambuca, which I've not been able to touch since that night), Cashy (could party with the best of them), Macca (also good when he gets going), John Alexander (the life of any party), Pernfors (crazy without trying), Charlie (trying to be sensible), my brother Brian (looking out for me, as always), and a bunch more great blokes from my playing days and guys from Lesley's basketball scene. It was quite a night.

The ceremony was held at the beautiful St Michael's in Leederville and a reception followed in the Burswood ballroom. (Johnny Mac and Tatum were perhaps focused on a little too much in the video!) A honeymoon beckoned, but we put off the main one until May, when we would cruise the Nile.

We had a mini-honeymoon on Victoria's Mornington Peninsula, where we rented a house with a view over the bay at Portsea. On the drive back to Melbourne something caught my attention on the radio—I was tuning in to the action at the Australian Open. News was breaking: 'John McEnroe is in the process of being defaulted.' I knew exactly what that meant.

We were outside the Mordialloc Hotel, so I stopped the car and ran in to watch TV, muttering, 'He doesn't know the rule, he doesn't know the rule…'

Inside the pub Lesley and I watched as supervisor Ken Ferrar read the last rites on Johnny Mac's Open campaign. I was numb.

It came as no surprise to me when John revealed in the post-match media conference that he thought he had one more 'life'. He wasn't aware that the rule had changed. And he'd just played a tournament over in Perth under the old system.

That was the only time in his career that John was defaulted, and Ken Ferrar got a bit of celebrity status for being the man who stared him down. Many years later, when I was running the Australian Open, the ITF asked me if there could be a special on-court presentation to Ken, who was retiring. 'Not at this tournament,' I said, without divulging my guilt.

John, you got the short straw—it was not all your doing. I apologise for my role in it, mate.

15.
THE NEXT BIG THING

AT THE third Hopman Cup we witnessed the emergence of a superstar. She was a sixteen-year-old innocent from Yugoslavia, with an infectious personality, a broad smile and lovely parents. As we soon found out, she also had an indomitable spirit, the like of which I've never seen in anyone else. She became, in my opinion, the best female player of all time—with all due respect to Court, Navratilova, Evert and Graf.

Monica Seles was just learning the ropes, and her father was overseeing her progress. He'd introduced Monica to tennis when she was very young, famously painting cartoon characters on the tennis balls she practised with. He was a warm man with a big heart, proud of his exceptional daughter.

It was easy to see that Monica was special over the three weeks she spent in Perth. Playing two-handed on both sides, she had an incredible return of serve, but it was her competitive spirit that blazed most fiercely. She took the Hopman Cup by storm, and although her partner, Goran Prpic, was—relatively speaking—a far more modest talent, they became a formidable team.

In the semis against France it came down to the mixed doubles, where an imposing Guy Forget rifled back Monica's serve and engaged in lashing cross-court rallies with her. She never gave an inch, and those who witnessed the breathtaking baseline exchanges will never forget it. Monica didn't lose her serve in mixed doubles the entire week, and the understated Prpic was a perfect foil for her brilliance. They swept to the Hopman title, beating David Wheaton and Zina Garrison from the United States in the final.

Come Melbourne, the others didn't have a chance. Monica had prepared for the Australian Open under the radar but in perfect conditions in Perth: outdoors on the only other Rebound Ace surface in town, at the Vines Resort. At sixteen she stormed through to her first Grand Slam title—greatness, and regrettably sadness, were not far off.

The fourth Hopman Cup saw the return of Steffi Graf, who was involved in the most dramatic off-court moment for me in my 24-year involvement in the event. We'd managed to assemble a dream team. The two biggest stars of their generation, both German, were Steffi Graf and Boris Becker. It was the ultimate male and female combination in international sport. And they'd never played together before.

I pursued my mission of bringing this pair to Perth relentlessly. I knew this would be a coup for the cup. The only way the venture could be funded, I reasoned, was if German television underwrote it.

Boris's manager, Ion Tiriac, was heavily involved in the negotiations, as was Phil di Picciotto from Octagon for Steffi. The stars aligned and Sat.1, a new German sports cable network, agreed. They'd send a team of almost twenty people to cover this historic moment.

Sat.1 only had one condition: Boris and Steffi had to play together on court at least once. Straightforward, or so I believed.

Steffi arrived out of sorts, visibly struggling in her first match. She defeated Pascale Paradis, and Boris backed it up by beating Henri Leconte. Steffi decided she was too sick to play the mixed doubles, given Germany had already won the tie. No problem, I thought: there was the semi-final against the Czechs, and probably the final after that.

Steffi took the court a couple of nights later against Helena Sukova. She won the first set easily, then faded away to lose the second. I was a little shocked when she defaulted the match at a set apiece. I went straight to Boris: 'Mate,' I said. 'You need to talk to Steffi. You need to tell her she must play the mixed.'

Boris went to the women's locker room, knocked on the door, and the two had a chat.

Anxious, I asked Boris how it went. He'd told Steffi not to worry. He would beat Novacek and she just needed to rest up. Was he sure Steffi would play the mixed? He hadn't asked her directly. *O-kay*...but perhaps he was right to skirt around the issue.

Steffi certainly decided to rest—she went back to the Burswood hotel and straight to bed. This caused me great concern, as I knew getting her out of her bedroom was tougher than getting her out of the locker room or player lounge.

I didn't know what to do. Eventually I went back to the hotel myself to chill out and avoid the endless enquiries. It's not the first time I've had a nap in response to a stressful situation—I knew I'd need a clear head when the crunch came.

I set my alarm for half an hour hence, then woke to irate messages like, 'Where the hell are you? We have a crisis here!' I checked the score: Boris was up a set.

It was time. I went and knocked on Steffi's door. She had a small entourage with her and I was ushered into the room. At least she was out of bed, but she didn't look at all well. Taking a cue from Boris, I suspected it was advisable to dodge the question of whether she would play the mixed, as I might not get the answer I wanted. Instead I told her that Boris was winning well and I'd let her know when his match was finished.

Boris went on to win in straight sets, and I duly headed back to tell Steffi that the mixed was due to start in twenty minutes. The mood in her room was all doom and gloom. There was a strong vibe that Steffi would not be playing; I didn't need to speak German to figure that out.

I chose to ignore it and said, 'I'll see you over in the Dome in fifteen minutes. *Danke*, Steffi.' Then I waited in the hotel lobby nervously watching the descending lifts, willing Steffi to appear in tennis attire. If she didn't set foot on court we'd not be paid the German TV fee:

a substantial blow to the tournament. The clock was ticking.

At last, just as I was about to head back upstairs, Steffi and her trainer emerged from the elevator. I didn't want Steffi to think I was second-guessing her, so I quickly hid behind a pillar.

She walked towards the Dome, with me following fifty metres behind her. I felt like a spy.

The best route from the hotel to the courts is through a forty-metre-long tunnel. When Steffi got to the far end of the tunnel, she suddenly stopped and began a conversation with her trainer. It got louder and more animated. This wasn't a good sign. There was a fair chance Steffi was about to do a U-turn and head back to her room.

I was at the other end of the tunnel, and the only way back to the hotel was past me. I remember thinking with absolute clarity: If Steffi tries to go back to the hotel, I swear I am going to block her path.

It seemed an eternity before Steffi finally headed off for a little jog and then, without fuss, entered the Dome. I followed hastily and said to all and sundry, 'Sorry, I'll explain later where I've been,' and escorted the four players to the court.

My relief was palpable, but the match was sadly an anticlimax. Steffi could hardly play, and although Boris tried to cover for her the Germans lost the decisive match in two quick sets to the Czechs, who the next day lost the final to Switzerland's Jakob Hlasek and Manuela Maleeva.

Chatting with Steffi Graf, 1992.

Steffi withdrew from the Australian Open. She'd contracted, of all things, German measles. No wonder she felt so ill. Amazingly, that was the only occasion in their careers that the two greats graced the court together.

Around this time I made a foray into coaching. The head of the Western Australian Institute of Sport, Wally Foreman, introduced a tennis program, appointing me as head coach, and supported funding for two clay courts to be laid at the McGillivray Oval complex. I recommended Har-Tru, the pre-eminent clay-court surface in America, which had been used at the US Open. I had no doubt it would be more suited than European clay to our climate, especially given the wind in Perth.

The courts were fabulous, and we were able to expose a string of fine up-and-coming players to the nuances of clay. I'd also invite down more advanced players. Jenny Byrne, a former tour player, was a welcome visitor—she'd been top 100 in singles and a quality doubles player, but injuries and other challenges had taken their toll, and her career appeared over.

Jenny, now in her late twenties, confided that she wanted to make a comeback. Would I be her coach? I knew it was a tall order for her to get back to the tour, as she had no ranking, but I could tell she was sincere. My first piece of advice was, 'You won't get your game back until you've played fifty matches. We need to find somewhere for you to play.'

This is easier said than done, as even the lowest levels of tournaments require ranking points for entry. But we found an exception. Japan had a series of $10,000 ITF tournaments (the lowest category to carry ranking points) with open qualifying. Anyone who showed up would get a game.

When Jenny arrived at the first event she discovered that these Japanese tournaments had 128 draws in qualifying. She was required to win five matches just to qualify. Still, this was just what she needed.

Jenny qualified and won main draw matches every week, and after three events she gained a humble WTA ranking of around 700. And she quickly ticked off thirty matches, a fair slab of the fifty I believed she needed to play to find her game again.

Japan is not a cheap destination and Jenny had to run an extremely tight budget. Somehow she survived the trip, rationing meals and sharing abodes with girls in a similar situation. When she got home, Jenny revealed the close call she had at the end of her trip. She'd forgotten there was departure tax at Narita airport and, to her horror, she added up all the money she had left and was 100 yen short.

She was sitting distraught on her luggage in the middle of the airport when out of the corner of her eye she spotted a coin rolling across the floor. She jumped up and put her foot on it, hoping no one had noticed. When a little time had passed, she bent down and picked it up…100 yen. Yes!

After a period of training it was time for Jenny to play more matches, this time in the Australian challengers ($25,000 events). Now that she had a ranking, she could get into the qualifying for these higher-level events. In her first attempt Jenny qualified in week one and made it all the way to the final of the main draw. In the second week she won the tournament.

By the end of that series of challenger events Jenny's ranking had jumped substantially, and she'd racked up the magic fifty matches, or close enough. More importantly, she'd been the best performer on the overall Australian circuit, earning her on merit a main-draw wildcard entry to the Australian Open.

I sat proudly in Margaret Court Arena as Jenny played the superstar Gabriella Sabatini. A win was out of the question in this encounter—but we're not talking about the first round here. Jenny had already passed two rounds in style, and the cheque that came for playing the third round at the Australian Open was gratefully received.

She went on to have a very good year on the WTA tour, and at the year-end WTA Awards won Comeback Player of the Year. It was a fitting honour for Jenny Byrne, who'd experienced the highs and lows of an elite sporting career. She went on to become a highly respected coach in New York City.

In the middle of the following year I was in Paris when I received a call out of the blue from Stefano Capriati, father of the very talented Jennifer Capriati. Jen, only seventeen, was already an Olympic gold medallist, having defeated Steffi Graf in the final in Barcelona, and had broken into the top ten. Stefano asked if I'd help Jen with her grass-court game, with Wimbledon on the horizon. I'd need to go to the new Hopman camp at Saddlebrook Resort in Florida. Lesley, who was in Europe in the middle of a bus tour with her mother, Margaret, swapped with her sister Stephanie and came to Florida too.

Jen was a great ball striker. It was obvious that her game didn't require much refining for success on grass. The wide serve, a *sine qua non* on the surface, needed some work, but mainly she needed to up the ante in her off-court training. I made her go for a run each day, something she wasn't accustomed to. It was a little concerning that Jen was going into Wimbledon without a grass-court warm-up event; nevertheless, she was in good shape.

At Wimbledon, Jen marched through to the quarter-finals, where she lost a tough match with the world number one, Steffi Graf—a decent result. That night we all went to dinner in Piccadilly, after which Jen asked her dad for some change so she could play the coin machines at the Trocadero. She was still a minor, and had to ask her parents for spending money.

I was asked to help get Jen ready for the US Open. There was significant expectation: Jen had lost a brutal semi-final against Monica Seles in a previous Open and was now being marketed as the future of American tennis.

Stefano intimated to me that Jen was becoming less focused. I didn't think that was overly surprising, as she'd soon be turning eighteen. Maybe she was yearning for more independence. In addition, it seemed Stefano and Denise, Jen's mother, were not on the same page about Jen's future. Perhaps I was naive, but Jen was training well and I decided to do no more than be watchful.

The night before we were leaving for the Premier WTA tournament in Toronto I asked Stefano if he was coming, as Jen always had a parent along. 'Jen hasn't decided yet,' he said.

Although I tried not to show it, I was taken aback. Jen needed to ask permission to get a small amount of play money, yet she decided which of her parents would travel with her.

The next day I was picked up and taken to the Capriati residence. I was ushered inside the front door and, to my surprise, noticed there were two sets of luggage packed and ready to go—Stefano's on the left and Denise's on the right. Were both parents coming? Who would be looking after Jen's younger brother?

The family assembled at the front door. 'Jen,' Stefano asked, 'who's going to Toronto?'

'I want…' Jen said, looking at Stefano, then at Denise, then back to Stefano. This went on for some time. Finally, she announced, 'I want Mommy to come.'

As we departed, not really knowing what to say, I mumbled to Stefano, 'See you in a week.'

In Toronto, Jen stormed to the semis, where she met the defending champ, Arantxa Sanchez-Vicario. This would be a stern test, as Arantxa was ranked three, higher than Jen.

It was a tough encounter, but Jen powered her way through in straight sets. She had a natural strength—she could step up in the crunch, as top players can do. It was impressive, but the final would be harder. Waiting there was Steffi Graf.

Jen was up a notch from Wimbledon, but Steffi played faultlessly and took the first set. She was a super athlete. In the second set Jen's game came together superbly, and she won 6–0, a stunner. The third was hard-fought, and in the end Steffi just edged Jen out.

This was the perfect lead-in to New York. Jen had made the final of a big event, and had given Steffi Graf a lot to think about. After all, Steffi was not in the habit of losing a set 6–0.

It was time to go to New York. The whole family was coming on this trip. The hype around Jen was huge. Many commentators were tipping her to win her first Grand Slam.

The day before Jen's first-round match she had a clinic

ABOVE: *With the victorious Cashy at the 1987 Wimbledon Champions' Dinner.*

Off to practise with Charlie Fancutt, mid-1980s.

With Dallas Dempster, owner of Perth's Burswood Resort, in the air-conditioned Dome, 1988.

At Hoad's with the great Ken Rosewall, 1994.

Roger Federer's maiden pro victory—the 2001 Hopman Cup, partnered by Martina Hingis.

At the 2000 Open, Pistol Pete was on a crusade to break Emmo's record for Grand Slam singles wins.

With the Rocket and his statue at Melbourne Park in 2002.

Hosting Serena Williams at the 2003 Hopman Cup Ball.

With Johnny Mac, Jim Courier, Layne Beachley and members of INXS in the Australian Open club, 2003.

Bringing Jelena Dokic back into the Aussie fold, 2005.

As sweet as a Wimbledon victory: celebrating El Segundo's 2007 Cox Plate win alongside Rowan and Lesley in Melbourne.
© *Russell Tindale / Newspix.*

In the player box at Wimbledon, watching Su-wei Hsieh win the 2013 women's doubles final. (Photo by Chuan Chung.)

Arriving with the victorious Su-wei for the 2013 Wimbledon Champions' Dinner. (Photo by Chuan Chung.)

for kids organised by Prince, her racquet manufacturer. I weighed up whether I should go to Flushing Meadows to scout her first-round opponent, Russia's Leila Meskhi.

'I know her well,' Jen said. 'I've played her before and know what she does. I'll be fine.'

I went to the Prince clinic, figuring that I could help Jen out there and step in if the media or fans got too intrusive.

The first match was at Armstrong Stadium—Jen would be front and centre for the Open. She won the first set easily. Then, in the second, Meskhi picked up a bit and Jen went down. In a close set, Meskhi pipped Jen. Disappointing—but I knew Jen had too much game for her opponent and would come back in the third.

Early in the third set Jen began fidgeting with her bra, continually looking over to Denise, who was sitting next to me, and complaining about it. This went on for game after game. I couldn't believe Jen wasn't taking a bathroom break and getting it sorted out.

The match was slipping away, I was getting frustrated, and finally I called out to Jen—as discreetly as possible, but bluntly—'Take it off. Who cares?'

That was probably inappropriate, but there was a big match on the line and sometimes you've just gotta do what you've gotta do, and hang the consequences. Jen, out there in front of sixteen thousand fans, unsurprisingly didn't take my advice.

There was a bigger concern. Jen was over-playing Meskhi's backhand, the Russian's stronger side. Meskhi's forehand would be the side that would break under pressure—but only if Jen noticed and switched her focus.

She didn't, and Meskhi hung on to score a massive upset. It was shattering; there's no other way to describe it.

As a coach I'd made a fatal error. I'd not prepped Jen properly for Meskhi. It's easy for a coach to scout in preparation. All you need to do is watch one set of a prospective opponent's previous match, and you'll have a handle on their strengths and weaknesses.

However, a first-round opponent is different, as she hasn't played a match yet, so you need to find out their practice time and try unobtrusively to watch them hit. In addition, or if all else fails (and these days there is YouTube), ask another player or coach whom you trust to give you the inside running, especially on whether they favour the forehand or backhand, and anything else of value—second serve is vulnerable under pressure, that kind of thing. You may need to return the favour down the track. No information comes free.

I shouldn't have accompanied Jen to the clinic—I should have been scouring the courts at Flushing Meadows doing homework on Leila Meskhi. I'd let down Jennifer Capriati, a serious talent, and learnt another unforgettable lesson.

Later that day, after the shock exit, Jen called me to her room. 'I need to tell you something,' she said. 'I'm quitting tennis.'

'Why?' I protested. 'It's not the end of the world. Everyone has a loss like that now and then. And I didn't do my...'

'It's not about that. I've got something I need to deal

with, and I can't say what it is but I can't go on until I deal with it.'

And that was that. I was then—and still remain—in the dark about the situation, but for me it was a sad end to a promising partnership.

At the next Hopman Cup, Steffi Graf returned, not with Boris Becker but with another former Wimbledon champion, Michael Stich. The Germans swept to the title. The highlight of the week was when they took on the brother–sister team of Natalia Medvedeva and Andrei Medvedev of the Ukraine, with some awesome power tennis on display in the men's match.

The year after saw the Hopman Cup introduce a world first: new technology that could call every line on the court. Previously, service line calls were made by Cyclops, a camera-based system emitting a beep when a serve was long. This new system, TEL (for Tennis Electronic Lines), relied instead on an electromagnetic field beneath all the court's lines and metal filings inserted into balls during the manufacturing process. It was designed by an Adelaide weapons researcher, Brian Williams.

The sixth Hopman Cup unveiled this revolutionary technology—quite an operation, as we had to re-lay the entire court to incorporate the electromagnetic wiring. Only time would tell whether it would be used elsewhere, and whether lines people would become redundant.

We soon encountered a problem no one had predicted. Cedric Pioline was representing France with Mary Pierce. In Pioline's first match, TEL started making inexplicable calls. We were forced to bring out a full crew of lines people, to the bemusement of the crowd.

The system was perfect in the next matches—until Cedric Pioline played again. This was unfathomable.

The TEL team undertook extensive testing and discovered the cause of the problem. Pioline's racquet was an antique aluminium model, unlike those used by any other player. And the metal in it created the same electromagnetic frequency as TEL's iron filings in the tennis balls. Whenever Pioline swung his racquet near the baseline, TEL recognised the metal and beeped 'out'.

There was also a predictable backlash against the 'dehumanising' of the sport. After all, wouldn't it be the death knell of serial 'umpire bashers', colourful characters such as John McEnroe? That could hardly be good for tennis.

I could see the merits of these arguments. But I was a strident supporter of TEL. The theatre of sport should not override the carriage of justice in the most critical moments of a player's career. Line calls need to be as accurate as possible—everyone benefits from that. Our experience was not without teething problems, but we felt overall it had been a success and an indication of how the Hopman could be a game changer in the sport.

The tournament that year was won by the wonderful Czech pairing of Petr Korda and Jana Novotna, victorious over Germany's Anke Huber, a future Australian Open finalist, and Bernd Karbacher, who had a notable win over Ivan Lendl during the week.

Huber was once more in the spotlight the following

year, 1995, the year Boris Becker returned to Perth. Again the highlight of the week was Germany versus Ukraine, featuring the Medvedevs, this time in the final. The unusual thing about this match was that Andrei Medvedev and Anke Huber were an item. Andrei had to watch his sister play against his girlfriend—he was definitely between a rock and a hard place.

It was a torrid match, with the higher-ranked Anke eventually winning in three sets. It was obvious that Anke was irritated by Andrei in the match, as she kept a close watch on him. Boris then had another hard-fought win over Andrei, giving Germany the honours.

The courtside atmosphere was frosty, and Andrei chose not to play the 'dead' mixed against his girlfriend. I ended up filling in with his sister, playing an exhibition match against Boris and Anke. Andrei's romance with Huber was, regrettably, on borrowed time. Proof, perhaps, that blood is thicker than water.

16.
OPEN FOR BUSINESS

MY HOPMAN exploits and forays into coaching had been testing; after humble beginnings in the west, a bigger challenge was lurking around the corner. The Hopman Cup had caught the attention of Tennis Australia and in particular its president, Geoff Pollard. He was impressed by its growing stature, by how quickly it had become part of the fabric of the city, and especially by the plaudits players were giving the event.

On the last, much of the credit should go to Lesley. She believed that every person in a player's entourage should be looked after like the players themselves: transport, hotel room, sightseeing and the highlight, access to a courtside box laden with gourmet food and fine wine. That did not go unnoticed by the players. A regular visitor, Amanda Coetzer, was moved to say, 'Every player is treated like they're Steffi Graf.'

Lesley's other major influence was the concept of the Hopman family. Anyone who worked on the tournament was treated as family, and in return they upheld the Hopman spirit of friendship and service, ever loyal to the event. This extended to contractors—the Burswood catering staff, trays overflowing, would kneel on the stairwells of the corporate stand, daring not to move in case they interrupted play. They would return year after year and wait on the same boxes, getting on a first-name basis with many of the corporate clients.

During 1993 Geoff Pollard had sounded me out about the Australian Open. The incumbent tournament director was Colin Stubs. Stubsy knew his stuff (he still oversees the AAMI Classic at Kooyong), and stayed close to the players. He'd been very good to me in my junior days. I made it clear to Geoff that I was not interested in the role while Colin was in it.

Another year passed before Geoff informed me that Stubsy's contract had not been renewed and the position was open. In early 1994 I applied and shortly after was appointed by the board. Given the financial challenges of the Open at that time, and the lack of funds at Tennis Australia (under a million dollars in the bank), the initial salary was modest. But it was a rare opportunity and an honour. I caught up with Stubsy, who generously wished me well, adding, 'Watch out, there's always something unexpected that happens.'

Geoff's brief was simple. 'I want you to bring the sparkle of the Hopman Cup to the Australian Open. And I want you to help elevate the tournament to be a full and equal partner of the other Grand Slams.'

When I arrived, in March 1994, the Australian Open had all the ingredients of a marquee event—but it seemed to be lacking atmosphere. In marketing speak, the event had no position that presented a unique identity to locals or to the rest of the world. Having only seven full-time staff didn't help.

Sweeney's had conducted research which showed that the Australian Open was Australia's third most important sporting event. It was no embarrassment to be ranked behind the Melbourne Cup and the AFL Grand Final, but neither was being third going to constitute our public identity. We commissioned the National Institute of Economic and Industry Research to undertake an economic-impact study. This would not only give us a benchmark for future years, but provide valuable information on visitor attendance and demographics.

We needed a market position, and fast. Melbourne, much to Adelaide's chagrin, had just secured the rights to the Australian Formula 1 Grand Prix. If we were aspiring to pole position on Australia's major-events calendar, we had some serious competition across the Yarra. When Premier Jeff Kennett donned the black-and-white-checked jacket at the Grand Prix launch, I knew we were up against it.

Many keywords could describe the characteristics of the Open: prestigious, big, great, global, Melbourne, Australia, and so on. The marketing director of Tennis Australia, John Brown, quite reasonably suggested that we should be 'Australia's premier international sporting event'. Our positioning statement needed to be bold yet credible. I reckoned that there was only one prize worth going for in our sports-crazy nation, and that was to be 'Australia's biggest sporting event'.

The Open spans two weeks (three, if you count the

qualifying competition), and has many hundreds of competitors and thousands of staff. I passionately believed that the tournament needed to go for it, so we decided to raise some eyebrows and stake out the claim. But if we were going to be Australia's biggest sporting event, we needed to start behaving like it, for only a change in behaviour can alter perceptions—which, in marketing, are reality. We needed to be big, and we needed to be truly Australian.

I was always impressed by how Wimbledon could incorporate a brilliant new development, making it look like it had been part of the complex for decades. And by the aesthetics of Roland Garros, where a haute-couture-collection feel complemented the burst of springtime in Paris. New York just needed to be itself—an exciting, in-your-face city and event. We needed to follow suit: to reflect our identity, to project our own vibe. To be Aussies, not shackled by English traditions.

Which brought me to a bone of contention during my first year on the job. Why was the Australian Open's schedule a carbon copy of Wimbledon's? Understandable, I suppose, to imitate the world's most prestigious event, but surely the set-up was designed for English weather and grass courts—neither of which was relevant to us.

We designed a new schedule that provided a combination of men's and women's singles in as many sessions as possible. From my Hopman Cup experience, I thought this diversity was essential. And part of being accepted as the equal of others is unashamedly being yourself.

Lesley and I, while still guiding the Hopman Cup with Charlie Fancutt, took on another project. One of our favourite visitors to the tournament, the Aussie great Lew Hoad, who attended with his wife, Jenny, was very sick. For Lew to have any chance, he needed the best treatment, and it became clear that the medical bills were starting to add up.

Lesley and I had visited their beautiful tennis club in Mijas, near Malaga in southern Spain. We felt it would be the ideal setting for a fundraising tournament that summer, and set about inviting as many as possible of Lew's tennis mates, past and present. All who could possibly make it put their hands up straight away to play in the Lew Hoad Classic.

Lesley and I made several trips to the Campo de Tenis, setting about the myriad details of running a tournament and, especially, raising sponsorship. Lew and Jenny's abode was a humble hacienda, walking distance from the clubhouse, and we shared some great times there. Lew's health was deteriorating, but he still loved holding court in the bar, surrounded by his photos of Frank Sinatra, Grace Kelly, Ava Gardner and the rest.

He'd tell me how he was employed by the Spanish Federation to coach the coaches, and about how the Campo was formed. He'd done a fair bit of wheelbarrow pushing himself, and there were many touches of Jenny, also a former player, around the club. She'd designed the logo, visible on the floor of the swimming pool and hand-painted on souvenirs.

An unbelievable line-up of players was ready to congregate—among them Laver, Buchholz, Santana, Stolle, Orantes, Carmichael, Davies, Taylor, Mottram,

Relaxing with Rod 'Rocket' Laver after playing golf at Lew Hoad's Campo de Tenis, Spain, in 1994.

McNamara, and Trevor, Daphne and Charlie Fancutt. And Lew's tennis 'twin', Ken Rosewall, of course. Even Mrs Lucy Hopman was coming. The event was scheduled for just after Wimbledon. Everybody was keen to help, and we reckoned we could raise some decent money to help with Lew's treatment.

In London on the day of the Wimbledon final I got one of those phone calls you dread. Lew had passed away. We were gutted—we'd lost an iconic and much-loved Australian. We let things sit for a day or two, then I contacted Jenny. She was keen for the tournament to go ahead: Lew would have wanted that.

So the Lew Hoad Memorial Classic was played as a dedication to Lew and his life. The matches, held in the cooler twilight hours, were fabulous. Everyone played their hearts out with a wonderful spirit. The most emotional moment of the week was a memorial service for Lew. One of Lew's friends played the music. It was a simple yet moving yet send-off for an irreplaceable man.

I'll never forget the sumptuous paella and sangria, the music and wonderful company, and all of us gathered to rejoice in our love of Lew and of tennis. We enjoyed every balmy night into the wee hours at the Hoads' club. I have precious memories of that week and, with the help of a generous donation by the ATP, the money raised would assist Jenny through the difficult times to come. We headed home feeling sad, yet knowing we'd done our bit.

Not long after, we had cause for celebration. 'Paul,' Lesley said one day, 'I'm pregnant.' I was as excited as I'd ever been, and like all first-time parents we frantically started making arrangements.

Meanwhile, at the Australian Open, there was much that needed to be done. The TV situation was dire. In the preceding five years the sport had seen its prime-time coverage systematically eroded in all of the lead-in events. If the Open followed suit, mainstream irrelevance beckoned.

We needed to assess the product and see how to tweak it. That Andre Agassi, currently the biggest star in men's tennis, was playing the event for the first time was certainly going to help, but I knew Agassi alone couldn't save us.

The 1995 Open's TV schedule guaranteed tennis until at least midnight, which was good for racking up advertising minutes. But everything was shown on a one-hour delay from 8.30. The format was a women's singles match followed by a men's. We needed to change direction, and it seemed to me that the only way to improve the ratings was to go live in prime time, ideally with a big men's match. The network had never entertained this idea. And, in order to test it, I needed the women's match to be over by 8.30.

On my first night as tournament director I knew I had a chance. There was a first-round match between the popular Swede Stefan Edberg and an eighteen-year-old Melbourne talent, Mark Philippoussis. This was scheduled at night, to follow a match I handpicked between Steffi Graf and a qualifier—one that shouldn't take long.

I went to the executive producer of Seven Sport, Gordon Bennett, and played my hand. Gordon responded that Seven was committed to its schedule, promoting the women's match followed by the men's, on a one-hour delay, and would not be changing the longstanding protocol. I was disappointed but not dejected—I knew I had to press on.

As expected, Steffi delivered. The German superstar was on song, and off court by 8.15. Now came the moment of truth.

I placed my second call to Gordon Bennett, to politely double check that they didn't want to go live with the men's match. He didn't dismiss me out of hand, and asked if I'd hold the players for a few minutes so he could confer with the programmers in Sydney.

Gordon called back shortly after with a message I've always been grateful for. 'Paul, we'd like to go live with the men's. Can you hold them in the locker room until we go on air at 8.30?'

When Seven's tennis coverage came on air that night, the television audience was treated for the first time to a week-one live telecast of a men's match. The unflappable Swede took on the gangly, guns-blazing Aussie. The Scud was erratic but often breathtaking, and that night he managed to snare a set. Here was a match that offered the pure joy of sport, contrasting styles and personalities in high-quality battle, and I prayed it captured the TV viewers as it did the patrons.

Next day, Gordon was on the phone summoning me to his office in the TV compound to discuss the previous night. I felt like a naughty schoolboy about to be reprimanded.

'Paul,' Gordon greeted me. 'It rated 21!'

I was gobsmacked. Prior to that, the best they could hope for was a 14. And this was my first night in the job. I was ecstatic.

To fuel this new approach I needed more marquee men's matches. We'd have to revoke our long-standing tournament protocol which dictated that players only had to play one night match, a throwback to Bjorn Borg's distaste for nights at the US Open. But all the players were aware of this limited obligation. All except one—the only star player who'd never participated in the tournament, Andre Agassi.

I sidled up to him in the corner of the locker room

(which was to be dubbed Andre's Corner) and said, 'Andre, you know you're going to have to play twice at night?'

'Can you make it once in the first week,' he replied, 'and once the second week?'

I knew that if the biggest star in the sport was willing to play more than once at night, no other player would complain. It was a gamble, like the Edberg–Philippoussis match, but it paid off.

Andre played his first night match early on, then had a fourth-round match against an athletic young Aussie from Mount Isa, Patrick Rafter, on the second Monday. When I think about that night I can feel the electricity in the air as Pat serve-volleyed the first point of the match. It was like a world-title fight, with the two athletes punching and counter-punching on a floodlit court, a cheering crowd willing them on.

Andre's far greater experience carried him to an emphatic victory, yet in TV land we rated 39. That was close to the ratings of the 1988 Open final between Mats Wilander and Pat Cash—the highest-rating match in tournament history. And we were only in the fourth round.

In one week, we had irrevocably altered the prime-time program, its subsequent appeal to advertisers and sponsors, and indeed the future direction of the Australian Open. Nights would now be televised live, featuring a battle that would informally be known as Match of the Day.

That year Pete Sampras was numero uno and the defending champion. No one could have foreseen the tragedy that almost derailed his campaign.

His coach was an affable bloke who'd been a top-ten player, and his twin brother had also been a very good player. Tim and Tom Gullikson were the pair Macca and I had beaten in what turned out to be our last title, the US Indoors in Memphis. The Gullies were identical twins, one left-handed (Tom) and the other right-handed (Tim). They were popular and influential in American men's tennis.

At the '95 Open, Sampras, coached by Tim, raced through to the quarter-finals, where he was up against the former world number one and dual Australian Open champion Jim Courier. This was on the second Tuesday, a fantastic follow-up to Agassi and Rafter. Pete and Jim went toe to toe for hours, all the way to the fifth set, when Pete was seen wiping tears from his eyes between points. Nobody, Courier included, knew why.

These emotional scenes continued for some time, with Jim at one stage calling over the net to Pete, 'We can play this out tomorrow if you want.' It was a strange and unnerving sight.

Tim Gullikson, it transpired, had taken a bad turn the previous night and been sent to hospital for tests. He'd just received the diagnosis—he had an aggressive brain tumour and not long to live. Pete, a private bloke, had kept the news to himself as he took to the court. But as the match progressed Pete's thoughts turned to his mentor's fate.

Still, he pressed on. He managed to pull himself together in the most critical moments. At one stage, after seeming to take more than the legal time limit to wipe away his tears and compose himself on break point, he peeled off an ace.

Against the odds he won that fifth set. Many pundits still believe it was the greatest quarter-final ever played in the sport. Pete was back on track, but his revered coach would pass away just over a year later.

On the women's side, even before the tournament had started I was in a situation I hadn't encountered on the men's tour. Mary Pierce, the statuesque French player, came into my office.

'Paul,' she said, 'is it okay if I practise without a top, just in a sports bra?'

My inner bloke had me say, 'Of course,' before I'd had a chance to really think about the ramifications. My mind started racing, recalling all the times kids, myself included, had been warned at tennis clubs for wearing 'non-conforming attire'. Imagine the havoc if this occurred at the All England Club at Wimbledon, where I don't think even the bra being white would excuse the breach of decorum.

I realised that I should be referring matters of attire to the tournament referee, Peter Bellenger, rather than winging it—but by that time Mary was already out on a show court and word had spread to the media room.

Bellenger was a wise man, not at all prone to sudden shifts of mood. I informed him about Mary.

'We're not actually a tennis club here,' Peter said calmly. 'It's a public venue, so club rules technically don't apply. We should be okay if it becomes a big deal. But Paul, next time, can you give me a bit more notice?'

No surprises about the front-page photo of the following day's *Herald Sun*. It probably was something that could only happen in Australia, given the combination of hot weather and irreverence. And the publicity certainly did Mary no harm.

Over in the men's draw Sampras won his semi, and in the final would come up against the winner of the match between Andre Agassi and another American, Aaron Krickstein. That semi-final was a battle royal with an odd conclusion. Agassi was leading when the roof was shut due to a heavy storm. Then, early in the third set, Krickstein retired due to injury.

Later, by chance, I noticed on a TV screen that there was water on Centre Court. Why on earth, I wondered, has a conservative chap like Peter Bellenger opened the roof? He's got to be kidding.

I ducked down to Centre Court. When I arrived, to my horror I saw that the roof was still shut: water was entering from floor level, and quickly. It was a flood, on the eve of the women's final. All I could think of was Stubsy's warning about the unexpected happening. Too right!

The venue is managed by the state government's Melbourne and Olympic Parks Trust. Its events crew kicked into gear, unplugging all electrical equipment and ensuring the safety of spectators. Centre Court was now a swimming pool, so one chap dived in and starting doing laps. A few players, including Natasha Zvereva and Rennae Stubbs, starting frolicking in the makeshift pool.

The water started subsiding a couple of hours later,

and the massive clean-up operation could start. But there was no telling whether we could get things back to working order in time—or what damage the water might have done.

Geoff Pollard was certain that there'd been significant flooding during an ice show six years before at Flinders Park, and the Rebound Ace tennis surface had not been adversely affected. This gave us some hope, enough for me to attend the media dinner that night and proclaim that we had every reason to believe there would be no hold-up to the women's singles final, scheduled for 1.30 the next afternoon. I was not at all confident, but erred on the positive side—there'd be enough bad news tomorrow if we couldn't pull it off.

After a restless night I stepped onto Centre Court with trepidation. I looked for evidence of bubbling. Nothing. Armed with racquet and balls, I proceeded to rally a few. My shoes weren't squelching—a huge relief.

The roof was open, the fixtures and fittings were aired and dry, the electrics were operable, and the stench was almost gone. We had a match. I contacted Mary Pierce and Arantxa Sanchez-Vicario. After warming up, neither was concerned by the surface in the slightest. It was game on.

For the record, Pierce won the Open, her maiden Grand Slam singles title, beating Sanchez-Vicario in two sets. We'd dodged a bullet.

Come Sunday, the Sampras–Agassi contest was the Grand Slam final the sport had been waiting a long time for. It was a set all in a riveting encounter when they headed to a tiebreak in the third. I remember Sampras hitting a second-serve ace as hard as I've seen, at more than two hundred kilometres an hour.

Pete was arguably the best server the game has ever seen, and he had an awesome standing-jump smash, but there was no more dangerous shot than his running forehand. If you came in and hit a volley wide to his forehand, you had to hope it was out of his reach. Pete would give you the room and almost dare you to go there, and once you took the bait he seemed to come alive—his eyes widened, his body seemed to explode into action and he began the backswing while in full flight. And then the forehand destroyed his prey in one fell swoop. I guarantee you, no ball would be struck again in the rally.

At 3–2 in that tiebreak Pete smashed a running forehand cross court—it was breathtaking, and everyone swore he was on top. And he would have been, against anyone other than Andre. A net cord went against Pete, and somehow Andre squeezed out the tiebreak and they headed to the fourth set. And that was it for Pete. All the anguish of Tim's hardship seemed to catch up with him—he was a spent force.

The 1995 Open had been a watershed. With two weeks full of drama, unprecedented prime-time ratings and a dream final, the Open had begun the process of becoming Australia's biggest sporting event. We were coping (just) with the local climate, taking a chance or two, even being a bit risqué. We were doing things the Aussie way.

17.
THE GREAT AUSTRALIAN DREAM

THERE WAS one critical difference between the women's and men's finals at the Australian Open: the ranking points on offer. In the women's events at the four Grand Slams, players received the same points. The men's ranking points, though, were allocated according to prize money at all levels, including Grand Slams. And we offered considerably less money than the other majors, meaning fewer points.

Growth in prize money was linked to our overall business success. Geoff Pollard's aim was to increase the pool of cash, then around $8 million, by $1 million each year. This was an ambitious target—and even with these annual rises we'd stay way behind the other three Grand Slams. Wimbledon was already at $14 million.

But a major is a major, and surely the rankings should be viewed differently? After all, we were in the highest category—shouldn't the points reflect the event's status?

I knew Geoff saw things the same way as I did. 'Now's the moment to make our move with the ATP,' I told him. 'We've just had *the* men's final.'

Geoff didn't need convincing, but it needed to be discussed by the ATP, and at the Grand Slam Committee, a forum of the four Grand Slams. For any change to occur the chairmen, who alone can vote, need to be unanimous. This committee stretches diplomacy to its limits, as it brings together the English and the French, Americans and Australians.

The other Grand Slams and the ATP were accommodating and supportive: they worked on a formula whereby the Grand Slams would receive the same points, based on average prize money. Therefore, it wasn't just the Australian Open that would be affected: equal points would mean equalisation in the other three Grand Slams, all of which had slightly different prize purses.

Even though we were the weak link, we received the acquiescence of the other Grand Slams, and for that we were most grateful to their chairmen: Christian Bimes at Roland Garros, Lester Snyder at the US Open and, particularly, John Currie at Wimbledon. For the first time since rankings were introduced in 1973, the Australian Open would receive points equal to the other Grand Slams for men and women.

In this my second year as tournament director, I was appointed head of marketing. I became jointly in charge of the Open with the general manager, Jim Reid. Jim was from a construction background and a stickler for process. 'In big events there's no such thing as a small thing,' he'd say. Together I think we made a fine team—he chaired the management committee, freeing me up to go for it on the marketing side.

A bigger change in circumstances occurred on 4 April 1995, when our son was born. Lesley and I had made a deal. If it was a girl, Lesley would choose the first name and I'd choose the middle one. If it was a boy, the reverse would apply.

I wanted Lenny, as my dad's best mate was Lenny Ramm. They went to school together at Tarnagulla Primary, played footy and cricket on the same team, played doubles together, and in later years Lenny introduced Dad to golf. Lenny, a lifelong Tarna man, was a great friend and mentor to my brothers and sister, and to me. We were all shattered when he died, especially Dad.

So when our son was born, at St John of God hospital in Perth, the first thing I said was, 'Hello, Lenny.'

'I can't call him that,' Lesley said.

I picked Mum and Dad up at the airport, and the name problem came up. 'I really want to call him Lenny, but Lesley's not that keen.'

'Lenny was my best mate,' Dad said, 'but you know something? I never really liked his name.'

'That settles it, then. He'll be Rowan Frederick Hateley McNamee.'

This had come from a conversation Lesley had with my mum, who'd dreamt that we had a curly-haired blond boy called Rowan. Lesley liked the name, and so did I—especially, from my perspective, the connection to Glenrowan, where the bushranger Ned Kelly made his last stand. Fred was from Brian's and my nicknames for each other, and we added Lesley's maiden name as the six sisters ended the name on her side of the family tree.

Life was going well: I was a proud dad, in my first year as head of marketing, and preparing for the 1996 Open. Responsibility for the event was being transferred from the umbrella organisation, Tennis Australia, to the Australian Open team headed by Jim Reid and me. The process of 'Australianisation', the next step in establishing the brand, began in earnest. Every decision we made needed to reflect the essence of Australia—the sights, sounds and smells of our nation.

I pinched the very capable Meghan Tozer from elsewhere in Tennis Australia and hired an ad agency to help, headed by Digby Nancarrow. We set about creating a blueprint for converting the Open from a big, friendly and professionally run tennis tournament to a major event, and ultimately a major brand.

Meghan and I worked annually on a marketing plan, and this formed the building blocks of my tenure at the Open. Central to the Australianisation push was a spectator-friendly policy to reflect the egalitarian Australian character. That of course needed to reverberate through the hundreds of tournament staff and thousands of contractors—a bit like the Hopman spirit in Perth. Above all, we wanted the Open to be affordable and accessible to fans.

Our logo was the Ford emblem sitting above a tennis net and the words 'Ford Australian Open'. That's normal: the major sponsor is underwriting proceedings and would expect to mesh the company brand into the event's logo. But the other three Grand Slams—Wimbledon, the

French Open and the US Open—had no commercial entity in their names.

It seemed to me that for financial reasons an unencumbered brand name, the Australian Open, was a long way off. We'd need to get creative if we didn't think the logo was fully representative of our event. On the other hand, the last thing we'd want to do is risk alienating our longstanding and biggest sponsor.

Changing the logo was not an option, so instead we'd endeavour to capture the essence of the tournament and its local character through a distinctive look. Five advertising agencies put forward designs, but one stood out. It showed the sun, the earth and the sky, overscored with the silhouette of a player serving. I loved it: the sun, in sync with our summer; the earth, represented by the ochre of the country's red centre; and the sky, the blue so dominant nationwide.

We consulted Ford who, appreciative of the unchanged logo, approved the new look. This was liberating—now we had a palette of colours to use in signage, advertising, floral displays and, especially, merchandising.

There was an appetite for it. The number of international visitors was growing rapidly, led by the Swedes, who flocked to support Wilander, Edberg and Johansson, and the Germans, supporting Graf, Becker and Stich. They'd fly over the red centre of Australia to bask in the summer sunshine under blue skies—and want a souvenir to take home.

The nomenclature around the grounds needed to reflect our identity too: for example, the Courtside Bar was renamed the Beach Bar & BBQ. We used native flowers where possible, and the soundtracks for our advertising came from Aussie acts like INXS, Men at Work and GANGgajang. We could see the Open coming into its own—and making it happen was a lot of fun.

That year, 1996, was the first using the Stage Two development at Melbourne Park. This included the new Show Court Three, eleven new outdoor match courts on the western side, a function centre and a large outdoor area smack in the middle named Garden Square.

Garden Square was ideally placed for patrons to meet and hang out. If you didn't have a Centre Court ticket, you could relax and enjoy the action on the big screen. Free outdoor concerts featuring rising Aussie bands became part of a day at the Open, attracting younger people. I've always believed that 'the better the atmosphere, the luckier you get.'

We dubbed our ground pass 'the best value sports ticket in the world'. We meant it. I was determined that we would not deny access to any spectator, and that this pass would become a unique asset we could promote to the tennis world.

Stage Two, doubling the footprint of the site, would help elevate the Open to the next level—and this became the centrepiece of our marketing campaign. The slogan for the 1996 Open was 'Double the Action'. Digby Nancarrow wrote some lyrics and got Mike Brady (of 'Up there Cazaly' fame) to sing the jingle for radio and TV ads.

Digby had also written lyrics for a song about the

Open: 'That's What You Mean to Me'. It was emotive, but it went for went for a minute and a half—hard to see how we could use it. Then Digby said he could get a ninety-second spot in the TV coverage of the AFL's Brownlow Medal count.

'How much, Digby?' I asked, a little nervously.

'Twenty-seven thousand.'

That was nearly a third of our entire advertising spend. And yet...how audacious to have an ad that long on prime-time TV, during such high-rating coverage of footy's famous night. Now that's behaviour befitting Australia's biggest sporting event. It sent the perfect message, so we went ahead.

Meanwhile, in Perth, the eighth Hopman was eventful, to say the least. It unveiled another female superstar to Australian audiences. Martina Hingis was only fifteen, and that year she was involved in the biggest on-court drama the tournament ever experienced.

I'd seen her play as a thirteen-year-old, when she won the French Open Juniors—open to players eighteen and under. Martina had extraordinary talent that belied her slight stature, and her gifts would enchant the next generation of players and spectators alike.

At that Hopman Cup, Martina was partnering Marc Rosset, who'd won the Olympic gold medal at Barcelona. The Swiss pair swept to the final, where they came up against another great team in Croatia's Goran Ivanisevic, who later won Wimbledon over Pat Rafter, and Iva Majoli, who'd go on to win the French Open. The singles were split, with wins to

Martina and Goran—the final would be decided by the mixed doubles.

It's rare in international sport for men and women to determine a country's fate, side by side. Ted Tingling, a women's tennis fashion pioneer who often visited the tournament, observed: 'The Hopman Cup has singlehandedly resurrected mixed doubles from the tennis graveyard.'

This mixed doubles was a ripper that went into a third set. Martina was seemingly untroubled by Ivanisevic's lethal serving, and on more than one occasion rifled a return winner off his first serve. Post-match, Goran said, 'She's one of the best returners I've ever played against, and I'm talking about the men too!'

Everything was tense at 4–4 in the third set. 'It's been a great match,' Lesley whispered to me. 'It doesn't matter who wins. Nothing can go wrong now.'

At 4–5 and love–40 down, the Croats were in huge trouble. The Swiss pair had three Hopman Cup points on Goran's serve. He hit a second serve to Marc Rosset that was clearly long—match over.

Except there was no call from the lines person and no over-rule from the chair umpire, who said, '15–40.' I couldn't believe it, and neither could Rosset.

Goran proceeded to serve his way out of the predicament, to 5–5.

In the moment when we needed it most, TEL wasn't available. It had malfunctioned early in the tournament due to a resonator problem, so we'd relied on lines people for the remainder of the matches.

It was too much for Marc Rosset. He turned around and punched the back wall hoardings, hard. You could tell right away he was hurt. He'd inadvertently hit the place where the board is steel-reinforced. Self-inflicted, but horrible luck. He tried to play another point, yet writhed in pain. He had to default, handing the Hopman Cup to the Croatians.

Not only was there more than $100,000 in additional prize money on the line: there was also the matter of the gold and silver tennis balls encrusted in Argyle diamonds, designed by Doris Brinkhaus. These added considerable glamour to the event, and became one of the sport's most sought-after trophies.

Martina's mother, Melanie Molitor, was incredulous: how could Rosset could do that to her daughter? I tried to suggest that it demonstrated Marc was fully committed to winning, but the plea fell on deaf ears. The two times Martina returned to play the Hopman Cup, there was no chance her partner would be Marc Rosset.

The Hopman Cup had flourished in its first eight years, supported by loyal Perth crowds and the media, and the spike of worldwide publicity generated by the Rosset wall incident meant we were on the international tennis radar. Yet the Hopman Cup had no home in the sport. Owned and operated by my company, PME, it was vulnerable to any tour rule changes. There was talk of Hong Kong wanting to put on a blockbuster women's WTA event in our week, which would jeopardise our ability to attract top players.

As an invitation event for men and women, it wasn't

an option to be either a men's-only ATP or women's-only WTA event. It was time to sound out the ITF about whether the Hopman Cup could join the other major team events in its stable, the Davis Cup and Fed Cup—to complete the trinity of team events, as we'd envisioned way back at the start.

After much discussion Charlie and I agreed it was the right time to make the move. Soon a proposal for transition of ownership was put to the ITF. A final decision on the Hopman Cup's fate would be made at an ITF board meeting in Barcelona in April 1996. Leading up to that, I enlisted Neale Fraser's help in lobbying a couple of the ITF board members.

I had the surreal experience of flying from Perth to Barcelona for a fifteen-minute presentation to the ITF board, then straight back to Perth. At Barcelona airport I took a call from Brian Tobin, now the ITF president, who said, 'It was a very close vote, but congratulations.' I was ecstatic: it looked like our dream of the Hopman Cup standing alongside the Davis Cup and Fed Cup was becoming a reality.

The deed of transfer outlined a nine-year transition, with the ITF assuming ownership after the first six years. PME would retain a profit share for the transition period. Charlie and I transferred the Hopman Cup to the ITF with no money changing hands. PME retained a management agreement, which included securing the field, and I retained a board position for a minimum of a decade after the ownership transitioned.

One condition in the agreement was that the ITF

could never sell the event. (Charlie and I could have done this in the past, as Octagon and IMG, for example, had made overtures.)

At the time it seemed the event would be sustainable and would have a true home in the sport—immensely satisfying. And I know Mrs Lucy Hopman, who gave Charlie and me her blessing, felt the same way. Well into her seventies, she was making the long trip from Florida each year to add her special touches and considerable grace to the tournament. She was the event's royalty.

At the Australian Open that year Mark Philippoussis took on Pete Sampras in an extraordinary night match. The Melburnian, still a teenager, produced a devastating display of raw power rarely seen before or since, dumping the world number one in three mesmerising sets. Awesome for those lucky enough to witness it first-hand, but also the catalyst for a party for the thousands of people watching in Garden Square.

Another cracker night match that year was between Arantxa Sanchez-Vicario and Chanda Rubin. They played an epic that Rubin finally won 16–14 in the third. That meant it was well after 11 p.m. before Agassi and Courier hit the court for their quarter-final. The women had played a wonderful match, but it didn't sit well with me that, with the ranking of world number one on the line, the two male players would be on court in the wee hours.

Deep into an epic first set, the heavens opened. I took that as a sign…despite the roof, the match wasn't meant to be completed that night. We suspended proceedings with the players' approval. There were a few disgruntled fans, but they'd witnessed an epic women's quarter and almost five hours' tennis.

The next day Agassi came back from two sets to love down to beat Courier in five sets. In the semis he played Michael Chang and was favoured to win. Andre lost the first set 6–1, and was losing the second badly. I noticed he didn't seem to be chasing some balls within his reach. One point he'd work hard, the next he'd not bother. I called Lesley. 'I can't believe it—Agassi is tanking. It's the semi of a Grand Slam, so no one will ever believe it, but I swear he's tanking.'

Andre lost in three straight sets to Michael Chang, and it was only in his recent autobiography that he admitted he tanked in that match—because he didn't want to face Boris Becker in the final. Figure that out, if you can.

Boris Becker overpowered Chang to win his second Australian Open. Agassi may have gone to number one, but Becker got the chocolates.

That Open saw the return of Monica Seles who, prior to a devastating stabbing in Hamburg, was the world number one and destined for history-book greatness. Her attacker, Gunter Bosch, admitted that his motive was to see Steffi Graf regain the top ranking, yet he never spent a day in prison. This was unfathomable to most fair-minded people, but particularly to Monica. She vowed never to play another German tournament, and she kept her word.

There was more humiliation in store for Monica. She assumed the special circumstances of her break from tennis would mean her number-one ranking would be reinstated when she returned. The WTA, in a drawn-out compromise, decided that Monica would share the top ranking with Steffi Graf. Monica naturally regarded the protracted discussions as a slight, adding to her physical and psychological turmoil.

The '96 Australian Open saw her battle through to the final, where she came up against the German Anke Huber. It was not a final that reached great heights, but Monica, with her superior talent, did enough to win in three sets. At last, she'd won another Grand Slam.

The victory media conference was travelling smoothly until an Aussie journalist asked Monica if she was likely to play again in Germany. This triggered an understandably emotional reaction—Monica did not wish to answer the question, and the press conference hastily wrapped up.

About ten minutes later one of our staff told me that Monica was slumped by herself in the corridor near Centre Court, sobbing uncontrollably. Imagine that—despondent within an hour of winning a major. I was with Lesley and wasn't sure what to do, but I knew I had to go to Monica. 'Take Rowan,' Lesley said, 'it'll help.'

I carried our little boy, who by then was nine months old, down to where the champion was slumped on the floor. 'Monica, I'm so, so sorry about what happened... This is my son, Rowan.'

She straightened herself up and held the little fella, and it seemed to assuage her grief. We chatted for a while, until she was able to regroup and face people again.

Monica Seles never got her tennis mojo back. I witnessed the brunt of her power and prowess again in practice, but not in a match. It was as if she didn't want that single-minded intensity to be on public display. Her father talked of the pain of watching his daughter trying to fly again with clipped wings.

I'm so happy she won that Australian Open—she never won another Grand Slam title. At her peak, Monica's brutal two-handed ground strokes and irrepressible spirit were overwhelming, even for Steffi Graf. It was a privilege to see her play and to spend a little time in her company.

That was a melancholy end to an otherwise upbeat event. Australianness was becoming fundamental to the Open's identity, a bit like the tradition of Wimbledon, the chicness of Roland Garros and the brashness of the US Open. If there was one way to be Australian, it was to be part of a giant outdoor party in summer, and what better location than Garden Square at the Open.

18.
LEGENDS OF THE GAME

NOTWITHSTANDING OUR egalitarian focus at the Open, there was one group of individuals whom we had a duty to enshrine: our legends of the sport. We needed to embrace Australia's tennis greats, without whom we would not have a Grand Slam.

In 1933 the Australian Jack Crawford won the national titles of Australia and France, and the championships at Wimbledon. He made the final of the American championships that same year. On the eve of the match a New York journalist, John Kieran, co-opted a phrase used in bridge. If Jack Crawford (an avid bridge player, by the way) were to win that day, Kieran wrote, he would achieve an unprecedented 'Grand Slam'. He would be simultaneously holding the championships of the only four nations who had hitherto won the Davis Cup. And so the tennis term was born.

Alas, Jack Crawford was unsuccessful, and it wasn't until 1938 that a player—the American Don Budge—won the Grand Slam. In fact, the calendar-year Grand Slam has only been won by five players: Budge, Maureen

Connolly, Margaret Court (the first Aussie), Steffi Graf and Rod Laver (the second Aussie, and the only player to do it twice). Australia would never have hosted a coveted Grand Slam event if our greats of the past, like John Bromwich, Don Turnbull, Adrian Quist, Daphne Akhurst (after whom the women's trophy is named) and Sir Norman Brookes (whose name is on the men's trophy) had not voyaged by boat to the far side of the world to put this nation on the tennis map.

There is a dynasty of Aussie male champions, from Crawford to Bromwich to Sedgman and McGregor, Hoad and Rosewall, Laver and Cooper, Emerson and Stolle, Newcombe and Roche, Cash and Rafter, Philippoussis and Hewitt—to name only a few. And the women, led by Akhurst, Nancye Wynne Bolton, Court and Evonne Goolagong Cawley. They needed to be recognised and celebrated. While we'd been a little irreverent, it was important to see the Open being respectful too.

Geoff Pollard led the charge to establish an Australian Tennis Hall of Fame, and to induct all those who'd already been inducted into the International Tennis Hall of Fame in Newport, Rhode Island. He commissioned a local sculptor, Barbara McLean, to create busts annually for the legends to be inducted each year. The ceremony would take place on Centre Court on Australia Day, and be celebrated at an annual Hall of Fame Ball on the eve of the tournament finale, the men's singles final.

The induction ceremony is now a feature of every Open. And from 1997, beginning with Rod Laver and Margaret Court, followed by Roy Emerson and Evonne

Goolagong Cawley, the sculptures have been on permanent display in Garden Square. It's credited as being the second-largest display of bronze busts in the world.

Now we were paying homage to our Aussie champions, it was time for the Open to look at supporting the sport in our region. For the 1997 Open we offered a wildcard to the highest-ranked Asian player from a nation not represented in the singles main draws. The recipients that year were Leander Paes from India and Chen Li, who became the first Chinese player to receive direct entry into a Grand Slam singles event. It was a start, albeit a humble one.

Over on the west coast Ivanisevic and Majoli had returned to defend their Hopman title, but were derailed by the American team of Chanda Rubin and the unlikely Justin Gimelstob, who'd answered a last-minute SOS on a Miami beach. They defeated South Africa's Wayne Ferreira and Amanda Coetzer in a riveting three-set mixed doubles. One pivotal point was extraordinary and, given it lasted thirty seconds, was a no-brainer to be the TV ad for the next event. It seemed Ferreira and Coetzer, who'd come to Perth six and eight times respectively, seemed destined never to lift the cup.

The '97 Open was a scorcher. Top seeds were dropping like flies, with Steffi Graf's loss to Amanda Coetzer a prime example. Martina Hingis, who'd been unveiled to Australia the year before at the Hopman Cup and had reached the Australian Open quarter-finals, was now sixteen and ready to break through. She didn't lose a seat, beating Mary Pierce 6–2, 6–2 to win her first Grand Slam title. That year, she also won Wimbledon and the US Open, and only a surprise loss to Iva Majoli in the final at Roland Garros prevented her winning the calendar-year Grand Slam.

The men's final that year was a memorable occasion, and I can't imagine the prelude will ever be repeated. We'd chosen James Blundell to perform a country song on Centre Court for the pre-match entertainment. It would be televised live around the world as the curtain-raiser to the match between Pete Sampras and Carlos Moya.

I'd read that Blundell was an accomplished horseman: here was an ideal opportunity to Australianise what would otherwise be universal, a song performed on a tennis court. The script notes in my mind were: James, a rugged Aussie bloke, rides a stockhorse into Centre Court, jumps off, looks around, sees a guitar lying around, picks it up, walks to the mike, sings an Aussie tune, jumps back on the horse and rides off into the yonder. Pretty you-beaut Australian, I thought. However, I hadn't factored in the old show-business adage about working with animals...

My father-in-law, Laurie Hateley, was a real man of the land in Western Australia. He had difficulty passing on his guns and hunting equipment to his six progeny, as they were all girls and had no interest. Laurie was head of the WA branch of the Stock Horse Society, so I sought his help in sourcing a reliable nag. Laurie arranged a stockman, Bill, and his horse Quamby Mirrabooka.

Bill was a man of few words and Quamby a very placid horse. Okay with us—James Blundell was the star.

'I reckon it'll be okay,' was all Bill would reveal prior to the gig. But he was the sort of bloke you just trusted.

It came round to rehearsal on the day before the final. This took a fair amount of organising by my PA, Katrina Caris, who went on to become the tournament's general manager of administration. (Katrina, a country girl from Murtoa, would often arrange what I'd need before I'd even thought of it. I trusted her—and her assistant, Stacca—completely.) Quamby would need to come down the stairs, like the players: we'd need to erect a ramp. Hopefully Quamby would be okay with that?

Bill didn't have a strong view. We'd have to see.

Thankfully, Quamby came down the ramp okay, James jumped on and rode him around the court, jumped off and rehearsed his song—all fine. Then Quamby decided that going back up the ramp was not his idea of fun. After fifteen minutes of futility we got in six tradies, who were pushing and shoving for over half an hour before Quamby would leave the arena.

I had a sleepless night. What if Quamby pulled that stunt tomorrow and we had to delay the men's final for an hour? We'd be a worldwide laughing stock—no pun intended.

Pushing crazy ideas out of my head—Quamby lying on hay in a room beside the court while the men's final played out, that kind of thing—I made my way to Melbourne Park. If we went ahead we were taking a huge risk. And this was only my third event as tournament director—surely I'd be sacked if the gig (or horse) went belly up.

To me, this was not a stunt. It was another statement of who we were and what we stood for, and another step in the journey to realising our vision. But I realised that we were probably biting off more than we could chew and would most likely have to abandon the plan. But how, I wondered, did horses get in for shows like *The Man from Snowy River*?

As I drove in to the grounds it occurred to me that there must be a way to partially dismantle the temporary southern side of the arena, so the horse could exit at ground level if need be. The question was, how many seats would we need to dismantle and how long would it take? I figured a twenty-minute delay before the match would be acceptable, but no longer than that.

Glen Sharam was a production manager at Melbourne Park. He surmised there'd need to be four rows of six seats removed to provide enough head height for the horse to trot out. It would take about fifteen minutes to dismantle the seating, and there was one caveat—the high-paying front-row patrons would need to vacate their seats. I'd need to speak to all of them and get their co-operation.

I went to the locker room before the final, and told Sampras and Moya about the horse. Pete gave me one of his meaningful sideways looks, but I assured him that the horse would not leave any 'evidence' on the court.

As I waited with the guys in the locker room I watched on the TV screens the performance by James Blundell, with Quamby Mirrabooka waiting patiently. It was quite the sight.

I listened anxiously for the message that would update me on whether Quamby had gone up the ramp. Over the walkie-talkie came Glen's voice: 'The horse has left. Bring the players.' It had all gone smoothly.

I turned to Pete and Carlos: 'All's set—let's go.' Publicly, I was delighted. Privately, I was a touch disappointed our contingency plan wouldn't be activated—what a twenty minutes of chaos it would've been, and the worldwide publicity would have been invaluable!

Sampras duly defeated Moya in straight sets, a clinical display. He later remarked that the '97 Open was the toughest major he'd endured, due to the searing heat. I suspect our Aussie forefathers—in tennis and beyond, right back to the earliest arrivals from the northern hemisphere—could relate to that.

19.
THE ROOF, THE WHOLE ROOF, AND NOTHING BUT THE ROOF

AS A multi-purpose venue Melbourne Park needs a retractable roof. Concerts need to be indoors and the Australian Open to be outdoors—most of the time. But what if it rains: wouldn't it make sense to close the roof and play the match indoors? What if it was so hot it was unbearable for the players: would that be a case for closing the roof? And what about the spectators, and officials, and ball kids? These are the various considerations that the Australian Open's management has grappled with since the retractable roof was built for the 1988 Open, my last tournament as a player.

Back in '88 the roof policy was that the referee could close the roof at his discretion if it rained or the temperature exceeded 35 degrees. During that inaugural Melbourne Park tournament there wasn't any sign of either until the women's final, between Chris Evert and Steffi Graf. They were locked in a tussle mid-match when it began to rain. Chrissie was a product of the Florida system, and had grown up outdoors in hot and sometimes windy conditions. Steffi, being German, was raised with an abundance of indoor tennis.

Peter Bellenger informed them that the roof would be closed and, after a short delay to dry the court, the final would be completed indoors. Chrissie wasn't happy, and said so in post-match media comments. It being a Grand Slam first, the indoor final understandably ruffled feathers in the upper echelons of the sport.

That final established a precedent. After all, you can't play on a hard court in the rain, and you could be waiting hours for a break in the weather. It would seem odd and wasteful not to play a match when patrons have paid money, there's a global TV audience and taxpayers have forked out $15 million for a roof.

Heat was a different matter. It's not like you can't play. It's just relentlessly hot. Isn't that what players have trained for in preparation for the Australian Open? And anyway, when it's a stinker what do you do on the outside courts—are they to be treated differently because there's no roof?

To answer that last question, it was quickly and correctly established that if the Centre Court roof was closed due to extreme heat, play on all of the outside courts would be suspended. Good for health and safety— yet it meant shutting down the entire tournament outside Centre Court. Many patrons had travelled to Australia to enjoy exactly that type of weather...and so the list of complications went on.

Up until 1993, though, when Jim Courier and Stefan Edberg met in the men's final, the heat policy had not been put to the test. On that day, a scorcher, Peter Bellenger informed Courier and Edberg that the tournament organisers were going to close the roof and play the match indoors. It being a final, no other matches or patrons would be affected.

Both Courier and Edberg refused to play an indoor match. So Peter, very reasonably in my view, relented and the final was played outdoors. This set a different and difficult second precedent.

That was the way the roof issue was treated for the next few years, to the frustration of tournament management. I knew the chances of two players agreeing to closing the roof was remote. One player always believes they are fitter than their opponent (sometimes both players believe it) and would be losing a valuable edge in hot conditions. And once one player found out that the opponent wanted to play indoors, that would be enough to sway them in the opposite direction.

In really hot weather the quality of the tennis was greatly reduced. Players opted for shorter points, bailing out of sets when they were down a break, looking for respite. It seemed to me that extreme heat led to lousy play and had too much bearing on the result of a match.

You can say that's all part of the sport. But if there's one match in a player's career that determines his or her place in history, as occurs in Grand Slams, I don't think 40 degrees on a hard court in Australia gives the opportunity to bring your A-game to match up against your opponent's A-game.

THE ROOF, THE WHOLE ROOF, AND NOTHING BUT... | 223

I went to the WTA and ATP, who were staunchly opposed to suspending play or closing the roof during extreme heat. I understood that there were consequences for other events on the tour. But few tournaments in the world were subject to climatic conditions akin to the Australian summer. And the players were arguably at less risk medically than the ball kids. Data consistently showed that children, like the elderly, have a lower tolerance of heat. The duty of care to ball kids was a factor that was difficult for the players' associations to argue with.

The defining moment arrived during the 1997 Open. It was brutally hot, particularly at the quarter-finals stage. The forecast temperature was 40 degrees. One quarter involved Pete Sampras, perhaps not the best person on whom to test a new interpretation of the rule.

Another featured Carlos Moya against his Spanish compatriot Felix Mantilla, who were scheduled for the first match. I went to Peter Bellenger the night before and asked him whether he had any plans to close the roof. Under the rule he had the right to do so, but he knew that it was far easier said than done.

'Look,' he said, 'I'll have to ask the two players. And if they both agree, no problem.'

'Peter,' I replied. 'There's virtually no chance that two Spanish players will agree. Let's plan on closing the roof. But if we tell them tonight, the ATP will rally all the guys overnight and it won't happen. Is it okay if we tell them before they practise tomorrow? That way at least they'll be preparing in the same conditions as the match, indoors.' As the forecast could be different in the morning, it seemed fair to wait until then.

Peter agreed. The only other person privy to our plans was Geoff Pollard, president of Tennis Australia, and we determined to keep it that way.

'You know,' Peter told me, 'if I tell the players we're closing the roof and don't ask their permission, if one of them refuses to play I'll have to default him. And if they both refuse to play I'll have to default them both, so there'll be no semi-final either.'

That pushed my ex-player buttons. I knew that if we defaulted one or both players, all the others would revolt. They'd stand united until the original defaulted player was reinstated to the draw.

'This is how we can do it,' I said. 'You tell Carlos and Felix before they practise tomorrow that you're closing the roof—no ifs or buts. If one of them refuses to play, you tell him he will be defaulted. And see what happens. If he still won't play, you follow through with the default. Then I'll call an emergency tournament management meeting and we'll overrule your decision. That's the only way a referee's decision can be overturned.'

'So you'll overturn it?'

'Yes,' I said, 'as I can't be party to a player being defaulted in the quarter-final of a Grand Slam like that. Peter, I know it will be embarrassing for you. You'll be humiliated. Are you prepared for that, if it comes to it?'

'Yes,' Peter replied. 'I believe this is in the best interests of the tournament, so that's what I'll do.'

THE ROOF, THE WHOLE ROOF, AND NOTHING BUT... | 225

Peter Bellenger is that sort of bloke—a man of integrity, prepared to be hung out to dry.

The morning arrived with no change to the forecast. Peter, in his usual mild-mannered way, went out to Centre Court, directed the roof to be closed, and informed Moya and Mantilla before practice that the match would be played indoors.

Neither was pleased, and there was a late flurry of activity in the men's locker room, with entourages and ATP officials none too pleased with the rule suddenly being invoked. It looked dicey, so I kept my distance, fearing a standoff.

Right on 11 a.m. I went to the locker room to get the players. I saw Moya shrug and heard him say: 'Same for both.' Mantilla, the less senior of the two, was I think influenced by Carlos's approach and not enticed by the alternative—being defaulted on his lonesome. He decided to take the court as well.

The match was played with the roof shut and without further ado (Moya won in four sets, as it turned out), as was the remainder of the Centre Court schedule that day. No matches were played outside until much later, when conditions cooled. And so, for the first time in 120 years of Grand Slam tennis, matches were played indoors due to extreme heat.

I think history will judge the Australian Open kindly for the stance we took. Vindication of sorts came much later, when Wimbledon unveiled its new roof to the world in 2009. Matches were played indoors for the first time in the tournament's history. Not due to extreme heat, though!

20.
STAR POWER

IN 1997 the Australian Open, having won the annual award in the Major Festivals and Events category for three years in a row, became the first sporting event to be inducted into Tourism Australia's Hall of Fame. We were delighted—and out of the blue came another award. Coopers and Lybrand conducted a survey, the Great Sporting Cities Index, to determine Australia's biggest sporting event, and we received the accolade. To think we'd come so far in a few years—this was one of the most fulfilling periods in my working life.

But you can't rest on your laurels. Wimbledon had just completed its sensational new Court One and, in its traditional understated fashion, made it look like it had been there all along. It was brilliant, both in operational terms and in brand execution.

I knew that we too had to do something about our size and space. There were now too many stars to get them all on Centre Court, and crowd levels had increased to more than four hundred thousand, up by more than one hundred thousand from when I started.

We'd soon be bursting at the seams. I wrote to Premier Jeff Kennett about supporting a new Court One—and the timing was good, as Melbourne was going to bid for the 2006 Commonwealth Games, necessitating further infrastructure. These things take time, but at least the conversation was underway.

Each year we'd sit down with Channel Seven and talk about the next event, including the commentary team. It wasn't as if there was any major problem, as the team led by Bruce McAvaney was formidable. Nevertheless, I suggested we throw John McEnroe into the mix. 'He'll cost too much,' came the response—and it was a fair point. John was already a star of the coverage at Wimbledon and the US Open.

'Look, we only need him for Match of the Day, and why not just limit it to the second week? That's got to reduce the price,' I countered.

Seven responded with a reasonable but challenging budget, and my job was to convince John. I saw him at Wimbledon. I knew he'd regretted not playing the Australian Open more, so I said, 'You're really Mr Tennis—you need to be there. And besides, you won't recognise the tournament from when you played it.'

John seemed interested. I followed up with what I hoped would seal the deal: 'You only need to come for one week, and only call one match a day.'

'Really?'

We had an agreement in no time. I was ecstatic.

Over in Perth, the Hopman Cup encountered more problems with TEL. After the Pioline racquet problem in the first year, and the line-resonator failure a couple of years later, the system was playing up again. As the lines people defiantly marched on to the court during the final, won by the qualifiers Karol Kucera and Karina Habsudova from the Slovak Republic, they received a huge ovation from the crowd. The Perth public, so supportive of a world-first, had given its verdict on TEL.

I felt that if we could not use TEL in a final, and this not being the first time, we couldn't use it at all. With a heavy heart I decided that the Hopman Cup was done with the technology. I suspect other event managers around the world saw things the same way and, regrettably, TEL never got off the ground.

The 1998 Australian Open began in earnest, with almost all of the top men's and women's players competing, and a record $10 million in prize money. Scheduling was difficult, and I mentioned early on to Andre Agassi that he'd need to play a match on an outside court. He agreed and in the second round was scheduled for Court One, which seats five thousand people. It was the same day that the hugely popular Anna Kournikova was to play there—and, as it turned out, that Premier Kennett would attend the Open. Court One was full to bursting. Crowd control had become a major issue, and it didn't go unnoticed by the government.

The theme for that year's Open was 'Come to the Party'. We lined up celebrities with front-row seats, opposite a Seven camera. One night we had Sir Cliff Richard, Michael Klim and Brooke Shields seated together. Brooke was married to Andre Agassi and in the middle of filming the TV show *Suddenly Susan* in New York. She was arguably a bigger star than Andre, so we gave him the cheeky nickname Suddenly (behind his back, of course).

Brooke was able to come for the second week of the Open. We sent two cars—one for Brooke, one for her luggage—to the airport on the Monday morning. I asked if it all went smoothly; it had, except that Ms Shields, according to the driver, had come with around ten suitcases. I guess she'd heard about Melbourne's changeable weather.

That night Andre was playing Alberto Berasategui from Spain, who'd beaten Pat Rafter in a gruelling match in the previous round. Up two sets to love, the American had put on quite a show. But the match was starting to tighten up, and Andre dropped the third set. Brooke, who'd been beaming for the cameras, started to look a little worried and when it went into a fifth set her mood was decidedly subdued. The next morning Brooke, suitcases in tow, headed back to the airport for New York. Andre had lost, so it was a one-night visit to Melbourne.

John McEnroe revolutionised prime-time coverage that year. He sat in the little commentary box we constructed right on the court's edge, copying Wimbledon (ironic, I admit), and the players couldn't help gesturing to him during the match. John became part of the on-court action, and his post-match interviews were pure theatre. Say what you like about Johnny Mac, but he knows and loves the game more than anyone I know, has the ability to call it as he sees it without ever being patronising and,

Reviewing the 'Talking Tennis' running sheet with the legendary Seven commentator Bruce McAvaney, 2004.

as a New Yorker—well, he has that self-deprecating edge that Aussies like.

Every year Seven had asked to get inside the men's locker room before the men's singles final. I'd never thought the finalists would be comfortable with having cameras in their faces once they were in the countdown, but I knew if anyone could pull it off it was Johnny Mac.

'John,' I said. 'The network wants you in the locker room with the players'—this year, Petr Korda and Marcelo Rios—'before the men's final.'

John stared at me. 'You're kidding me! Look, no way I'm going to interview them.' He paused. 'I gotta have a reason to be in there.

'I tell you what,' he said. 'I'll go in and play a hand of poker with them, and the winner can choose to serve or receive.'

Stealing his most famous line, I said, 'John, you cannot be serious! Thank you for embracing the concept, but mate, you've lost it. How would you feel being asked to play poker with your opponent before a Grand Slam final?'

He thought about it for a moment. 'Yeah. That won't work. That'd suck. Look, I'll just go in and figure somethin' out.'

'Just don't cross the line,' I cautioned.

In went Johnny Mac and a camera twenty minutes before the 1998 Australian Open men's final. He sneaked around the backs of the lockers, spying on each player (I had warned them) and commentating in hushed tones on what we were witnessing.

Marcelo was in a huddle with his coach, Larry Stefanki, who used to coach John. So John was able to speculate about what was being said. Then he moved seamlessly to the training room, where viewers watched Petr Korda's ankles being strapped for two minutes. Sounds strange, I know, but it was revealing for viewers, who for the first time were taken into the inner sanctum minutes before players' dates with destiny.

On the women's side, Martina Hingis defended her title, defeating Conchita Martinez in the final. The women's doubles and mixed doubles were both won by wildcards: Martina Hingis and Mirjana Lucic in the women's, and Venus Williams and Justin Gimelstob in the mixed.

It's well known that the Williams sisters bypassed junior tournaments, preferring to train under the watchful eye of their father, Richard. After the presentation ceremony Venus said to me excitedly, 'Wow, my first tennis trophy.' Imagine your first trophy being a Grand Slam.

We'd had a huge tournament, with seventeen of the twenty-three sessions setting an attendance record, and a total of almost 435,000 patrons, surpassing Wimbledon. And the McEnroe factor led to a double-digit jump in prime-time TV ratings, and helped Seven win the ratings in the tournament's second week, the only week the network won for the entire year. Love him or not, Johnny Mac had made for riveting TV.

But outside the Open things weren't so rosy. Australian tennis was entering turbulent times.

21.
TROUBLE IN THE RANKS

WHEN I arrived at Tennis Australia in 1994 it was amid upheavals in the Davis Cup world. Neale Fraser was in his sixties and had an outstanding record across his twenty-four years in the role, following Mr Hopman's historic tenure. In fact, Australia had reached at least the semi-finals in all but five of his years in charge, had won it four times, and had never left the elite World Group of sixteen nations.

Frase had a readymade replacement: someone who'd been in a winning team, played for next to nothing, always believed he had to earn his singles spot, and was a wonderful mentor to younger guys like Macca and me when we entered the fray. It was John Alexander.

JA had understandably wondered about the prospects of a transition from Neale Fraser, but Frase didn't seem to pick up on it. So JA changed tack and asked if there was a process for selecting a captain and, if so, how he could apply. This put the cat among the pigeons at Tennis Australia, especially as Frase's brother, John, was vice-president. When matters came to a head,

JA came up just short. Perhaps he pushed too hard, too soon—something I may have been guilty of myself later on—but it was a great pity he did not become captain, a role he was eminently qualified for and deserved.

John Newcombe was appointed captain, with Tony Roche as coach. This was a break with tradition, as under Frase and Mr Hopman there was one boss and a clear chain of command.

Australia did not make a great start under the new arrangement in 1995, with losses to South Africa and Hungary, bringing relegation from the World Group for the first time in our history. But we rebounded into the World Group in 1996, and the following year went to the semis, familiar territory, losing to a strong American team in Washington, DC.

For whatever reason, and I do not know all the facts, in early 1998 our two big guns, Pat Rafter and Mark Philippoussis, were no longer pointed in the same direction. They'd been doubles partners through 1996, reaching the semis of Wimbledon and the US Open—where they lost to the Woodies, their fellow Aussies Mark Woodforde and Todd Woodbridge. They continued in 1997, beating the Woodies to win at Queen's Club, and reaching the finals of Indian Wells and Cincinnati.

However, the partnership had ended at the Australian Open in January 1998, and Rafter began playing with Jonas Bjorkman (with whom he would win the 1999 Open). There'd obviously been a falling out. It was a pity, as they were a terrific pair to watch—a lot of young women mentioned how much they enjoyed seeing them play!

TROUBLE IN THE RANKS | 235

After the 1998 Australian Open, our first Davis Cup tie was against Zimbabwe, to be played on grass in Mildura. Pat Rafter, having won the previous US Open over Greg Rusedski, was the mainstay and team leader. Mark had made himself unavailable—and he certainly wasn't the first Australian to do this over the years, for one reason or another. There was an enormous backlash in the Australian media.

Premier Kennett tried to aid Mark's cause, organising a private plane to fly him to Mildura so that, even though he wouldn't be playing, he was showing support. Jeff Kennett had a right to intervene, as the Victorian government had just committed to building a 10,000-seat multi-purpose venue at Melbourne Park, suitable for cycling at the Commonwealth Games, and becoming our new Court One.

Mildura was a disaster. From all reports, Mark was ostracised. Rafter lost on the opening day, then Australia recovered to gain a 2–1 lead. But Rafter withdrew through illness on the last day, and Jason Stoltenberg and Mark Woodforde, thrown in at the last minute, lost their singles matches against brothers Wayne and Byron Black. Australia, at home and on our chosen surface, had lost to the lowly ranked Zimbabwe.

Rafter headed off immediately to India, where he won the ATP event in Chennai. That left Mark Philippoussis to face the recriminations. His presence in Mildura was deemed a distraction, and he was blamed for the loss. This did enormous damage to the fabric of the Davis Cup team—no longer did Australia close ranks as a matter of course. Later that year Rafter and Philippoussis squared off in the US Open singles final. This too had terrible consequences.

I'd been in contact with Mark and his father, Nick—I saw it as my business to have a direct line of communication with every player if possible, for the good of the Australian Open and the Hopman Cup. Nick let me know that Mark was open to rejoining the Davis Cup fold, but he was now pretty much persona non grata. Even in the media conference after his semi-final win at the US Open, Mark stated his desire to play Davis Cup again. This offer seemed to fall on deaf ears.

In the final, with the two Aussies facing off, all of us would be in the neutral corner. It is tennis tradition not to be seen to be supporting one countryman over another. There was a complicating factor. Rochie, who'd originally been coaching Philippoussis, was now privately helping Rafter. And given he was the Davis Cup coach, he had a decision to make. After much pondering, he concluded that he felt comfortable sitting in Rafter's box. Mark, he reasoned, wasn't currently in the Davis Cup team.

Rafter, under considerable pressure from Mark mid-match, defended his title, winning in four sets. The aftermath in the locker room and player lounge was ugly. Mark later remarked that the first thing he noticed when he went to the court was the Davis Cup coach (and his own former coach) sitting in Rafter's box. He was not impressed. John Newcombe naturally backed Rochie, Pat Cash took the opposite view and told Rochie as much in the locker room, and others were divided. It was a polarising moment. Rochie, a great servant of the sport, faced a dilemma—but I believe he made the wrong call.

Australian tennis was split, and a wounded Mark was further isolated from the Davis Cup fold. The breach, I feared, could be terminal. However, I had no hesitation in inviting Mark to represent Australia at the Hopman Cup in January 1999.

That was a special year for the cup, as a talented teenager made her debut and another unheralded teenager came as a hitting partner before going on to rewrite tennis history. The latter had an Aussie coach, Peter Carter, who was helping the Swiss Federation and had brought the young bloke along to help out and to gain some experience.

You could see by the way this guy hit the ball that he had raw talent, but he was definitely a work in progress. He cruised around nonchalantly, he had funky hair with a tinge of artificial colour and, although only seventeen, he tried his luck getting into some nightclubs. Carts really looked out for this kid, and reckoned he had a big future ahead of him. He was right: the hitting partner was Roger Federer.

The female debutant was a fifteen-year-old Australian, Jelena Dokic. She'd emigrated from Serbia with her family when she was eleven. Lesley Bowrey, a former multiple Grand Slam singles winner, guided Jelena's tennis once she settled in Sydney.

Jelena was a delight to behold on court. Though she was smashed by South Africa's Amanda Coetzer in her first match, she shook it off and stuck bravely to her task all week. Mark Philippoussis did an excellent job of protecting and encouraging Jelena in the mixed doubles. Wayne Ferreira was injured in the last round-robin match, so South Africa's misfortune gifted Australia the opportunity to take on Sweden's Jonas Bjorkman and Asa Carlsson in the final. Jelena came of age, winning her singles, and Philippoussis completed the job by defeating Bjorkman. It was a most unlikely victory by the host nation, and it's the only time Australia has won the Hopman Cup.

In early 1999 I became chief executive of the Australian Open. Jim Reid, turning seventy, chose to relinquish joint stewardship and continued as chairman of the management group. He'd made a mighty contribution, and it was great to have his quiet wisdom to tap into, as he'd been involved from the earliest days of the Open.

For me, nothing was off limits in trying to build the reputation of the tournament. I started wondering again whether our ultimate objective, an unencumbered brand, a la Wimbledon or the Masters in golf, was now achievable. Did we now have the financial muscle to pull off a tournament without the sponsor having naming rights? It was risky—Ford might react badly—but it could break the hold of a sole sponsor and entice others, given the attractiveness of a 'clean' brand.

The timing to consider such a transition was right, as we were entering renewal discussions with Ford. Geoff Pollard had handled the previous negotiation, so this was my first entry into the fray. We were armed with figures about the huge growth of the Open.

Its economic impact, measured by the National Institute of Economic and Industry Research, had been rising. I'd been reticent to do another study, as inevitably we'd be compared with the Formula 1 Grand Prix. Its impact was now close to $90 million, more than our results from the survey two years prior. And I knew only too well the way that statistics can work for you and also against you. But the new figures, which I would have ensured did not see the light of day if they were inferior to the Grand Prix, showed that the Open's impact had increased from a baseline of $50 million after the 1995 tournament to $114 million.

Slightly apprehensive, Geoff and I sat down with Geoff Polites, the new boss of Ford Australia. Our naming preference was the 'Australian Open presented by Ford', but we were under pressure to raise more prize money to keep up with the other Grand Slams. We decided to wing it. The price for retaining naming rights (the Ford Australian Open) would come at a steep premium, whereas the price for major sponsorship—the Australian Open presented by Ford, allowing new sponsors—would be similar to Ford's previous fee.

Geoff Polites and his team deliberated for some weeks. The Australian Open was extremely important to Ford, that was clear—but their sponsorship was funded by the company's local office without any cash injection from its Detroit headquarters. They chose to relinquish naming rights and renew as a major sponsor for three years, to 2001. We gratefully accepted.

This was a game changer for the Australian Open,

as we had taken another critical step to becoming a full and equal partner to the other Grand Slams. A bigger financial deal would have been attractive, but in business and marketing terms this outcome was liberating. With Ford's acquiescence, the look we had created—the silhouette of the serving person—would be the official logo. We could embark on a new and unconstrained marketing campaign, exploiting an unencumbered brand. And we were now in the market for other significant contributors, including an associate sponsor.

At a Davis Cup tie, Geoff Pollard had watched the action in a cap bearing Heineken's logo, courtesy of the cup's official beer. He got talking to the brewer's global marketing director, and before long Heineken became our associate sponsor and official beer. And our big suppliers, Nike, IBM and Rado, all took the opportunity to upgrade to being sponsors.

This was a new benchmark in funding for the Open—and outside the management offices we were hitting other targets. On the first Wednesday of the 1999 Open I heard Julia Singleton (who'd replaced Meghan Tozer as marketing manager) scream with delight. We'd broken the fifty-thousand mark for a single day's attendance for the first time in Grand Slam history.

On court our top-tenners Rafter and Philippoussis lost, in the third and fourth rounds respectively, to Thomas Enqvist. The Swede's run lasted all the way to the final, where he was stopped by Russia's Yevgeny Kafelnikov.

In the women's, Martina Hingis won her third consecutive title, beating Amelie Mauresmo of France.

Hingis also won her third consecutive doubles title, this time with Anna Kournikova.

I'd received a letter from the three-time doubles winner Kim Warwick saying that he'd never received a trophy for his wins at the Open. I knew that was true, as I too didn't have anything in the pool room alongside my Wimbledon trophies. When professional tennis began, thanks to Wimbledon in 1968, the Australian Open introduced prize money but had felt no need to present trophies to doubles winners.

I decided to correct that historical aberration, and at our Hall of Fame Ball all doubles winners since 1969 were presented with a trophy. Like the others, I was chuffed to receive mine.

We also honoured Martina Hingis's 1998 doubles Grand Slam (achieved not with the same partner) with a trophy presented by the only men ever to win a doubles Grand Slam. They were the Aussies Frank Sedgman and Ken McGregor, who completed the clean sweep in 1952—two wonderful gentlemen, and living reminders of our sport's grand tradition.

22.
THE MILLENNIUM

WE'D HAD huge success with the Match of the Day TV coverage at night, and my dream was one day to have a live prime-time men's singles final. It would require snaring the Holy Grail of prime-time viewing, the Sunday night movie. This time slot was sacrosanct to TV executives, as it was considered an institution for Australian families.

'Don't even think about it—it won't happen,' was the network's reply when I mentioned the idea. So the night final became my special mission, needing considerable clandestine planning. I didn't discuss the idea with anyone, other than divulging it to Lesley and two of our closest friends, Mike and Debbie Clayton. Mike was a successful professional golfer, and like me a little non-conformist.

I came up with a three-part plan. We had two men's quarter-finals at night; the semis and finals were in the day. I figured that if we could split the Friday men's semis up and get one on the previous night (part one), at some point it would be conceivable to get the other semi to the Friday night (part two). Ideally the conditions of the final should replicate the semis, so there would then be a strong case for the final also being played at night (part three).

We justified moving the first semi as a way to add a session, with the extra revenue to help keep prize money growing. And, as things were going well and it wasn't overly disruptive, after raising an eyebrow or two Seven agreed.

Part one was done: the easiest bit. I knew a night final would be many years away, but I figured so long as we had a good semi or two played on the Thursday night I could get the second semi to the Friday night. I was playing the long game.

With help from a gun management team and outstanding staff, the Open was going from strength to strength, and we were looking forward to the Millennium Open. Yet it wasn't all Heineken and skittles. There were a couple of tricky issues about to hit hard. Ford gave us notice that the 2001 Open would be its last as major sponsor. The company had decided to concentrate on its core auto industry, and move resources into that area. I'd suspected that the change in naming rights would whack us on the head at some stage.

Jeff Kennett was no longer the state premier, and had set up a sponsorship consulting business with the golf impresario Tony Roosenburg. Kennett offered to help us replace Ford. 'All I need is six weeks,' he said. 'I'll know by then if you'll get the money.' His logic was sound: there was only a handful of companies in Australia who had the money, and international reach, to justify such a big investment.

Anyone Jeff didn't know at CEO level in Australia probably wasn't worth knowing—his network was impressive, although he'd probably burned a bridge or two along the way! But he found the Open challenge tough going: he couldn't detect sufficient interest. The arrangement ended and Jeff warned, 'You won't find the money in Australia—you need to get it from Asia.'

We hired IMG to assist us in the global search, but Kennett's parting words kept ringing in my ears over the next year. They seemed prophetic.

The second issue, which came out of left field, was the so-called Y2K bug. As the Open takes place in January, the worry was that a New Year computer meltdown in Australia would disrupt essential services. One contingency being discussed related to water shortage. I kid you not, there was talk of building a dam on Old Scotch Oval, part of the Melbourne Park precinct. That's how far the risk-assessment process was taking us.

Power outage was a greater fear. We would probably lose TV coverage, our scoring systems would crash and our communications systems would not be operable. A back-up generator made sense, but it could be commandeered by government if required. Then I had—appropriately enough—a light-bulb moment. 'When the Australian Open was first played nearly a hundred years ago,' I said to the committee dealing with Y2K, 'the officials didn't worry about power…All you need to play a tennis match are the players, daylight and a can of balls. The show will go on, Y2K or not.'

We decided not to spend much money combating the possible bug, and instead get on with running the tournament.

In Davis Cup, Australia's dramas showed no signs of ending. Newk had announced that, after the problems of 1998 and discussions with his team, players would only be eligible for selection if they made themselves available for every tie. With Mark Philippoussis on the outer, feeling unloved and unprepared to confirm his unconditional availability for every tie, this move was effectively banishing him from the team.

Nick Philippoussis sought me out, wondering if there was anything I could do to help. I was sympathetic. I asked Nick if Mark would be available for the first tie, away to Zimbabwe in April, and the answer was an unequivocal yes. That was a start. I said I would try, but couldn't promise anything.

At Tennis Australia we had a cross-organisational forum (Executive Management) that dealt with issues affecting the whole organisation. Along with many others inside and outside Tennis Australia, I felt the bad blood in Davis Cup was harming the sport. Though it was obviously not my area of responsibility, I put the cup on the agenda at the next monthly meeting.

Australia has a proud Davis Cup history, I said, so the infighting and the ostracising of one player, whatever the rights and wrongs of the situation, are at odds with our traditions. I completely disagreed with the new policy on availability and selection, which was really an ultimatum.

Frase, my captain, had always believed that he had a duty to pick the best Australian team for each tie, irrespective of players' past disposition or behaviour, and he did so without exception. Davis Cup selection needed to be above personalities, and Frase's doctrine had served us well.

I put a resolution to that effect, and it was unanimously passed, minuted, and distributed to all managers and the board. I knew it was a pivotal moment, and it wouldn't go down well with Newk.

I spoke to Nick and Mark, who were in Florida, explaining that Tennis Australia was changing the every-tie commitment. Mark reiterated that he was available for the Zimbabwe matches.

It was Geoff's job to inform Newk. I wasn't privy to the conversation, but to Newk's credit he accepted the situation. I called Mark to tell him it was all sorted. He was back on the Australian Davis Cup team.

The powerful unit of Rafter, Philippoussis and the Woodies went to Zimbabwe, and without incident exacted revenge for the Mildura debacle. The following tie, a quarter-final, would celebrate the centenary of the Davis Cup, with the combatants fittingly being Australia and the United States, the two most successful Davis Cup nations, playing at the original setting, the Longwood Cricket Club in Massachusetts.

At Wimbledon that year Philippoussis was one set up and in command against Pete Sampras in the quarter-final. Then he moved the wrong way, twisted his knee and had no chance. Sampras, still the world number one, marched on to another Wimbledon title. It meant Mark missed the centenary Davis Cup quarter-final, but the young gun Lleyton Hewitt would make his debut.

And what a debut it was. He took out the highly credentialled Todd Martin in his first match. Rafter lost to Jim Courier, while the Woodies beat Sampras and Alex O'Brien, so Australia led two matches to one going into the last day. The American camp was saying that Martin was sick, and would need to be replaced by Pete Sampras—a handy substitute. After some colourful exchanges during the Aussie protest, the neutral referee, Stefan Fransson, forced Martin to play. He was ill but still dangerous, and Pat Rafter only just won, taking us through.

Now it was Rafter's turn to be injured. Philippoussis was still out, so the semis saw Hewitt and Wayne Arthurs, on debut, take on a strong Russian team in Brisbane. Arthurs, a leftie with a potent serve, did an excellent supporting job, and the Russians were frustrated from the outset, likening the makeshift grass court to a 'potato patch'. The Aussies stormed through to the final, away to France, on clay in Nice.

Rafter was still injured, but by now Philippoussis had recovered and was ready to rejoin the team—he and Hewitt in singles, the Woodies in doubles. On day one Mark destroyed Sebastien Grosjean while Cedric Pioline squared the ledger with a victory over Hewitt. In the doubles the Woodies bounced back from a set down to put Australia up two matches to one.

Mark Philippoussis got up the next morning needing

to play the match of his life. Against the French number one, Cedric Pioline, a dual Grand Slam singles finalist and top-ten player, and on clay, Mark's worst surface, the Aussie was the heavy underdog.

Mark started well, winning the first set, but when Pioline evened the match up the signs were ominous. Under pressure, Mark suddenly went into the zone. His power and precision were extraordinary. There was no place on the court from where he couldn't strike a cold winner. He'd had that year's Wimbledon within his grasp, and this time he wouldn't be denied. Playing like a man possessed, Philippoussis took Pioline apart, winning the third and fourth sets 6–1, 6–2, leading Australia to victory.

Given the occasion, the opponent and the surface, it must be one of the greatest matches ever played by an Australian in Davis Cup tennis. The team had risen above personality differences and our observance of our traditions had been rewarded.

I was at the Hopman Cup Ball in Perth to see in the millennium—and whether the Y2K bug would spell doom. Lesley, with able support from Katrina Hunter and our colleagues, put on another extravaganza. That year's theme was 'your favourite rock superstar', and I was kitted out in gear straight from the Beatles' *Sgt. Pepper's* album cover. Y2K was a flop…but the party was not. The next day a photo of Lesley and me partying to bring in the millennium was smack bang on the front page of Perth's *Sunday Times*. One for the grandkids!

Hopman Cup 2000 showcased a new format in elite tennis. The mixed doubles was now the best of two sets, with a match tiebreak (up to ten) at one set all. This format emerged from a Tennis Australia committee called Brand Tennis, which I chaired, and which was discussing new formats being workshopped around the world. It aimed to provide tennis with a time-friendly format, which I hoped could then be adopted in junior competitions, in order to compete with parent-friendly sports that can schedule at fixed times. But I also knew doubles was becoming a problem on the ATP and WTA tours, with many tournament directors preferring not to have doubles at all if they had a choice. This trend bothered me greatly, as doubles well played is one of the fundamentals of our great sport, at all levels and stages in life. May it never be a forgotten art. Perhaps a shorter format would stop the exodus of players to singles only?

To use this format at the Hopman Cup we needed approval by the ITF. This was granted initially on a trial basis, before being fully approved. I wasn't in favour of using the format in men's or women's doubles at the Australian Open, but felt it could also be introduced for mixed doubles there, which we did in 2001. The format was also adopted by both the ATP and WTA tours for doubles, and is still used today.

It was also used at the US Open mixed doubles that year, where the final was between the Aussies Todd Woodbridge and Rennae Stubbs, and Lisa Raymond and Leander Paes. It was strategically scheduled before the Hewitt–Roddick singles quarter-final, and Todd and Rennae won the title after a seesawing match tiebreak. They took the microphone to say they felt they'd won a 'chook raffle'. Asked my opinion, I said, 'It's the most successful chook raffle in history—live in front of twenty thousand people!'

At Tennis Australia I was subsequently given a consulting role for the lead-in events to the Open, backed by the assistant tournament director, Peter Johnston, who would go on to head the WTA's Asia office. Another format change I pushed was to schedule the finals of the lead-in events on Friday nights, rather than at weekends.

Around the world tournaments commence on a Monday morning, when everyone's gone back to work and kids are in school. Why not begin them at the weekend, when there are the most matches spread out on the most courts, with the cheapest ticket prices and the maximum number of parents and children? Then, scheduling the semis and finals on Thursday and Friday nights exploits the value of prime time. Tennis is one of the rare sports where you can schedule matches at any time of the day, any day of the week. Why schedule finals in the clutter of the weekend, competing for media attention with every other pro sport?

I'd already been starting the Hopman Cup on a Saturday, to packed houses, and moved the final to a Friday night. With Johnno's critical support, my push led to the Hobart and Sydney women's events moving to a Friday night final. The idea has not caught on more widely yet, but I'm still a firm believer that this simple change can be transformational, helping to unlock the commercial value of the sport and responding to the needs of its fans.

The tennis in Perth that year saw some surprises. As defending champions, Philippoussis and Dokic were expected to do well, but lost their opening tie to qualifiers Thailand, represented by Paradorn Srichaphan and Tamarine Tanasugarn, and never recovered. The efforts of Paradorn and Tammy, in defeating Australia and then making it through to the final, created headlines in Thailand. Even the King, a tennis lover, sent a message.

Their opponents were the South African duo of Wayne Ferreira and Amanda Coetzer. In Wayne's seventh attempt and Amanda's ninth, the pair finally broke their jinx and won the cup. It was a popular victory, and a just reward for two loyal supporters of the event.

Over at the Australian Open our new multi-purpose venue was running behind schedule, and we had to pull the plug for that year. This was a blow, as we'd used it in our marketing campaign. Then the court surface, Rebound Ace, similar to the US Open's hard court but with a more cushioned base, came under scrutiny.

Using Rebound Ace differentiated us from our American counterpart, and ensured the four Grand Slams were played on four different surfaces. Our management committee had resolved to produce a surface that was medium to medium-fast, a little slower than New York, so we could lay claim to having the fairest conditions.

In 1999 there was consensus that the courts were too slow. There was also chatter from our top player, Pat Rafter, who preferred something a little quicker. (A few years later the same thing happened with Lleyton Hewitt.) I went to Rebound Ace with a directive to speed up the surface. Rebound Ace already had a varietal referred to as FastTop, and this seemed a good choice for the 2000 Open.

Until the overseas players hit town. The Europeans and South Americans were ropeable. Even Marat Safin, not normally interested in such issues, was complaining. But the more damning indictment came from the Americans. Sampras let it be known (by more than his usual sideways glance) that even he, who liked medium-fast courts, found he couldn't play his normal game. Michael Chang, the world number two, said, 'This is quicker for sure than the US Open.'

I faced the annual men's ATP player meeting the day before the Open and apologised to all the players for the speed of the courts, promising it would never happen again. It wasn't an easy thing to do, and the players knew I meant what I said. That year's Open was played in very quick conditions and FastTop would not see the light of day again.

The action was furious as well as fast. Australia was well represented internationally, with eight men now ranked in the top 100. But things weren't going well for our highest-ranked woman, Jelena Dokic. Having beaten Martina Hingis at the previous Wimbledon for the loss of only two games, and going from qualifying all the way to the quarters there, she was attracting a lot of attention locally. Expectations were high.

She lost in the first round to the unheralded Hungarian Rita Kuti-Kis. In her post-match conference Jelena talked about her own poor play and was accused of giving little credit to her opponent. This didn't track well in the media, and by extension among the public. There was no love lost between our rising star and the press, Melbourne's *Herald Sun* in particular.

Jelena subsequently announced that she was reconsidering whether she'd represent Australia at the Sydney Olympics that year. This spelt big trouble for her, and was potentially embarrassing for Tennis Australia.

On the men's side Pete Sampras was looking for his thirteenth major. We invited Roy Emerson, a legend of Aussie tennis, to the tournament, as he held the Grand Slam record for singles majors. But Pete couldn't break Emmo's record in Melbourne—Andre Agassi came out victorious on the men's side, with his compatriot Lindsay Davenport winning the women's singles. Andre's victory probably camouflaged any lingering player disdain about the too-fast surface.

The new multi-purpose venue might not have been unveiled, but the crowds had swarmed to Melbourne Park. The Millennium Australian Open cracked the magical mark of half a million patrons, becoming arguably the highest-attended annual sporting event in the world. Australia's Grand Slam had, we felt, navigated difficult times with aplomb.

Sadly, the same would not be true of our best hope in women's tennis.

23.
THE DOKIC FACTOR

WITH ALL eyes on Sydney, which was ready to host the Olympic Games, Tennis Australia had to deal with the uncertainty over Dokic. It was decided that I would go to Sydney to talk with Jelena and her father, Damir.

The Dokic family home, in Fairfield, was humble—they weren't living on easy street. Damir was welcoming, offering me a drink on arrival. However, he soon cut to the chase: 'Jelena's not playing Olympics.' Yet she'd agreed, along with the cricketer Mark Taylor and other notable sporting figures, to be an ambassador of the Olympics—how could she justify her non-participation and not be ridiculed?

The best I could hope for was damage control. 'This is how I see it,' I said to Damir (and Jelena, who was watching us).

'If Jelena's not playing, then giving the reason that she's upset with the media, in particular a newspaper not even in Sydney but in Melbourne, is just not going to cut it. She'll need a much better excuse...

'If she doesn't defend her quarter-final at Wimbledon

she can say she's down on confidence, and needs to focus on her form and her ranking. That would work, I reckon. For the record, Tennis Australia obviously cannot endorse her declining to play in the Olympics, but we will be sympathetic and supportive. And if we all stick together, the PR damage will at least be minimised.'

Damir and Jelena seemed comfortable with this approach. I think they appreciated that I'd come to their turf, and that I wasn't trying to change their minds, or Damir's anyway. He and his wife, Liliana, were perfect hosts, and we hovered around the BBQ as Damir cooked up a sumptuous fish meal. I felt like the visit had been good for the relationship.

Just as I was about to order a taxi, Damir said, 'You have one glass whisky with me, she play Olympics.' I could tell he was serious. I've never been a Scotch drinker, but in the scheme of things that seemed a minor issue. The dram was drunk and the decision made, just like that—Jelena Dokic *would* be playing the Sydney Olympics.

And she played so well, getting to the semi-finals, where she met Russia's Elena Dementieva. She led 4–1 in the third set and had two break points for 5–1. If she wins one of those points, I said to myself, there's no doubt she'll close out the match and be playing Venus Williams for the gold medal. This would be fantastic: worst case, Jelena was winning a silver medal for Australia and, just maybe, a historic first tennis gold in singles beckoned.

Not for the last time, fate did not go her way. Jelena lost those break points, and Dementieva scrambled back and won the match. Now Jelena was in a bronze medal play-off against Monica Seles. She lost that match too, and came away empty-handed. This was a bitter pill to swallow. A medal of any colour would have fostered a far better relationship between Jelena and the Australian public.

Dokic dramas aside, the Sydney Olympics were a wonderful celebration of sport, technology and entertainment, all done in an Aussie way. In essence, what we were trying to do at the Australian Open on a slightly smaller budget!

I headed back west to prepare for the 2001 Hopman Cup. I had an inkling that the 21-year-old Martina Hingis (who'd won three Australian Opens in a row) was a little in awe of her teenage partner, Roger Federer. Roger, in turn, was shy around his celebrated doubles partner. At one point during the tournament he said to me, 'I'm not quite sure how to behave around Martina. She's so famous!'

Their prodigious talents were on full display, and they stormed into the final. Waiting there was the formidable American pairing of Monica Seles (who'd changed citizenship) and Jan-Michael Gambill.

Martina, at the peak of her powers, beat Monica in two hard-fought sets. The heavy-hitting Gambill, like his partner two-handed on both sides, went in as slight favourite to level the tie. The kid Federer was making plenty of errors, yet he'd produce a sublime forehand, or a flick backhand, at just the right time. Roger won in straight sets, sealing victory for Switzerland. That tournament was his maiden professional win, and I guess you could say he's gone on to have a decent career.

Once Hopman was concluded, as usual I was on the first plane to Melbourne. We would have the new multi-purpose Vodafone Arena open for the first time. The attention to operational detail by the Melbourne Park management and my team, headed by Sarah Clements, was exemplary. We'd invited Rod Laver out and he had a hit with Lleyton Hewitt. Lleyton, with his keen sense of tennis history, was chuffed to be on court with one of his heroes.

A statue of Rod had already been commissioned for the forecourt of Rod Laver Arena. It was a stunning sculpture and would soon become the public's meeting point, but initially it had a slight flaw. Rod is captured hitting his one-handed backhand, but it looked like a slice.

I asked if anything could be done so that it looked like a topspin backhand. After all, Rod's flowing top-spin backhand was his signature shot. The sculptor kindly obliged by simply rotating the racquet in Rod's hand, though I'm sure only connoisseurs were any the wiser.

Rod liked the statue. But when he looked up and saw his name in huge illuminated letters adorning the stadium, he just stood there overwhelmed and shook his head with amazement. 'To think of all the great Aussie players like Lew and Muscles and Sedg and Newk, and it gets dedicated to me,' he said. 'I'm so honoured.'

The dedication to Rod was one of the most satisfying contributions I was able to make to the Open, without a doubt.

When the tournament began I was near Vodafone Arena when Stefano Capriati collared me. 'Paul, Jen's hitting in there. Come with me and watch her practise. She's hitting the ball great.'

It had been eight years since I'd coached Jen. It was wonderful to see her back on the tour and happy.

Stefano was often vilified for his role in his daughter's career, and perhaps, as he admitted, he did push her hard as a teenager. I'd caught up with him from time to time after Jen left the tour. He'd say, 'People criticised me for helping Jen take the money when she was young, and for giving her limited access to it. But I was making sure she was set up for life, so I don't regret that part of it at all.'

'This time, I'm not raising a finger,' he'd told me. 'If Jen decides to play again, it will be her decision. Then, and only if she asks me, will I help her come back.'

As we watched Jen practise that day, he whispered to me, 'I think she can win the whole thing, I really do.' A huge call, I thought.

When the draw came out Jelena Dokic was scheduled to play the defending champion, Lindsay Davenport, in the first round. This was terrible luck, and Damir unwisely claimed the draw was rigged. After Jelena lost in three battling sets on the opening night she did an interview with the *Herald Sun*. The resulting article claimed that Jelena herself had suggested the draw was rigged.

This led to intense media scrutiny of the Dokics as they tried to go about their business. It seemed that everywhere Jelena and her father went a camera was in their face. We at Tennis Australia were alarmed at the treatment she was receiving, and Jelena—who was only seventeen—was adamant that she'd never made the accusation.

Geoff Pollard and I took up her case directly with the newspaper, but they stood by their story. We persisted and, with Jelena's consent, asked that the transcript from the interview be produced. The *Herald Sun* refused, citing it was not newspaper policy to pass on or publish transcripts.

True to Stefano's prediction, Jennifer Capriati stormed to the title, her first Grand Slam, beating Martina Hingis 6–4, 6–3 in the final. She also won the French Open that year, and her world ranking went to number one. Some comeback!

On the men's side Pat Rafter made his best run at the title. In the semis he led defending champion Andre Agassi two sets to one, but was overcome by cramps and had no chance in the fifth set. Andre went on to win his third title over the Frenchman Arnaud Clement.

Not long after the tournament, rumours began surfacing that Jelena Dokic wanted to represent Serbia in the Fed Cup. Initially I found that hard to believe, but it was clear that Damir was making moves in his old stomping ground.

Unfortunately the rumours were true, and Jelena, still a minor, would be representing the country of her birth. Serbia was at that time completely unheard of in the tennis world. A decade later, they've produced three world number ones: Novak Djokovic, Ana Ivanovic and Jelena Jankovic.

Jelena representing Serbia made her off-limits from a Tennis Australia perspective. I'm sorry to say I didn't see her often after that. When I did we were friendly, despite her shutters being up. It would be five years before she played the Australian Open again.

24.
EMBRACING ASIA

PAUL KEATING'S famous manifesto while he was prime minister about the importance of Asia to Australia's future was, for me, timely and inspiring. There were compelling reasons to engage with the continent. It made sense to connect with a market 150 times bigger than our own.

The region was on the rise in many sports, while Australia was the natural leader in tennis. I thought we had a duty to share our expertise. This didn't resonate with everyone at Tennis Australia. There were some who felt, for example, that it didn't make sense to help the Chinese, given that that one day they might be better than us.

Yet there was a bigger picture—surely engaging through sport, sharing knowledge, was part of a broader global realignment. True, from our perspective it might not turn out well in business or even in tennis, but engaging with Asia was the right thing to do. Growing tennis in Asia meant growing the sport worldwide.

We needed to temper our pitch to suit this market,

rather than assuming it would simply accept us. And what worked for one country might be offensive to another. John McEnroe's post-match TV interviews were made available to the world feed. While acclaimed elsewhere, his interviewing style was, we were told, a little abrasive for Thai tastes.

First things first. We needed a new positioning statement—Australia's Biggest Sporting Event had served us well, but would not suit this new mission. The Department of Foreign Affairs warned, in response to our query about 'Asia's Grand Slam': 'Remember, technically we are not actually part of Asia, so this may cause some offence.' So we decided to go with 'Australian Open—the Grand Slam of Asia/Pacific'.

Early in 2001 I met with Anil Khanna, president of the Asian Tennis Federation. I asked what we could do to help the federation. While appreciative of the two Asian wildcards we'd been offering each year since 1997, he told me they were having difficulties with sponsorship of the Asian Tennis Championships, their most prestigious annual event.

'Maybe,' I suggested, 'We can change the Australian Open wildcards from being the highest-ranked Asian players not in the draw to being the winners of the Asian Tennis Championships?'

Anil didn't hesitate to accept, as this would elevate the championships, attracting sponsorship dollars and a quality field of Asian players keen to vie for direct entry to the Australian Open. The proposal was passed unanimously by Australian Open management group.

We'd made a start on reinforcing our new position as the Grand Slam of Asia/Pacific.

Our commercial priority, meanwhile, was finding a new major sponsor. We'd been looking for over a year without success and were getting to the pointy end. As the year went on, our value to a sponsor, and hence the price we'd receive, was heading south. Compounding the predicament, for the 2002 Open, due to the fall in the Australian dollar, we'd been forced to put up prize money by 17 per cent to hold ground with the other majors.

Finally, there came a real nibble. IMG delivered the news that there was a prospect and, true to Jeff Kennett's prophecy, it was an Asian company: the giant Korean automaker Kia Motors.

After much negotiation, Kia were prepared to do a look-see for two years, but the price they were offering was well under Ford's. Notwithstanding our desperation, I knew that if we accepted the deal as offered we'd have enormous trouble getting the level back up in years to come. We countered with the proposition that the annual fee was non-negotiable but, given the lateness of the engagement, we'd only require the full price for the second full year, with the far smaller balance being the fee in the first year. It didn't change the total, but it protected the integrity of the sponsorship value. Although we were taking a hit in the short term, Kia was a great fit for the Open.

In the Hopman Cup that summer Spain, represented by Arantxa Sanchez-Vicario and Tommy Robredo, upset the more fancied American duo of Monica Seles and

Handing over the Hopman Cup, 2002.

Jan-Michael Gambill after saving cup point. This was the last Hopman Cup before its ownership transferred to the ITF under the 1997 deed of transfer. That was pretty emotional, especially for Lesley and me, after all the years we'd put in. Although we would continue in management roles, the post-tournament party was wrenching—along with then general manager Rick Williams, who'd been involved since the first year, we symbolically handed over the Hopman Cup trophy to the ITF president, Francesco Ricci Bitti.

Lesley, in a moving speech to the ITF representatives, said: 'The Hopman Cup is given to you with much love. Please make sure you look after it.' How telling those words would turn out to be.

It was back to the east coast, where the Open was soon in full swing. The Aussie men, after a disappointing loss at home in the Davis Cup final to France, really struggled. Pat Rafter was unable to recover from a shoulder injury; Lleyton Hewitt, who had just won the US Open over Pete Sampras on the eve of September 11, bravely played with a bout of chickenpox, losing in five sets in the first round to Spain's Alberto Martin; and Mark Philippoussis lost in a tough second-round match to Greg Rusedski.

The men's final pitted the Swede Thomas Johansson against the overwhelming favourite, Marat Safin. As always, there was a bevy of beauties in Marat's player box, but they had little to celebrate that night as Johansson won in four sets.

The women's final was dramatic. Melbourne threw up a wickedly hot day, fuelled by a scorching northerly wind. We had the heat policy in place, but the required level hadn't been reached when the players took to the court at 1.30 p.m. Martina Hingis was playing her sixth consecutive Australian Open final, against Jennifer Capriati, the reigning champion.

It was spellbinding. Both players, especially Martina, were reduced to a shadow of themselves by the heat. Martina was well on top, but couldn't convert any of her championship points, and it went to a set apiece. With that, she staggered like a drunk to the locker room, where she was immediately covered from head to toe in an ice bath to try to get her core body temperature down.

We all feared Martina might damage her health. We had an ambulance on standby as she went through the motions in the third set. There were no rallies—Martina had run her race. Not to take anything away from Jen, but her Latin roots probably stood her in good stead against the Northern European in those searing conditions.

Away from the action there was a standout Open moment in 2002. We dedicated the 5000-seat outside arena, adjacent to Rod Laver Arena, to Australia's other Grand Slam singles champion: Margaret Court. Now the two giants of Australian tennis were being honoured side by side at the heart of every Open.

With our new emphasis on being a truly regional tournament, I appointed an Asia/Pacific marketing manager, Richie Gee, then began affirmative action. Looking ahead to 2003, we wanted Asia/Pacific representation in as many facets of the tournament as possible, including ball kids and officials. This was easier said than done, as the head of the ball-kids program, Jan Howse, was very strict in her standards (even my own goddaughter Stephanie didn't make the cut!).

We conducted trials to find talented youngsters in Seoul and Singapore, and later in Shanghai. This was not cheap, nor simple to organise, though the tennis federations were helpful and it engendered enormous goodwill. The ball kids needed to be chaperoned and accommodated in Melbourne. We took them on all manner of excursions, so they could feel like they got a taste of Australia—the zoo, the beach, the Sovereign Hill goldfields—and made sure they had a great time.

Likewise, Wayne Spencer, head of officials for the Open, ensured that there was a growing number of Asia/Pacific lines people. It was satisfying to see a couple of the ball kids and officials from this program making the elite squads for the Australian Open finals. But we weren't offering support in the player development area. So we piggybacked junior clinics on the ball-kids trials whenever we went to Asia, with Peter McNamara as head coach.

The engagement went deeper. After seeking advice from Anil Khanna, we targeted our efforts in the fourteen-and-under demographic. This, according to the ATF, was the group most in need of support. The Open became the sponsor of a group of Asian junior tournaments that ran year-round. We flew in and accommodated the top fourteen-and-under boys and girls: they played the Masters final event at Melbourne Park, then stayed for a couple of days at the Australian Open.

We were determined to make sure that the Asian players, officials, juniors and ball kids felt at home. That was the ultimate test—not how happy we were with our efforts, but how they were received. There was a sense of achievement when Anil said he would like to host an Asian Tennis Federation board meeting on site during the Open. This was a symbolic gesture about our continents' integration in tennis, and it subsequently became an annual event. At that meeting I was awarded a plaque for services to tennis in Asia, which meant a lot to me.

Anil had a vision for more tournaments in Asia. The region was, and still is, a poor cousin to the main tennis continents of Europe, North and South America, and Australia. Although there'd been a big event on the ATP tour in Japan, backed up by the Sydney Indoors, those had been downgraded in a tour realignment, and

Sydney disappeared. This was partially addressed later on, with the Tennis Masters Cup going to Shanghai and its subsequent Masters 1000 Series status, but at the time of writing there are only five men's tour events in Asia each year, played in a three-week period.

Compare that with golf, where there are more than fifty annual men's events at tour level. Which sport has engaged Asia more effectively? Golf has multiple tours, whereas tennis has only one. Tennis needs to look seriously at its tournament model, particularly on the men's side, as the growth in jobs and money, outside the top-fifty players and at the Grand Slams, has not kept pace with other professional sports.

The Open's other big play was in TV. In endeavouring to compete with the other Grand Slams in the global market, we would come off second best in Europe and the United States. But we had a strategic Asian advantage over the other majors. It was the only region where prime time at a Grand Slam meant prime time in Asia.

Taking advantage of our time zone was an imperative, but I felt there was a natural synergy we hadn't yet explored. Surely, as the Grand Slam of Asia/Pacific, we should be televised by a pan-Asian broadcaster, like Rupert Murdoch's Star Sports?

The Open's head of TV was Daniel Chambon. He had brought the European Champions League football and the Tour de France to Australian audiences in a deal with Les Murray at SBS—in fact, Les, Daniel and I remain good friends. Daniel was my go-to guy for TV negotiations, with the switched-on and loyal Lysette Shaw my go-to for bouncing ideas, and was the boss of the sometimes chaotic 'TV land' during the Open.

We had an excellent relationship with our American broadcaster, ESPN, and we'd subsequently forged broadcast ties with their South American equivalent, ESPN International, which also had a strong presence in Asia. ESPN International and the aforementioned Star Sports were merging in the region, resulting in ESPN Star Sports, or ESS.

This was now by far the biggest player in that market. I called on ESPN for assistance, in particular their chief negotiator Len DeLuca, a real character, and he convened a meeting with Russell Wolfe, the head of ESPN in Asia. At a dinner in Paris during the French Open, Daniel and I made our pitch. Russell was supportive and steered me towards the executives of the News Limited business arm, who we invited to the Australian Open to witness first-hand our Asia/Pacific engagement.

We were assisted by IMG's TV arm, TWI. The outcome, after this long chain of negotiations, was successful—both financially and in audience reach. To give you an idea of the kind of growth, in 1998 Asian TV coverage of the Open—770 broadcast hours—represented just over one-third of our global reach. In the first year of the new ESS coverage we received almost 1,600 broadcast hours in the region, nearly half our global reach.

Another TV development for the 2003 Open was part two of my plan to have a prime-time final.

There'd been a bit of grumbling from the media, who were speculating about whether the second men's semi-final, which was being played in the heat of the day on Friday, disadvantaged the winner. Perhaps it should be held in cooler conditions, like the Thursday night semi?

I informed the network that we wanted to schedule the second men's semi on Friday evening—and the bosses agreed. Now part two of the plan, both men's semis at night, was in place, and it was game on for the last part of my plan, securing the Sunday night. But I needed to be patient…

25.
THE HOLY GRAIL

THE LEAD-UP to 2003 was a rugged time for the McNamee family. Dad had been bravely struggling against Merkel cancer, a rare form, and by December 2002 it was taking over his body.

A couple of months earlier Mum had called me to a specialist's consulting rooms at St Vincent's Private Hospital in Melbourne. She and Dad had received some results, and the specialist wanted to explain it further with a son or daughter present.

I went in and Dad shook his head. 'It's bad news. There's nothing we can do.'

The specialist explained the rapid advance in the cancer and said there was a risk that Dad could black out without warning. It was important that he didn't drive anymore. Dad took the news on the chin, stoic as ever.

We got home to Essendon, and Mum and I walked down to the pharmacy to get medicine for Dad. As we were walking back I asked, 'Today's Tuesday, isn't it? Mum, there's no way he'll jump in the car and head over to golf, is there?'

'I doubt it,' she replied—but I wasn't so sure.

As we got near home we saw Dad backing his car out of the driveway. I raced over. 'What are you up to?'

'I need to go now,' he said, 'or I'll be late for golf.' He had his routine and he'd stick to it, prognosis be damned.

'But Dad, you heard what the specialist said. You can't drive anymore.'

'I'll need to see that in writing.'

Dad loved his cars and his golf over the years, so not driving was a harsh punishment. I cancelled my appointments that afternoon and took him straight to his beloved Medway Golf Club, in Maidstone. On an early hole, as he executed a chip and run to within a metre from around seventy out, I said, 'Dad, do you know how amazing that is? For you it's no big deal, because it's second nature, but for the rest of us it's a treat to watch!' Tennis was the only sport I ever ended up being better at than Dad.

Rowan was now seven, and it was great that he got to spend time (always playing sport!) with his Dad Dad—Mum was and still is called Nan Nan, and she calls Rowan 'my ten out of ten', as he is the tenth grandchild.

As Lesley, Rowan and I needed to get to Perth well before Christmas each year to take care of Hopman Cup preparations, our tradition was to have the McNamee Christmas at my sister Mary's house in mid-December. It was always a special occasion but this one, Dad's last, was more so.

Mary and her husband, Mick, have a tennis court. After lunch Dad was getting fidgety. I knew what this

Dad in the family home at Tarnagulla, circa 1995.

meant—enough of the chatter, time for a hit. Dad wasn't one for too much chitchat, especially when there was the chance to play sport.

During the 2001 US Open, Lesley, Rowan, Mum and I had celebrated Dad's eighty-eighth birthday with him in Times Square. It's an enduring memory, though overshadowed by the catastrophic events of September 11, the day we arrived home from New York and exactly twenty-four hours before Brian had a meeting on a high floor of the World Trade Center.

Soon after, Dad and I had a hit with the Essendon seniors group, and I noticed he'd changed his serve. Was he having difficulty nowadays with a full backswing?

'No,' he said. 'I saw Andy Roddick serving and liked the look of it, so I copied it.' I guess you're never too old to try to improve your game!

Out we went onto the court at Mary and Mick's, mixing in as usual. I ended up rallying with Dad. I could tell he was in a lot of pain, but he wouldn't show it. He was a country boy still, and a tough one at that. I was aware this would be the last time we ever shared a court together.

After a while I called out, 'Have you had enough, Dad?'

'No, I want a few more.'

We kept going for a bit longer, and I hit a deep volley to Dad's forehand. Dad summoned up all his strength and ripped a forehand winner past me. At age eighty-nine!

I gave him a look, and he said, 'I think I'll stop on that one.'

When we departed for Perth I gave Dad a big hug in the lounge room at Bulla Road. He was now too weak to come out to the front gate to give his traditional wave goodbye. It hit me hard when I felt how bony he was—once strong in body, he was now only strong in spirit.

We hugged hard, I said my goodbyes, and knew in my heart I might never see my dad again.

We had Christmas in Perth with Lesley's huge family, which was always festive. The Hopman Cup got underway and, as ever, I devoted my energies to it. Although the tournament was now the property of the ITF, to all intents and purposes there was little change in day-to-day operations.

I was able to assemble a terrific field for that event, highlighted by the presence of the current world number ones: Lleyton Hewitt (partnered by Alicia Molik), coming off his victory at the 2002 Wimbledon, fifteen years after Pat Cash; and Serena Williams (with James Blake), who was the showstopper at the New Year's Eve Ball in a stunning white dress.

Early in the tournament, just after play began on New Year's Day, I got the call I'd dreaded. It was my older brother, Stan. Dad had just passed away. He was just short of his goal of reaching ninety.

Apparently, Dad had woken up and said, 'Maryborough.' New Year's Day was always a gala sports day at Maryborough, near Tarnagulla, and Dad wouldn't have missed too many of those in his life.

Although I had known it could come at any time, the news was so damn final. It knocked me about, as it did everyone in our family. But I had a tournament to run and I knew Dad wouldn't have been impressed if I dropped the ball, so to speak. If there was work to be done, he always got on with it, and he expected the same of us.

So, apart from missing the tennis for the rest of that day (I'm not quite Dad), I got on with it. The powerhouse teams of the United States and Australia, the two nations who used to dominate tennis, made their way to the final. Neither team had it all their way on the journey, with Australia needing a tiebreak in the mixed to defeat the Czech Republic, and Serena needing to beat Kim Clijsters to reach the final.

Once there the Americans prevailed, winning both singles matches. For Serena, this rounded out her preparation for Melbourne, where she would be endeavouring to win her fourth consecutive major, technically not a

Grand Slam (because of the change in calendar year) but historic nonetheless.

Dad's funeral was held over to the Monday following Hopman. We had the service at St Theresa's, Essendon, where Mum and Dad went every Sunday. The four children and grandkids all played a part, and the eulogy was delivered by the priest who'd attended to Dad, an Irishman, Father Gillooly. He said he'd never come across anyone so welcoming, and so accepting, despite his predicament. He said Dad was 'radiating', 'saintlike'. This was generous praise, and he meant it—my father had left quite an impression on him.

Dad was to be buried next to his parents at the cemetery at Tarnagulla (where my plot is pegged and waiting, by the way). On the journey there Lesley, Rowan and I were passed by a black car. It was the hearse—Dad would have loved that, as he sometimes had a lead foot himself. He was buried with some sporting mementos; a blue Hopman Cup hat was on his head.

The wake was at the Tarnagulla fire station, and the locals turned out and put on a spread. Stan McNamee was a decent man, honest as the day is long, a loving and loved husband and father. He was well known and respected in Central Victoria for his sporting prowess, and he was given a fitting send-off. Bye, Dad.

Right away Australian Open 2003 was upon us. After all our work to bring the Asian region into the fold, why not give the honour of the opening match on Rod Laver Arena to an Asian player? We picked Thailand's Paradorn Srichaphan, who was able to beat Austria's

Jurgen Melzer. Only the year before Paradorn had been ranked in the hundreds, winning the Asian wildcard to the Open, but then his career took off. By April 2003 he was ranked in the top ten, the first and so far only Asian man in history to achieve the milestone.

News of wildcards and other support from the Open had spread quickly through the region, and it wasn't long before we were getting requests not only for singles wildcards, but in doubles and mixed doubles. I'd reply as best as I could, trying not to give any false hope.

On the first day of Australian Open 2003 I received a phone call from the accreditation office saying that two Chinese girls had arrived and were only able to say in English, 'Here, doubles.' I knew what this meant. They were seeking a wildcard. I checked their names on the WTA rankings list, and they were reasonably ranked but well below the doubles cut-off.

I went to welcome the girls and gave them temporary accreditation. I had an idea, gesturing: 'Have racquets here? Good, practice court in one hour.' They looked at me hopefully.

An hour later I was hiding, seeing how these girls played. I was impressed, and felt compelled to go to Geoff Pollard and explain the turn of events—there was a case for a wildcard.

'Do you think they can win a match?' Geoff asked, looking me in the eyes.

'From what I've seen, I think they can. And it's pretty gutsy to come all this way on a wing and a prayer.'

'Okay,' Geoff responded, 'but this is not a precedent.'

I was nervous when the Chinese duo went out for their first-round match, against a seeded pair. Again I skulked at the periphery, taking in the action. The two wildcards gave it their all, but came up short in the third set. At least they won a set, I thought.

That year we had introduced a training camp in December, overseen by Macca, to help the Australian players prepare. The 'Aussie Assault' seemed to help produce some strong results across the board. Nicole Pratt reached the fourth round; Peter Luczak, Sam Stosur and Evie Dominikovic the third; and Jaymon Crabb won a round too.

After some gentle prodding from former colleagues I introduced the Legends event and talked Ken Rosewall into playing, as it was the fiftieth anniversary of his winning the title as an eighteen-year-old. Incidentally, Muscles is not only the youngest male winner of the Open but also the oldest, at thirty-eight.

One encounter in this Open stood out. Andy Roddick and Younes El Aynaoui played the longest match in Grand Slam history (later blitzed by John Isner and Nicholas Mahut at Wimbledon), courtesy of an epic 21–19 fifth set that lasted two and a half hours.

Andre Agassi stormed to a fourth title, over Rainer Schuetler, but the big news was Serena Williams. She completed her crusade to win four consecutive Grand Slams, the 'Serena Slam', like Martina Navratilova before her.

And Martina was still questing for records. When she came to Melbourne that year I knew there was still one title missing from her CV. She'd won the singles, doubles and mixed doubles at all four Grand Slams, with one exception—mixed doubles at the Australian Open. Martina was turning forty-seven, but she was in incredible shape and had a good partner, India's Leander Paes.

Martina and Leander made their way to the final, where they defeated Todd Woodbridge and Greece's Eleni Daniilidou in straight sets. I was relieved it didn't go to a match tiebreak, as Martina (like Todd) was not a fan of the format. The victory clinched Martina's unique place in history: the winner of every event she could play in all Grand Slams. And she was true to herself all the way.

Not long after the 2003 Open, Kia agreed to a new five-year deal as major sponsor, surely the biggest of its kind in Australian sporting history. We'd well and truly shrugged off the post-Ford blues.

The pool of prize money for the 2004 Open had risen to $20 million, and we continued to roll out new initiatives to attract patrons. We introduced an 'After 5' ground pass to pull in city workers. The Heineken Beer Garden had live music every evening. And we introduced a 7.30 p.m. match on Margaret Court Arena, partly as a hook for the After 5 crowd.

Naturally, Seven was seeking as much local content as possible for its TV coverage—a Rafter, Philippoussis, Hewitt or Molik night match would be ideal. On the other hand, the European networks and America's ESPN sought their players in their preferred timeslots, daytime in Melbourne being prime time in the US and nights suiting Europe. As a rule, the views of the host broadcaster ought to hold sway. But I was becoming uneasy about our lack of flexibility. The evening match on Margaret Court Arena provided the option of non-Australian content in the evenings for the European networks, a move that would soon have wider ramifications.

Our Asia program continued to expand, with the wildcards extended to all main-draw events. This time, we didn't need to give those two Chinese girls a wildcard in the doubles—they were not only in the main draw but were seeded. They'd made big leaps up the rankings during 2003.

Two of the game's all-time greats, Roger Federer and Justine Henin, won the Open for the first time that year. It seemed an appropriate lead-in to the following tournament, which would be the centenary of the Australian Open.

Commercially, it was time to negotiate a new contract with the host broadcaster. Seven's representation was headed by the lawyer Bruce McWilliam, a hardball negotiator; Geoff Pollard and I represented the Open. The negotiations dragged on—we were seeking a considerable increase in price, commensurate with ratings growth, and to be fair we were being offered it, almost.

It came time to play the card I'd held close for so long, part three of my TV plan. 'Now both men's semis are at night,' I said, 'the final should really be at night too. For the players, it should replicate the conditions of the semis. We want a night final.'

I held my breath.

'I see,' Bruce replied. 'Okay—anything else?'

Just like that, it was done.

I'd have signed there and then, but we were still some way apart on the rights fees. 'There may be a way to resolve this,' I ventured.

It was always frustrating, and motivating, if another Grand Slam was doing something better than we were. I'd been hoping that in Australia technology and its attendant legislation would allow matches to be shown on multiple channels, as was occurring in the United Kingdom with the Wimbledon coverage on BBC Digital. But multi-channelling on free-to-air networks here was at least five years behind the UK.

With that off the agenda, would Seven let another Australian network into the tournament? Unlikely. Again I turned to the UK experience for guidance. The Nine Network and Fox Sports had shared the coverage of Wimbledon in Australia, with Nine securing the marquee matches its higher rights fees deserved. Some Aussie viewers were at least getting a choice when watching Wimbledon.

At a critical juncture in the Seven negotiations I raised this idea with Bruce McWilliam. 'The way to get this deal across the line,' I said, 'is if I go get extra dollars from Fox, just like Wimbledon does.'

Bruce right away said something unflattering, but factual, regarding Fox's limited audience at that time.

That was my opening: 'Well, if that's the case, it shouldn't bother you.'

Bruce thought about it, then said Seven must have exclusive rights to all matches on Rod Laver and Vodafone arenas. Anything else would be a deal-breaker. 'If that gets it done,' he said, 'okay.' We shook hands.

Within minutes I was on the phone to Fox Sports' Craig Dobbs and we agreed to meet. Without live access to either of the two main arenas Fox would arguably struggle, but in the end the value of TV rights is heavily linked to prime time, and we now had the new night match on Margaret Court Arena.

When I met with Craig at a cafe in East Melbourne, I told him that even though Fox would not have access to the main arenas, which he expected, they'd have an exclusive match in prime time. That was the clincher. We'd struck a deal by the time we finished our coffee.

Seven was paying an upgraded figure it was comfortable with, Fox was on board with its own prime-time match, and we would be getting the rights fees we were looking for, as well as the broader exposure we sought. Discerning tennis viewers would be getting a choice.

Plus, my Holy Grail: the prime-time final was now locked in.

At the Athens Olympics that year the tennis action came with a twist. Those Chinese girls whom I'd given the wildcard to in 2003 were selected to represent China in doubles. Would you believe it? Li Ting and Sun Tiantian won the gold medal, China's first Olympic medal in the sport.

26.
THE CENTENARY

THE 2005 Open, our centenary, was poignant for everyone involved in Australian tennis. There was a century of event history to draw upon, yet also an ever-present pressure to do justice to those years. We should celebrate our traditions as a great tennis nation, while setting the tone for the future.

One of my guiding beliefs is 'one eye on the ball and the other eye on the summit'. The challenge here was to balance the interests of looking back and looking forward. Discussion led to the theme '100 Years in the Making'.

We set about the task of turning Australian Open 2005 into a blockbuster. It needed to be much more than a tennis event, and more akin to the Sydney Olympics. I'd been moved by the unashamed celebration of sport and the goodwill on display in 2000—the atmosphere had been electric. I wanted this Australian Open to have its own celebration of sport, entertainment and technology.

First, we needed to pay homage to our tennis heritage. We commissioned a book, *Our Open*, for which we interviewed our legends about the various eras. The early years were covered by Len Schwartz, aged ninety-one, who talked about our champions—Brookes, Turnbull, Quist, Crawford and John Bromwich—and visitors such as Anthony Wilding, Jean Borotra, Fred Perry and Don Budge. Thelma Long, twice an Open champion, covered the women of the era, looking at Daphne Akhurst and Nancye Wynne Bolton, and visitors like Dorothy Bundy and Dorothy Round.

The foreword to *Our Open* was penned by Rod Laver. Rocket spoke about the 1959 championships in Adelaide, where it was so hot that the boys took their mattresses outside and slept under the stars. 'I was looked on as a bit of a hacker,' he said. 'Harry Hopman thought that I had potential, but there was still a lot to prove, and it was not until I won Wimbledon that I felt I could look people in the eye.' Our greatest champion—and always so modest.

Each chapter was dedicated to a postwar decade: Frank Sedgman covering the '40s, Ken Rosewall the '50s, Roy Emerson the '60s, John Newcombe the '70s, Pat Cash the '80s, Pat Rafter the '90s and Lleyton Hewitt the 2000s. Our two greatest female players, Margaret Court and Evonne Goolagong Cawley, covered the women's side.

No other nation can reel off names on par with those above. We were once a great tennis-playing nation—wouldn't it be something to be so again? It was a big ask to usher in an Aussie winner that particular year, though Lleyton Hewitt was ever ready as the world number three and Alicia Molik was soon to be top ten—they'd certainly have a crack.

The centenary was also good news commercially. We'd had a fillip with the entrance of Kia, and now the sponsorship frame was changing. Rob Dassie had taken over from Tony Duggan as commercial general manager; both were mighty contributors. Meanwhile, Heineken underwent a global shift in its marketing focus from sport to music, aimed at a younger demographic. That meant its tenure as associate sponsor had run its course, but they were staying on as the official beer.

This was a relief, as it meant the middle Saturday—our biggest day of attendance, and which had become known as Heineken Day—would not be affected. The company was replaced as associate sponsor by L'Oreal, using the Open to promote its brand Garnier. In the tournament grounds we soon saw queues hundreds of metres long of mainly teenage girls waiting for a facial or head massage and a gift pack. Garnier World became a destination in itself, and helped make the Open more appealing to a younger female—and, as night follows day, male—audience.

Sydney is the biggest market for visitors to the Open and in corporate terms the city had become a significant player. One of our sponsors, American Express, was in charge of our live site at Federation Square in Melbourne. Their ad agency, Momentum, suggested a similar site on the forecourt of the Sydney Opera House, where tennis fans could congregate free of charge and view the action from Melbourne Park on a giant screen. We received great support from the Seven Network to access the footage, and technological help. The rest we left to American Express.

The Opera House site started smoothly, with manageable and appreciative crowds, but no one predicted what a popular hub it would become. Because of the way the schedule panned out that year, both Lleyton and Alicia were playing singles matches on the same days.

I always felt the best way to approach it, being even-handed to the Rod Laver Arena patrons, was to ensure one played during the day and the other at night. Their fourth round matches fell on Australia Day. Lleyton was playing a young Spaniard called Rafael Nadal and Alicia was playing Venus Williams. Lleyton was scheduled in the day, and Alicia for 7.30 at night.

This was not the network's wish, as they believed that Lleyton versus Rafa would rate higher than Alicia versus Venus. I begged to differ, so Andy Kay from the network and I had a side bet. Lleyton and Rafa went on, and of course the match was a cracker. Lleyton won in five sets, well after 6 p.m.—smack-bang in prime time.

Channel Seven was all over the match, staying to the end, and kept crossing to the Sydney live site to capture shots of the burgeoning crowd assembling at the Opera House. The weather was beautiful in both cities. Lleyton was toughing it out with Alicia to follow—it didn't get much better than that. By the time Alicia was underway with Venus, there was a huge crowd on the Sydney foreshore. They got happier as Alicia rode the wave of euphoria to complete a stunning upset win.

We were thrilled, but couldn't have dreamt of the report we received from Amex the following day. Some seventy-five thousand people had attended the Sydney live site on Australia Day. Any sporting event in Sydney would kill to have that many fans—and the Open had achieved it on a video link-up to a Melbourne event. Proof, I think, that the Open is for all Australians. (Oh, and I won that little side bet with Andy at Seven.)

Some dared whisper that Alicia might go all the way in the Open. But her quarter-final was a difficult match-up, against the former champion and top-fiver Lindsay Davenport. This match will be long remembered, but not for the right reasons. The two ladies went at it full bore, blow for blow, to one set all, when you could feel the sheer willpower of a patriotic full house turning the tide in Alicia's favour. At 5–5 in the third Alicia had break point. On her second serve Lindsay clearly missed down the middle—Alicia to serve for the match. But the call wasn't made.

I try never to be biased, but as a former player I was pretty upset about this bad call. And, as history shows, Lindsay held on and ultimately won the match. Alicia was out, her only real chance of winning the Australian Open up in smoke.

TEL hadn't worked out at the Hopman Cup. But in the intervening years, there were new technologies being tested, not requiring adjustments to the composition of the balls. In time, the most prominent of the new electronic systems was Hawkeye, invented by a young Englishman, Paul Hawkins. By 2005 it had been successfully trialled in other sports, including cricket, and was being officially integrated into them.

After the Molik incident I started talking with Paul Hawkins. The Hopman Cup was the perfect place to test Hawkeye, and by the following January we had it in place. So, in another world first, the Hopman Cup introduced Hawkeye to elite tennis players, under the watchful eye of ATP and WTA officials. It was a resounding success, going on to be trialled at Miami in March, then used at the 2006 US Open. It debuted at the Australian Open in January 2007, and is now a fixture in the sport—too late, unfortunately, for Alicia.

Meanwhile, Lleyton had chalked up another epic win, this time 10–8 in the fifth over the Argentine David Nalbandian, to reach his first home Grand Slam semi-final, eight years after qualifying as a fifteen-year-old. His foe would be Andy Roddick. On the other side of the draw, Roger Federer was to play Marat Safin. These were dream match-ups: the top four men in the world all through to the semi-finals, a rare occurrence in the sport. It was just what we'd hoped for in our Centenary Open, especially as one player was Australian.

The first semi was Federer against Safin, the consummate champion against the consummate enigma. Sometimes Marat is distracted and ordinary; other times he's masterful. This day the mercurial Marat was in exquisite form. But Roger, with his eye always on history, displayed his wizardry. He went up two sets to one, and the tennis in the next set had to be seen to be believed. It went to a tiebreak, and Roger stood at match point.

The two got into a rally, and Roger came to the net and hit a net cord (at match point—it had to be!) that fell on Marat's side. I thought the big Russian wouldn't reach it, but he just got his outstretched racquet under the ball and spooned it over Roger's head. Roger ran back and, instead of hoisting a defensive lob, went for a reverse between-the-legs squash shot, which didn't come off.

I was surprised by Roger's choice of shot, and wondered if he'd do the same next time. Anyway, Marat went on to take the tiebreak—two sets all. Everyone was beside themselves with the tension, and in the men's room I ran into Gerard Tsobanian, Marat's agent, who'd just flown in from Madrid. 'What do you think, Gerard?' I asked.

'Marat's got him now,' he said. 'Roger can't play five sets, because he's so good he never needs to.'

I must admit, it had the ring of truth.

Out they went for the fifth set, and it went with serve until Marat struck, to serve for the match. He seemed stronger—but, inexplicably, or more likely due to Roger's genius, he was broken back. Sure enough, Marat broke again and this time he put Roger away.

It had been a match of stupendous quality. Gracious as always, Roger was moved to say: 'That's the best I've ever played in a losing match.' No greater compliment could be paid.

The second semi-final was just as tense and Lleyton came back from a precarious position, down in the third set at one set all, to win the tiebreak. The atmosphere was electric. Andy seemed flustered and, at two sets to one down, he left the court to go to the locker room, mumbling something about wet socks. This was not exactly kosher, and I noticed Peter Bellenger's response under the hut on Centre Court. It was obvious Andy would be facing a post-match sanction. Lleyton, driven on by an emotional crowd, stormed through the fourth set, then knelt down and kissed the court.

Straight after the match I went to the locker room and saw Andy slumped in a corner by himself. 'Bad luck, mate,' I said. He seemed consolable, so I brought up the matter of him wandering off during the match without permission. 'Andy, you're going to be in a bit of trouble for leaving the court...the ref and the supervisor are pretty upset.'

'Yeah, I figured that,' he said.

'Come with me to the ref's office and say you're sorry. It'll make a huge difference.' He looked at me. 'Now, no shower—let's go, get it done.'

Andy followed me to Peter Bellenger's office, walked in and said, 'Ref, I'm sorry I left the court. I shouldn't have.' You could see he meant it.

'Thank you, Andy,' Peter replied. That was that—no fine, no suspension. I wish this happened more in sport.

Now we had the men's final of the Centenary Open: Marat Safin versus Lleyton Hewitt, a giant of a player versus an Aussie with a huge heart. This would be a match for the ages, and it was fulfilling the decade-long mission I'd been passionately pursuing—against tradition, against the prevailing wisdom of the television industry. The Centenary Australian Open would have a night men's final on prime-time television, for the first time in the history of Grand Slam tennis.

Every first Tuesday in November, Australians stop whatever they're doing, go and find a TV, and watch the Melbourne Cup. This is what it felt like on that Sunday night. It seemed an eternity as we waited for the moment when Marat and Lleyton walked on to the court.

There was an eerie reverence early on, and the occasion threatened to overwhelm the match. Lleyton seemed to hit his stride quicker than the big man, and took the first set through a single break of serve. Early in the second set Lleyton took an injury time-out, and the Melbourne-based physio Ivan Guteritz attended to him. Unusually, both Lleyton and Marat had requested Ivan be assigned to them for this match. I asked him if Lleyton had anything to worry about. 'No, just a little niggle. He'll be fine.'

A couple of games later Marat asked for an injury time-out, without any obvious sign of impairment. Ivan came back to the little bunker on Rod Laver Arena and I asked the same question about Marat. 'There's nothing wrong,' Ivan said. 'But Marat says he's so nervous he can't feel the racquet in his hand. He's freaking out, and I guess he just wanted someone to talk to.'

The physio visit seemed to settle Marat down, and only a couple of games later he broke Lleyton's serve for the first time—a decisive moment, the catalyst for a release of uninhibited power tennis from the Russian. He was a different player. He took the second set, and the third, and the title was slipping from the Aussie's grasp.

The fourth set was an almighty struggle, with Lleyton digging ever so deep and refusing to accept defeat. But Marat broke serve; he had the best down-the-line backhand in the sport, a shot almost impossible to defend against, as the easier and more predictable shot is cross-court. Marat was up two sets to one and a break, and whenever he was in a tight situation on his serve he'd peel off an unreturnable strike.

He'd failed in his two previous Australian Open finals, understandably once against Federer and the second time when he was out of sorts against Thomas Johansson, but this time would be different. Marat served out the match and won the Centenary Australian Open. It was disappointing for Australians hoping to see our first men's winner since Mark Edmondson almost three decades earlier, but the big man won most people over.

His victory speech was classic Marat, thanking everyone he could identify (including, naturally, his attractive entourage). 'To everyone in Russia watching, thank you,' he said. 'I know there's a lot, because it's not 4.30 in the morning like last time.'

Russia had tuned in, but what about Australia? When I checked in with Seven's Andy Kay the next day, I wasn't feeling like a naughty schoolboy as I did during my first Open when I went to see Gordon Bennett. The match had peaked at more than five million viewers, but even more outstanding was the sustained viewership— the national audience averaged 4.04 million viewers for a four-hour program. We had created a new benchmark for a single program, and it still remains the highest-rating program in Australian television history. The Australian Open had transcended sport, morphing into blockbuster entertainment.

The Seven Network had blitzed the ratings in both weeks. Perennially the bridesmaid to Channel Nine, it became in the next survey the number-one network.

The Open's total attendance was a record 544,000, including a world-record attendance in the sport of more than sixty thousand patrons on Heineken Day. And its economic impact was calculated at $210 million, more than quadruple growth in a decade. The marketing department—led by Felicity Selkirk, who'd taken over from Julia Singleton, both of them key contributors—was overjoyed. The American Ted Schroeder, a fine former player and a gentleman, came up to me afterwards and said, 'Mac, I don't know if you understand how great that tournament was. Enjoy it, as there may never be another one like it.'

We'd enjoyed it, all right. There'd been much to celebrate at the Centenary Australian Open, but I doubt if anything could top that warm summer night in Melbourne when we showcased the men's final in prime time. It was the highlight of my post-playing career.

27.
MOVING ON

THE CENTENARY Australian Open might logically have been my last, but I decided to stay on. Nothing could surpass the 2005 event—yet the following year did produce incredible moments. There were also a couple of sadder notes.

Jelena Dokic had been absent from the Open, and from her former home, for five years. At the Tennis Masters Cup in Shanghai in November 2005, Heinz Gunthardt sought me out. He'd been in Monte Carlo working with Jelena, now twenty-two, who was trying to make a comeback.

Jelena had in 2001 renounced Australia in order to represent Serbia. The following year she had to all intents and purposes renounced Serbia by distancing herself from her father. For some time she'd effectively been stateless. Heinz had innocently asked Jelena where she felt she belonged. 'I feel like I'm an Aussie,' she'd replied.

When Heinz told me that, the words hit me like a sledgehammer. Could I help, Heinz wondered.

I tracked Jelena down in the mountains in Croatia, and suggested she consider reclaiming her status as an

Australian. She was sympathetic to the idea, so I continued the dialogue and looped in her London-based manager.

Reintegrating Jelena would not be straightforward, as most of the media, much of the public and one or two Aussie players had said good riddance. And Jelena's tennis had fallen a long way from lofty heights. By her own admission, she was not in good physical shape. A comeback would be a major challenge for someone with no nationality, no sponsors, little finances, almost no ranking, many psychological scars after her tumultuous life journey and ordinary fitness. Yet, if Jelena was willing to return to Australia, Tennis Australia had a duty of care to her.

I encouraged her to join the 2006 Australian Open Training Camp and the Open wildcard playoff. I knew Jelena needed time to adjust to being back in Australia, and the media scrutiny would be intense. Facing the press on day one, then spending significant time in Australia, would help counter the sceptics. We rented a small apartment for her in Melbourne—it was the least we could do to help her feel comfortable and secure.

Jelena approached training and the playoff with gusto. She was one of those rare athletes who could turn on the 'eye of the tiger' focus—intimidating, even in practice. She gutsed it out and won the playoff, giving her a spot in the Open. However, injuries started taking a toll and she struggled in the lead-up tournaments, missing Hobart the week before the Open.

However, come the Australian Open, she was ready to take her place, with the ITF and WTA granting her request to present her name in draws as Jelena Dokic (Australia). That was a welcome sight. Serena Williams, heading a field with all of the top twenty women for the first time, was asked in her pre-tournament media conference about Jelena's change of nationality. 'She sure sounds like an Aussie,' Serena replied. Way to go, Serena!

Jelena drew the French teenager Virginie Razzano in the first round. Although struggling on a few fronts, Jelena won the first set and fought through a tough second set, taking her to match point. Though I ought to have been impartial, I stood at the entrance to Margaret Court Arena willing her to win.

On match point Razzano hit a shot over the baseline (near where I was standing) to lose the match. Except the umpire didn't call it, and instead said, 'Deuce.' I was flabbergasted, and unfortunately Jelena was distraught. Too much physical and mental effort had been expended just to get there, and a shocker on match point broke her heart. She was gone.

I couldn't help bemoaning the injustice—how many more trials did this girl need to face?

The other disappointment came much later in the event. Down 6–1, 2–0 to Amelie Mauresmo in the women's final, Justine Henin defaulted the match. She was not well, that's beyond dispute, and in all likelihood she wouldn't have been able to win the match. But as a former player I felt that Justine should've hung in there and allowed Amelie the unbridled joy of experiencing winning match point for her first Grand Slam title.

After all, this is the moment that every kid dreams of

when they pick up a racquet, simulating it on a suburban court or against a brick wall, followed by arms raised in triumph. It's the essence of the sport. Justine, not unreasonably, protested in her media conference that she might've hurt herself if she'd continued to play.

While we were waiting for the trophy presentation I asked Justine if she was capable of getting through the long formalities. 'I'll be okay,' she said. I winced. In a way I wished she'd said she was too ill to stick around. (As it transpired, the two women played in the final of Wimbledon that same year. Amelie got to experience winning match point.)

The men's draw suffered the pre-event withdrawals of Agassi, Safin and Nadal, but this didn't stop a parade of actors, entertainers and sports stars attending. This couldn't have happened without my personal assistant Janine Doney's little black book of contacts. The presence of William Hurt, Billy Connolly, Michael Vartan, Kostya Tszyu, John Eales and Charlize Theron (who wrote me a personal thank-you note) was a feast for celebrity watchers.

But out on the court it was a young bloke from Cyprus who captivated the audience: Marcos Baghdatis. I was courtside when he completed a match in the early rounds, and the cheering, chanting and general noise was extraordinary.

Marcos saw me in the underground car park immediately afterwards and asked, 'Was it too rowdy? Do I need to temper it a bit?'

'No way,' I said. 'Marcos, you play with your heart on your sleeve and your fans love it. Actually, most players would love to be able to express themselves like you do. No worries.'

Marcos's semi-final, though, was not straightforward. He got to match point against David Nalbandian when it started to rain. I was hoping the match would be completed but the umpire was forced to suspend play, with Marcos stranded at the last hurdle. Lesley innocently suggested I go and give some counsel to the two players, especially Marcos.

'What could I possibly tell Marcos?' I protested. 'I lost from match point in the semis. I'm the last person to offer advice! I'm keeping right away from him.'

When play resumed Marcos didn't win that point, or that game, but he did win the match. He was through to meet Roger Federer in the final, and I think every Greek and Greek Cypriot in the city who could muster a ticket was there too! Marcos could just as easily have been playing at home.

He won the first set, and had a key point to go up a break in the second. Roger was in trouble, but he weathered the storm. He eventually won a hard four-setter.

The Rocket, Rod Laver, was on court to present the men's singles trophy to Roger. And right out of the blue the Swiss player started crying on Rod's shoulder—an outpouring of emotion from the man who will likely be regarded as the greatest ever, seeking comfort from the man many still regarded as deserving of that accolade.

If I had any lingering doubts about whether the Australian Open meant as much as the other majors, they were extinguished in that moment. The Australian Open

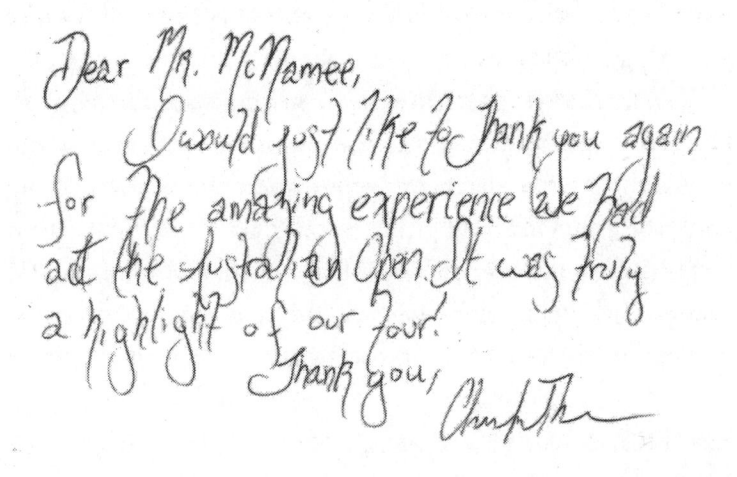

Dear Mr. McNamee,
I would just like to thank you again for the amazing experience we had at the Australian Open. It was truly a highlight of our tour!
Thank you,
Charlize Theron

A note from Charlize Theron, 2006.

was a full and equal partner of the other Grand Slams. Certainly there would be more challenges, but the DNA of the tournament had changed irreversibly. Prosperous times lay ahead.

As I made my way home from Melbourne Park that warm January night I wondered if I should remain part of the event in the future. And indeed, the 2006 Australian Open turned out to be my last as chief executive and tournament director. I felt I'd completed the job I'd been asked to do.

In the emotional farewell process, I penned a note to the management team: 'My heartfelt thanks for an amazing achievement against the odds. I cannot and ought not know the depth of your expertise, nor the length and breadth of your procedures. What I can suggest, with every confidence, is that you have provided

Tennis Australia with an enviable platform for future growth and a legacy for our players of all standards...'

After I left the Open I continued in my role as tournament director of the Hopman Cup. It was strong and stable, with the state government behind it, along with the longstanding title sponsor, Hyundai. We were lucky that the CEOs of Hyundai's southern region, Colin Naughton and Heinz Weisner, were part of the tournament fabric. Our highly capable sponsorship manager, Andrea Cavanagh, backed up by the irrepressible and ever loyal Jacinta Beros, did an incredible job of looking after Hyundai and the other sponsors. The Hopman family was alive and well.

The event had unearthed sublime talent over the years and in 2006 it had showcased two eighteen-year-olds who everyone agreed were something else. The first hint was at the Hopman Ball, where the female player turned heads, only to be outdone by her male counterpart, who took to the stage, grabbed the microphone and joined in with the band.

I'd seen this confident young guy play qualifying at the ATP event in Valencia on the recommendation of one of my great friends from my earliest tour days, the Italian Vittorio Selmi. Vito was a highly respected and long-serving player representative on the tour. He had an encyclopaedic knowledge of tennis—if he said someone could play, you took notice.

The young bloke Vito was praising had an Aussie coach, Dejan Petrovic, so I was an interested spectator as he ground out a three-set win to make the main draw. He wasn't mature in his game and was still lowly ranked, at around 150, but I saw enough to invite him to Hopman Cup. He was Novak Djokovic, and his partner was Ana Ivanovic.

The team from what was known as Serbia and Montenegro made a strong run at the Hopman Cup, beating Russia and Sweden (Novak defeated the former Australian Open champion Thomas Johansson), and only losing to the eventual champions, the United States. Ivanovic went on to win the French Open, the first Serbian to win a major, and become the world number one. At the time of writing Djokovic was still number one, having won four Australian Opens, three of those coming off preparations in Perth.

Ana and Novak are great players, and also great people. I'm delighted that the Perth public saw them as raw teenagers, like Seles, Hingis and Federer, and then while they were at the top of the sport.

In recent years more stars appeared, including Marat Safin and Dinara Safina, the only siblings in tennis history to both reach number one in the word. In 2011 Justine Henin came, as did Andy Murray. He partnered a teenager with a big future, Laura Robson, whose mother is a proud West Australian. In 2012 the world's number one and two women, Caroline Wozniacki and reigning Wimbledon champion Petra Kvitova, squared off in Perth, with Kvitova partnering Tomas Berdych to victory.

There had been a change in the TV broadcaster. After almost two decades, the ABC decided to focus on other endeavours. Its contribution had been enormous, and had seen the Hopman Cup broadcast to the most remote parts of Australia. The event was now on Network Ten and its offshoot One.

At the 2012 presentation ceremony, the ITF made a point of emphasising how vital the Hopman Cup had been in mixed doubles becoming an Olympics medal sport at London 2012. This was a proud moment for all involved in the tournament.

Meanwhile, another dream had been taking shape—to see a new multi-purpose venue become the cup's home. The genesis of the idea was the 2006 announcement by the CEO of Burswood International Resort Casino, John Schaap, that the Dome would be dismantled as part of a development. This came as not only a massive shock to me, but to the tens of thousands of West Australians who have a deep affection for the Hopman Cup. There was little time to act.

Andrew Firman was the cup's operations manager, and together we sought the assistance of a prominent Perth architect, Murray Cox. We commissioned some design work and a model was built for a potential venue kitted out with a retractable roof. The Burswood Dome had served us well, but if there was to be a new arena ideally it would be state of the art and enhance the event, and the city, for future generations.

Rather audaciously, we held a media conference showcasing the model venue, then put it on public display in the village area on site during the Hopman Cup. The wheels began to turn: the state government informed

Burswood, as they could legitimately under their gaming agreement, that the Dome could not be dismantled until a replacement venue for the cup was in place.

The concept gained momentum, and establishing a new multi-purpose arena in Perth became a matter of public policy. The Gallup government chose a CBD site, adjacent to the defunct Edgley Entertainment Centre, and called for tenders. This was an exhaustive and costly exercise, with significant budget overruns, but the Barnett government, on gaining power, committed to finishing the job.

This guaranteed that the arena would be built and it would have a retractable roof, replicating the conditions at Rod Laver Arena. Lesley and I, and Andrew Firman, along with all of our wonderful staff, were thrilled. Whatever the long-term fate of the Hopman Cup, it would leave a legacy in this wonderful city in the west.

Yet trouble was brewing. The Hopman Cup, being successful and independent, became a target for Tennis Australia. Over a number of years it courted the ITF, of which it is a powerful member nation, seeking control. The Hopman Cup is in the same week as Tennis Australia's Brisbane International, so the organisation had strategic interests in monopolising that period, the first week of the Australian lead-in tournaments to the Open (known as the Australian Open Series, from which the Hopman Cup had been unceremoniously removed by Tennis Australia in 2008).

At the same time the WTA had designated that the opening week would see a new Premier Series event.

Tennis Australia successfully bid on behalf of the Brisbane International for the sanction, which purported to protect the tournament through fines to any top player who played a non-tour event, such as the Hopman Cup, in that week.

I fought to stop what I felt was unfair treatment of an established tournament. The history of the Hopman Cup, boasting twenty-four world number ones over twenty-four years, seemed to count for little. Naturally, the ITF joined the fray, but—staggering as it seems for a governing body that attends WTA board meetings—making headway would still be difficult.

In the end a deal was struck between the ITF and WTA that is in full compliance with the WTA rules. I am not at liberty to discuss this agreement but I can now say that, from my perspective, it is disappointing.

One of the motivations Charlie Fancutt and I had in transferring the event to the ITF was that it be protected from such a scenario. We can only hope that the ITF will take all necessary steps to prevent any impost that may affect the future of the tournament.

The ITF arranged a tender process for the management of the Hopman Cup, a process Tennis Australia participated in—as I ultimately did, under protest. I was concerned about Tennis Australia's conflict of interest were it to manage the Hopman Cup, and feared that in the long run Perth would come off second best to Brisbane. The Barnett government was concerned too and joined the tender process, including me in its bid.

After a drawn-out process, in March 2012 Tennis Australia was awarded key rights by the ITF for the 2013 event and beyond. My association with the Hopman Cup was over, just like that.

For Lesley and me, and for Charlie Fancutt, it felt like a child that we'd loved and nurtured had been taken away. We'd put the cup in the hands of the ITF, true, but could not have imagined that this was how it would pan out. And I know many other members of the Hopman family, who'd given up their Christmas holidays year after year to make valuable contributions, and to whom we—and the event—owe so much, experienced the same emotions.

It would have been too hard to attend the twenty-fifth Hopman, especially given my intimate involvement in the myriad planning elements to ensure the new arena was optimised for tennis. Lesley, Rowan and I went instead to New York with Perth family friends, attending NBA games, Broadway theatre and the winter sales. We even squeezed in a side trip to Vegas en route, indulging my penchant for the craps tables at Caesars Palace.

Just prior to that, in late 2012, Perth Arena opened with a concert by Elton John. Premier Barnett invited us to attend and, difficult as it was in one way, I was so proud to see the new stadium open and glowing, and to witness the pride that West Australians have in this landmark building. That felt good.

28.
AND NOW

OVER THE period since I left, the Australian Open continued to grow in economic clout. The Tennis Australia PR machine was in full swing, boasting of 'unlocking the value offering'.

The rise in gross revenues and profitability was inevitable for one fact alone. The TV product had been transformed globally—after the 2005 blockbuster there would be a massive increase in rights revenues. In the next round of TV negotiations, conducted shortly after I departed the Open, over $10 million more was reportedly flowing directly to the bottom line each year. I have no reason to doubt this is true.

Add to that the more than 25 per cent increase in public and corporate ticket prices in successive years (straining the egalitarianism of the event) and Tennis Australia was seeing profits it had never dreamed of. Much of it was invested in player development, and you'd have thought that as a result more top players would be pushing through. However, Australian tennis has been, and still is, in dire straits. We've only just rejoined the World Group of the Davis Cup after six years in the wilderness yet, in late 2013, had only three men and one woman ranked in the top 100.

I spent a couple of years working in, among other things, golf—where a mate, Ian Hickey, talked me into purchasing a share of a horse. Incredibly, El Segundo went on to win the 2007 Cox Plate. The thrill was up there with my tennis victories, because I could share it with Lesley and Rowan.

Then, urged on by many stakeholders frustrated like me by Australia's fall from grace in world tennis, I decided to run for the Tennis Australia presidency, initially against the incumbent, Geoff Pollard. When Geoff retired the following year, I ran against a Sydney lawyer with a tennis background, Stephen Healy. These were difficult campaigns.

I made it my business to try to mend the damaged relationship between Lleyton Hewitt and Bernard Tomic, ostensibly caused by Bernard not practising with Lleyton at Wimbledon. Although Lleyton and I had not always seen eye to eye, the dwindling number of Aussies on the tour and the direction in which the game was heading had drawn us together. I had a good relationship with Lleyton and his manager, David Drysdale, and a sound relationship with Bernard and his father, John.

I felt it was vital to get the two players together: with Lleyton still playing and Bernard on the way up, this was the time to make a serious run at the Davis Cup. I met with Drysa and asked if he thought there was any way the two players could patch it up. I was happy to be the go-between. Drysa said he couldn't see it happening—he'd test the water with Lleyton and get back to me, but he wasn't optimistic.

A few days later Drysa rang me and said, 'Lleyton's fixed it up with Bernie. He called Bernie up, and they had a chat and sorted it out.'

This was great news for the sport in Australia—but it was greeted with incredulity in tennis circles, especially as it blindsided Tennis Australia. Shortly after, Lleyton was asked in a media interview about his relationship with Bernie. He revealed that all was fine, and made a point of thanking me for my role in helping bring the two together.

Tennis Australia then orchestrated a public denial, claiming that I had nothing to do with ending the rift. It was divisive and untrue, and Lleyton and I were shocked.

In the presidency bids I received votes from Victoria, South Australia and Western Australia, missing out in the northern states and territories. On both occasions Tasmania decided the presidency, and on the second occasion it came down to the vote of a single board member there. Healy was installed as president.

I was disappointed, naturally. But at least I'd put my hand up. I copped the loss and moved on, as I did in my playing days. Who knew what other doors might open?

A couple did. Frank Sedgman, a living legend, was Australia's president of the International Tennis Club, which fosters global friendship through the sport. Now in his eighties, Sedg asked me if I would take over. I didn't hesitate, as I was honoured to be asked. Last year Australia, with the support of Tennis South Australia, hosted the IC World Junior Challenge Finals, and helped twenty-four kids and managers from all parts of the world attend the Australian Open. My role in that organisation continues.

My mum got to be a president too—at the age of eighty-three. She became head of the Doutta Galla Lawn Bowls Club, adjacent to the tennis courts where I first learnt to play.

Then in late 2012 I was made a professorial fellow in the Enhanced Elite Athlete Friendly Program at Monash University. The program aims to combine academic and athletic enhancement, as occurs in the American college system, helping prepare athletes for international success in a range of sports. I'm excited by this opportunity, which draws on my playing and post-playing experience—and has brought me back to my alma mater.

Australia's player-development philosophy still worries me. So many talented boys and girls, top juniors, have been lured into the Tennis Australia system only to end up on the scrapheap. We have lost the art of aiding talent to make the leap to tour level.

Last year I penned an open letter to Australian coaches. I'd like to share some of it here:

> One of the common questions I get asked is, 'What happened to Australian tennis?', along with the follow-up, 'How can it be revived?'...
> The answer to the second question, and the key

to our renaissance as a great tennis nation, is surprisingly simple...

Most successful players can name the one person who made the difference—like Charlie Hollis for Rod Laver, or Ian Barclay for Pat Cash. Or Pete Smith for Lleyton Hewitt, the late 'Nails' Carmichael for Pat Rafter and Darren Cahill, or Barry Phillips Moore for Mark Woodforde, just to name a few...

It's fair to say that a coach may come from anywhere, and may pop up at any moment, but it's equally true that the most likely person to play that role is your coach in your formative teenage years, just like Ian Barclay was to Pat Cash. Well, at least that's how it used to be until the Tennis Australia (TA) juggernaut decided to engage in and endeavour to monopolise the coaching industry, including directly employing coaches itself and designating which talented players they work with...

At Wimbledon this year, I saw an Aussie player, part of the TA system, with the fourth coach in twelve months. I don't need to tell you that a mix of inputs like that, however knowledgeable and well meaning, is a recipe for disaster...Systems do not produce champions, people do. As a consequence, and I'm not alone in saying this, we've pretty much lost a generation of players who have not transitioned to the tour...

Early last year, I was in discussions in relation to working with a talented Australian female player... During an unrelated discussion I was having with a senior TA official, he said to me, 'I've heard that you

Coaching Su-wei Hsieh at the US Open. (Photo by Chuan Chung.)

might be working with such player. I've spoken to our guys and we're not approving that.' Simple as that. In other words, the player's financial support package would be pulled...

Shortly after that rebuff, I was asked by Su-wei Hsieh if I could help her at Wimbledon...At twenty-five years of age, her ranking at that time was so low that she didn't even get in qualifying for the singles, and she proceeded to lose first round in the doubles. I asked Australia's highest-ranked doubles player, Paul Hanley, if he would play mixed doubles with her. Paul obliged, and they went on a terrific run all the way to the Wimbledon semi-finals. That was just the boost she needed. Just over twelve months later, Su-wei Hsieh has won seven singles tournaments, including two career-first WTA titles, as well as reaching the semi-final of doubles at the 2012 US Open. In that time, her singles ranking has gone from 343 to 25... Why am I working with a Taiwanese player? Because she asked me and I was in a position to do so. It was a decision made not by a Federation but by Su-wei and myself, coach and player, without interference...

There are literally hundreds of you coaching around Australia who would walk over hot coals for your best talent...But I suspect you know from bitter experience that you will lose your player to the 'system'. After all, how can the parents turn down the inducements of heavily subsidised coaching, travel and other support...

A Melbourne coach recently said to me, 'I've got a really good kid who I love working with, but I know I'll eventually have to let him go to a better coach in the system...' I said to him, 'Stop right there... I guarantee you that by the time your kid is playing on Centre Court at Wimbledon, you will have acquired all the knowledge you need...The best chance for your kid to make it is if you guys go on the journey together.'

I say to any player (and parent), 'You ditch your personal coach at your peril. It may not be perfect but if your coach believes in you and unselfishly goes the extra yard, you're already well on your way.' So I say to you, the coaches, 'Do not give up the dream of sitting in the player box at Wimbledon.' A trusting bond between coach and player is the fundamental building block of a player making it to tour level. Our governing body sees it differently, but hopefully one day they'll be held to account...

> The revival of Australian tennis has as its cornerstone the liberation of the army of coaches...
> I urge you to hang in and believe in yourself, and start dreaming again.

I believe it would be more productive if Tennis Australia focused solely on providing support services for our talented players, and let go of directly coaching them. This goes to the heart of our National Sporting Organisations, their raison d'etre. Do they exist to rule or to serve? It's a debate worth having.

I trust that one day we'll start to spread our wings again. For the sake of those youngsters out there who are dreaming, as I did, of playing the Grand Slams in the great arenas of the world, and of representing their country in the Davis Cup, Fed Cup or Hopman Cup—to which, I'm proud to say, I could make my contribution.

It was tennis, as well as a loving family, that opened up so many different paths in my life. I was lucky, and I'm forever grateful for the opportunities I was given in the sport that I love.

POSTSCRIPT

AT WIMBLEDON this year I was out on Court Five warming up Su-wei Hsieh for the women's doubles final. Su-wei was using one of her new Yonex racquets, which I sourced for her through eBay and Twitter—she paid 130 euros for it, and she also bought her tennis outfit. Taiwan doesn't have the endorsement opportunities that you can take for granted in the major markets. Su-wei's partner was Peng Shuai from China, born just four days after her; their opponents were two Aussies, Ash Barty and Casey Dellacqua.

I hadn't said too much, which I thought was wise on such a big day. I knew Su-wei would be nervous, so I'd given her the advice I've always felt is sound in a high-pressure situation: 'Make sure you execute your strength.' It's far less stressful if you're focusing on that, rather than on your weakness.

That day Macca and I played our last match in the round-robin seniors' invitation event. After losing the other two matches, one to Patrick and John McEnroe (that man again!), we were up against Henri Leconte and Mansour Bahrami. The outcome might not seem important, but I couldn't help thinking that for Su-wei her coach losing would be a bad way to start the day. In a close match we eked out a win, and I felt much better for it.

Barty and Dellacqua started the final on top—Peng and Su-wei seemed more nervous. I was okay with that, until Su-wei got a put-away high volley, bread and butter for her. She didn't nail it. Dellacqua reflexed the ball back and won the point. Su-wei's glance to me in the player box, and no doubt my reaction, said it all.

Three times the Aussies went up a break, and each time their opponents broke back. Though Su-wei served for the set at 6–5 and was broken, the tide had turned. Peng had done an excellent job powering away at the baseline, getting them into the match, and Su-wei was starting to take over at the net. They won the tiebreak 7–1.

They jumped to a 2–0 lead in the second set, with Su-wei serving. Peng was not in the traditional net position and instead was camped on the baseline with Su-wei. They've been doing this on and off in their partnership for some time, and I'm sometimes asked by my Aussie peers if I condone it. I do: although it raises eyebrows, especially since it probably hasn't been seen on Centre Court at Wimbledon since the 1930s, I know it's comfortable for them.

I haven't forgotten the pressure I felt in the 1986 Davis Cup final to serve and volley 'like a true Aussie'. No player I coach will ever be subject to that pressure. The girls stayed in the formation that suits them and Su-wei held serve for 3–0—they were pretty much home.

Fifteen minutes later, with a 7–6, 6–1 scoreline, it was over. They had won Wimbledon with the loss of only one set.

I hope the Aussie girls will have their day soon, and it will be deserved, but on 6 July 2013 Su-wei Hsieh became the first Taiwanese player ever to win a Grand Slam title. Whatever happens in tennis, and in life, she will always be a Wimbledon champion—it's Su-wei's game changer.

ACKNOWLEDGEMENTS

I HAVE tried my utmost to be accurate in this book, but I realise that sometimes the memory plays tricks. To that end, I apologise for any mistakes or omissions herein.

Where a photograph's provenance has not been given, the image comes from my private collection. However, if any photographers or publications ought to have been credited, I am sorry. Please alert the publisher, and the omission will be rectified in future editions.

I would like to gratefully acknowledge the support I have received from Text Publishing over many years. To Michael Heyward and David Winter: thank you so much for your guidance and encouragement, especially in keeping me on track.

I also thank Andrew Jaspan, Russell Barlow and Elliot Swart, for their helping hand.

To the Hopman Cup family: no words can describe my lifelong gratitude to you. I can't name you all here, but the following represent a cross section of those who I am deeply indebted to: Ali, George, Hamish, Tina, Anthea, Jano, Roseanne, Ben and Mandy, Annette, Rosita, Anneliese, Liz, Fred, Gobble, Karen and Justin, Soren,

Mark H, Shaggy, Shaun, Noel, TC, PP and JG, Peter C, and Chook. To the entire family: you know who you are, and your contributions were real and enormously important. You can be so gratified by what you helped to create.

To the Australian Open team: I loved working with you all—whoa, you were a great bunch. Given there were so many of you over my years at the Open, I am not able to acknowledge you individually here, yet every one of you can be very proud of your work.

To my mum and my late dad: your love and support was unwavering. You allowed us all to believe we could fulfil our dreams.

Stan, you're a wonderful and kind big brother.

Mary, my sister, you've always been there for me. Your love and support for Mum and Dad—particularly in their later years, when it's meant so much—is admirable.

Brian, you're my enduring mate, the younger brother I always looked up to.

To the families of my siblings, and those on Lesley's side, thank you all for your unconditional help.

Lesley, thank you for your love and support. You've made many sacrifices to allow me to pursue my journey (including writing this book), while always being there for Rowan. Your own contribution to the sport of tennis, largely unheralded, has been huge.

Rowan, at the risk of being a touch embarrassing, we burst with parental love for you. You have taught me far more about myself, and about life, than you could imagine. May the wind be gently at your back as you pursue your life journey.